NOLO® Products & Services

Books & Software

Get in-depth information. Nolo publishes hundreds of great books and software programs for consumers and business owners. They're all available in print or as downloads at Nolo.com.

Legal Encyclopedia

Free at Nolo.com. Here are more than 1,400 free articles and answers to common questions about everyday legal issues including wills, bankruptcy, small business formation, divorce, patents, employment and much more.

Plain-English Legal Dictionary

Free at Nolo.com. Stumped by jargon? Look it up in America's most up-to-date source for definitions of legal terms.

Online Legal Documents

Create documents at your computer. Go online to make a will or living trust, form an LLC or corporation or obtain a trademark or provisional patent at Nolo.com. For simpler matters, download one of our hundreds of high-quality legal forms, including bills of sale, promissory notes, nondisclosure agreements and many more.

Lawyer Directory

Find an attorney at Nolo.com. Nolo's unique lawyer directory provides in-depth profiles of lawyers all over America. From fees and experience to legal philosophy, education and special expertise, you'll find all the information you need to pick a lawyer who's a good fit.

Free Legal Updates

Keep up to date. Check Nolo.com/updates for free updates to this book, and sign up for our free e-newsletters at Nolo.com/support/subscribe.cfm.

1st edition

The Essential Guide to Handling Workplace Harassment & Discrimination

By Attorney Deborah C. England

FIRST EDITION	SEPTEMBER 2009
Editor	LISA GUERIN
Cover Design	SUSAN PUTNEY
CD-ROM Preparation	ELLEN BITTER
Proofreading	SUSAN CARLSON GREENE
Index	VICTORIA BAKER
Printing	DELTA PRINTING SOLUTIONS, INC.

England, Deborah, 1959-
  The essential guide to handling workplace harassment & discrimination/ by Deborah C. England. -- 1st ed.
      p. cm.
  Includes bibliographical references and index.
  ISBN-13: 978-1-4133-1049-8 (pbk. : alk. paper)
  ISBN-10: 1-4133-1049-4 (pbk. : alk. paper)
  1. Discrimination in employment--Law and legislation--United States--Popular works. I. Title.
  KF3464.E54 2009
  344.7301'133--dc22

                              2009021415

Please note

We believe accurate, plain-English legal information should help you solve many of your own legal problems. But this text is not a substitute for personalized advice from a knowledgeable lawyer. If you want the help of a trained professional—and we'll always point out situations in which we think that's a good idea—consult an attorney licensed to practice in your state.

Dedication

To my nephew, Jake, and my nieces, Isabelle and Olivia. May your world be free of prejudice, with opportunity equally available to all. And if it's not, you know what to do.

Acknowledgments

The author wishes to thank everyone at Nolo who helped with this book, including:

Lisa Guerin, for her pithy, astute, and insightful editing. Also, for her unquenchable wit and enthusiasm for this inherited project.

Alayna Schroeder, for her diligent effort to pull this book into shape and clarify its many knotty concepts.

Janet Portman and Mary Randolph, for championing the book and staying with it.

Margaret Livingston, for making the book look great.

Sigrid Metson, Kelly Perri, and Tom Silva, for their strategic input.

About the Author

Deborah C. England has practiced employment law in San Francisco for more than 20 years, representing clients in litigation in state and federal courts. In addition to litigating, she regularly advises clients on employment issues, guides in efforts to informally resolve employment disputes, and has conducted discrimination and harassment training. Ms. England is the co-author, with Lisa Guerin, of *The Essential Guide to Family & Medical Leave*, published by Nolo, and frequently writes and speaks on employment and civil rights law.

Table of Contents

Introduction

What Are Harassment and Discrimination?.. 3

How Harassment and Discrimination Affect the Bottom Line 3

How This Book Can Help.. 4

PART I: Preventing Harassment and Discrimination

1 What Is Discrimination?

Laws Prohibiting Discrimination.. 10

What Is Discrimination? 13

When and How Discrimination Occurs... 33

2 What Is Harassment?

Which Laws Apply to Your Company?.. 44

What Is Harassment?... 48

Who Is a Harasser?... 58

Who Can Be Harassed?... 64

What Is Not Harassment?.. 65

3 Policies Prohibiting Harassment and Discrimination

Benefits of an Effective Policy.. 74

Elements of an Effective Policy 77

Complaint and Investigation Procedures... 82

Communicate the Policy to Employees.. 89

Review the Policy Regularly 92

4 Training

Benefits of Training 96

Combined Training Session for Supervisors and Employees 100

Separate Sessions 101

How to Conduct Training 106

Who Conducts Training 107

Diversity Training 109

PART II: Dealing With Harassment and Discrimination Claims

5 Investigating Complaints

Receiving a Complaint 118

Conducting an Investigation 124

Concluding Your Investigation 140

6 Documentation

What Your Documentation Should Look Like 155

What Documents You Should Have 158

Document Management 171

7 After the Investigation

Dealing With the Aftermath of a Complaint 176

Retaliation 184

Getting Others Involved 190

8 Dealing With Government Agencies

The Role of Fair Employment Agencies 197

The Complaint Process 199

Preparing for an Agency Investigation... 209

Mediation.. 213

Your Role in Dealing With Investigative Agencies.. 217

9 Lawsuits

Why Employees Sue... 229

How Lawsuits Work... 234

Alternatives to Litigation 250

Your Role in a Lawsuit 253

If You Are Sued Personally 269

Appendixes

A How to Use the CD-ROM

Installing the Files Onto Your Computer 279

Using the Word Processing Files to Create Documents.................................... 280

Listening to the Audio Files 282

Files on the CD-ROM... 284

B State Laws on Discrimination and Harassment

State Laws That Prohibit Discrimination and Harassment............................... 286

State Enforcement Agencies 298

C Forms

Policy Prohibiting Discrimination and Harassment

Acknowledgment of Receipt of Policy

Policy Distribution Log

Intake Form—Employee Complaint

Litigation Calendar

Index

Introduction

What Are Harassment and Discrimination? 3

How Harassment and Discrimination Affect the Bottom Line 3

How This Book Can Help 4

Diversity is among the great strengths of American society. Employers in this country are able to draw from a pool of workers of all races, religions, nationalities, abilities, and ages, and both genders. Diversity offers companies the broadest base of talent, the widest range of viewpoints, the deepest reach into potential client and customer communities, and the best chance of benefitting from our increasingly global economy.

Diversity can also present vexing challenges to employers, however. Managing a diverse workforce can be difficult. Sometimes, differences among employees can lead to conflict, misunderstanding, and, in the worst cases, hostility. The employers who enjoy the benefits of a multifaceted workforce also bear the responsibility of making sure that it functions harmoniously. It can, at times, be a daunting undertaking. This book is designed to help employers, and especially the human resources personnel, managers, and supervisors who work for them, negotiate some of the trickiest waters of the modern workplace: preventing and dealing with harassment and discrimination.

You may have turned to this book because you want to help your company avoid problems down the road by taking the right steps to prevent harassment and discrimination from occurring. Good for you! That kind of proactive initiative will help keep your company on the right track, using the strategies and tools provided here. On the other hand, you may have grabbed this book because your company just got hit with a harassment or discrimination complaint or even a lawsuit. You've come to the right place, too. The chapters that follow provide clear direction on how to help your company through the process and how to prevent similar problems in the future. You and your company can be confident that you're doing all you can to make the workplace welcoming to all employees, so they can focus on doing their jobs.

What Are Harassment and Discrimination?

Harassment and discrimination are terms that are used frequently and pretty loosely in everyday conversation. This book focuses on the kind of workplace harassment and discrimination that the law prohibits: illegal mistreatment of an employee because of that employee's race, color, national origin, gender, religion, age, or disability.

Harassment and discrimination are related but distinct concepts. An employer discriminates against an employee when it takes an action against the employee because of his or her membership in a protected group. For example, a company that refuses to hire Japanese American applicants is discriminating against those candidates because of their national origin.

Harassment is actually a type of discrimination, a particular way employers mistreat employees based on a protected trait. An employer harasses an employee when it targets someone in a protected category and subjects that person to unwelcome treatment that affects their job. Harassment can take the form of attempted sexual extortion, such as when a male supervisor pressures a female subordinate to consent to a physical relationship with him in order to keep her job. It can also take the form of conduct that poisons the working environment, such as when a coworker calls another employee racist names or displays sexual, racial, or other offensive materials in view of other employees.

How Harassment and Discrimination Affect the Bottom Line

The words "harassment" and "discrimination" may lead you to envision lawsuits, courtrooms, and lawyers—and those are certainly among the costs of failing to prevent and remedy these problems. Your company can be sued by an employee who faced illegal workplace discrimination or harassment. Lawsuits come with a very real price tag, from lost hours spent preparing a case to attorney fees to potentially huge damage awards. Of course, being sued can also have costs that are more difficult to quantify, including loss of goodwill, a poor reputation in the community, bad publicity, and poor morale.

But harassment and discrimination don't have to result in a lawsuit to cause serious problems for your company. Employees who work in an environment that is tolerant, free of slurs and offensive conduct, and welcoming to all are more content and productive than those who don't. Harassment and discrimination tear down morale, destroy loyalty, drain productivity, and harm your company's ability to attract and retain employees. Preventing and dealing appropriately with harassment and discrimination don't just fulfill your legal obligations; they also further your company's best interests.

How This Book Can Help

Many managers and human resources professionals have heard and read quite a bit about employment harassment and discrimination. Perhaps you've even attended a training session, participated in a webinar, or taken a professional development class on these topics. If so, here's something you may have noticed: There are innumerable ways problems can arise in a real workplace, most of which don't match the scenarios presented in training.

This book will help you make the leap from abstract rules to everyday workplace situations. It will help you recognize harassment and discrimination when they arise, and offer you proven strategies and tools for preventing and dealing with them. It's filled with examples, common questions, and real-world lessons that will help you apply the sometimes complicated legal principles of harassment and discrimination to the very real problems that come up in your workplace. Whether you're new to these topics or you're interested in refreshing your training, this book will help you understand the law and apply it at your company, in a way that makes sense on the ground in a functioning business.

Part One of this book focuses on prevention. It explains the legal ins and outs of harassment and discrimination, including what types of conduct are prohibited, when harassment and discrimination commonly occur, when your company can be held liable, and how to handle common problem areas, like conducting job interviews and managing workplace romance. This information will help you identify problems early on, so you can take quick action to stop potential misconduct.

Next, you'll learn how to develop an effective policy that prohibits harassment and discrimination. You'll find out how this type of policy can protect your company, what a good policy should include, and how to distribute the policy to employees. You'll also learn about the important role that employee and supervisor training can play in preventing violations, along with some tips on setting up an effective training program, whether you do the training yourself or hire someone else to handle it.

Part Two focuses on responding to harassment and discrimination that have already occurred. Here, you'll find information on investigations, including the importance of taking complaints seriously, how to investigate claims promptly and thoroughly, and how to document each step of the process. You'll learn how to handle the stresses to the working environment that complaints and investigations can cause, along with practical tips for healing any rifts that may have developed so that employees can continue to function professionally and collegially. Finally, the book explains the process of responding to complaints that employees file with governmental agencies and in court.

Although we as a society have come a long way, harassment and discrimination are still part of the landscape of the modern workplace. Armed with the information and tools provided in this book, including the resources and audio scenarios on the CD-ROM, you'll be ready to handle claims of harassment and discrimination from start to finish—and, better yet, to prevent those claims from arising in the first place.

Part I: Preventing Harassment and Discrimination

What Is Discrimination?

Laws Prohibiting Discrimination 10

What Is Discrimination? 13

    Sex-Based Discrimination 17

    Race Discrimination 22

    English-Only Rules 23

    Age-Based Discrimination 25

    Religious Discrimination 26

    Discrimination Based on Disability 30

    Genetic Discrimination 33

When and How Discrimination Occurs 33

    Hiring 33

    Decisions During Employment 36

    The End of Employment 40

You may hear the word "discrimination" used rather broadly in everyday speech. People who feel wronged may say things like, "He discriminated against me because he doesn't like people who speak their mind" or "It's so unfair that we have to go stand outside to smoke; this company really discriminates against smokers."

Statements like these get at only one important aspect of discrimination: It involves making a distinction between groups of people. But, as you probably know, discrimination is illegal only when the basis for the distinction has been declared off-limits by Congress, courts, or a state or local legislature. Not every decision, even every unfair or biased decision, is discriminatory. For discrimination to be illegal, it must be based on a "protected category," such as race or religion.

This chapter will cover:
- laws that prohibit discrimination
- what discrimination is, and
- how and when discrimination may occur.

This information will help you recognize the signs of discriminatory behavior. In later chapters, you'll learn what steps you can take to prevent discrimination and how to handle discrimination that has already taken place.

Laws Prohibiting Discrimination

There are many different laws, both federal and state, that protect employees from discrimination in the workplace. The most prominent federal antidiscrimination laws are:
- **Title VII of the Civil Rights Act of 1964 (Title VII).** This law prohibits discrimination on the basis of race, color, religion, sex, and national origin. Title VII applies to employers who have 15 or more employees.

⓪ CAUTION

If your company had 15 employees anytime in the last two years, Title VII may apply. Technically, Title VII applies only to entities with 15 or more employees for each working day in 20 or more calendar weeks in the current or preceding year. If your company's workforce fluctuates around 15 employees, talk with a legal adviser about whether the law applies to your company. Even if Title VII doesn't apply, your state's antidiscrimination laws may; state laws often apply to smaller employers. (See the chart in Appendix B for more information.)

- **Genetic Information Nondiscrimination Act (GINA).** This law prohibits discrimination on the basis of genetic information (beginning November 21, 2009). GINA applies to employers who have 15 or more employees.
- **The Age Discrimination in Employment Act (ADEA).** The ADEA prohibits discrimination against those age 40 or older on the basis of age.
- **The Americans with Disabilities Act (ADA).** The ADA protects workers with disabilities from discrimination in the workplace, and requires employers to offer reasonable accommodations to help those workers do their jobs.
- **The Equal Pay Act (EPA).** This law is designed to ensure that men and women receive equal compensation for their work. The jobs don't have to be exactly the same to require equal pay, but they must involve "equal work," meaning equal skill, effort, and responsibility and similar working conditions.
- **The Civil Rights Act of 1866, 42 U.S.C § 1981 (Section 1981).** Section 1981 prohibits discrimination on the basis of race in the making, enforcing, and performance of contracts. It also prohibits discrimination on the basis of ethnicity, if that discrimination is racial in character (for example, discrimination based on physical characteristics or skin color violates Section 1981; discrimination based on surname or accent generally doesn't). Section 1981 applies to all contracts,

including employment agreements, partnership agreements, and the like.

Most states also have their own laws prohibiting employment discrimination, and many extend greater protections than federal law. For example, they may apply to smaller employers or apply to other protected classes (such as marital status or sexual orientation). Finally, some local or county ordinances may also provide additional protection.

Which Antidiscrimination Laws Apply to Your Company?

Not every antidiscrimination law applies to every employer. For the most part, whether your company has to follow these laws depends on its size and location. Federal antidiscrimination laws (listed below) apply only to employers with more than a minimum number of employees—and this minimum number is different for each law.

Name of Law:	Discrimination Prohibited on the Basis of:	Applies to:
Title VII	Race, color, national origin, religion, sex	Employers with 15 or more employees
Age Discrimination in Employment Act	Age (against employees age 40 and older only)	Employers with 20 or more employees
Americans with Disabilities Act	Physical or mental disability	Employers with 15 or more employees
Equal Pay Act	Sex (applies only to wage discrimination)	All employers
Civil Rights Act of 1866 (Section 1981)	Race, ethnicity	All employers
Immigration Reform and Control Act	Citizenship status, national origin	Employers with four or more employees
Genetic Information Nondiscrimination Act	Genetic information	Employers with 15 or more employees

Common Questions

Q: We are a multistate employer, and our handbook says that we do not tolerate discrimination based on sexual orientation. An employee is now complaining of sexual orientation discrimination in a state that does not prohibit it. Do we have to do anything about it?

A: Yes. Arguably the company obligated itself, in its handbook, to protect employees from sexual orientation discrimination, regardless of where it occurs and whether it is illegal. And it's good business practice, too. Following this policy uniformly shows the company's sincere commitment to treating employees fairly and protecting them from discrimination no matter where they work.

What Is Discrimination?

In general, antidiscrimination laws are designed to keep an employer from making employment-related decisions that disadvantage employees based on the categories identified above (or other categories state or local governments find worthy of protection). It is illegal to discriminate when hiring, creating or applying policies, training, promoting, firing or laying off employees, or in any other terms and conditions of employment.

TIP

Conduct may be inappropriate even if it isn't illegal. This section explains how courts and legislatures define discrimination, including what an employee must prove in order to win a discrimination lawsuit. That doesn't mean, however, that you should ignore any behavior or conduct that falls short of these standards. For example, a supervisor might be able to show that the younger employee he promoted was truly the best qualified candidate for the position, even if that supervisor made inappropriate ageist remarks that led an older employee to mistakenly believe that the decision was based on age. That the older employee would find it hard to prove illegal discrimination doesn't make it acceptable for a supervisor to make biased comments. This is a situation where discipline is in order for violating company policy, even if no law has been broken.

Discrimination can take these forms:

- **Disparate treatment.** This is the textbook form of discrimination: intentionally treating people differently because of a protected characteristic. It can mean denying a job to someone because of his or her race, or giving promotions to men over equally qualified women based on gender.

- **Disparate impact.** Conduct that is fair on its face but affects a disproportionate number of employees in a protected class is also discriminatory. Unless the employer has a very good, job-related reason for the different treatment—for example, a strength requirement (which may disproportionately affect women) because the job regularly requires heavy lifting—the practice or policy won't pass legal muster. Even if an employer has a valid business reason for the practice, it may still constitute discrimination if an alternative exists that would not disproportionately affect the protected class.

- **Failure to accommodate.** When an employer is legally required to accommodate an employee (such as an employee with a disability or an employee whose religious practices require a change to workplace rules) and fails to do so, this is also a form of discrimination.

Discrimination doesn't often present itself in an extremely obvious way, like a supervisor admitting he won't promote women, refused to hire someone because of his race, or won't consider anyone older than 50 for certain positions. The rare occasions when something like this happens are called "smoking gun" cases, because employees have direct evidence of the discrimination that an employer will have a hard time refuting.

Much more often, however, an employee will have only an inkling or hunch that something isn't right. The employee may look at several different pieces of suggestive information (called "circumstantial evidence") and decide that discrimination is the logical conclusion. For example, an employee who claims that she didn't receive a promotion because of her gender might present evidence that her supervisor made sexist statements shortly before denying her the promotion, offered the promotion to a man whose qualifications were not as strong, and has a history of promoting only male employees.

An employee can't win a discrimination case simply by claiming that he or she experienced discrimination on the job. If an employee's discrimination case goes to court, the employee will have to show that:

- **He or she was qualified for the job in question.** An employee or applicant can't claim discrimination unless he or she had the necessary skills, qualifications, experience, and so on to do the job.

- **The employee is a member of a protected class.** Although this may seem like a fairly straightforward requirement to meet, it isn't always. For example, an employee who claims discrimination based on religion will have to show that the religious belief in question is "sincerely held."

- **The employee or applicant suffered an adverse action.** It isn't enough for an employee to claim that someone is prejudiced toward, or holds particular beliefs about, certain groups of people. The employee must also show that his or her job was affected negatively by these biased beliefs. For example, a female employee couldn't sue simply because her manager is a member of a private, male-only golf club; she would have to show that she suffered a negative employment action based on her gender.

- **There's some reason to suspect that the employer had an improper motive.** Essentially, it's up to the employee to show that there is some connection between his or her membership in a protected class and the adverse action the employer took. In other words, an employee who is fired and happens to be Black doesn't have a legal claim; an employee who is fired because he is Black does.

An employee doesn't necessarily win the case just by showing these elements, however. The employer has the opportunity to show that it took the job action for a legitimate business reason—for example, you didn't hire a qualified applicant because another applicant was more qualified. If you're able to do that, the employee will have to show that your rationale wasn't the real reason for the action (in legal terms, that it was just a "pretext" for discrimination). For example, if the employer claims that it never promoted anyone with fewer than two years of experience, and an employee bringing a gender discrimination case shows that several men with less experience were promoted, that might be proof of pretext.

Being a Jerk Isn't Illegal

Not every type of discrimination is illegal discrimination. Differences in personality, temperament, and taste can lead to friction in the workplace. And the law doesn't demand that employers force employees to like each other. If unfair treatment arises out of a personality dispute that is not based on membership in a protected class, it is not illegal. That means the "undiscriminating jerk"—the manager who treats everyone badly—isn't discriminating illegally if he's mean to everyone just because he's, well, mean. Even obvious favoritism or bias, such as refusing to hire fans of a particular baseball team, isn't illegal as long as it isn't actually based on race, gender, or some other protected status.

Of course, that doesn't mean the company has to put up with obnoxious behavior and foolish rationales for employment decisions. After all, it can affect employee morale and productivity. You'll probably want to put a stop to it; although the company shouldn't risk legal liability for it, it's hardly conducive to a good work environment.

Sex-Based Discrimination

Discrimination on the basis of sex means making decisions or adopting policies that appear to be neutral but disproportionately affect one gender. An employer discriminates when it gives men the plum assignments or gives women more paid leave than men, for example.

But there are more subtle ways to discriminate based on sex, too. For example, sexual harassment is a type of sex discrimination, as explained in Chapter 2. Here are some other forms sex discrimination may take.

Sexual Stereotyping

Sexual stereotyping, that is, holding men and women to different standards based on historic or traditional sex roles, is also sex-based discrimination. In one famous case, a female manager in an accounting firm was denied promotion to partner due to her "interpersonal skills," among other reasons. The partners making the decision wanted her to walk, talk, and dress more femininely and to wear make-up and jewelry. The Supreme Court recognized that this challenge to her "interpersonal skills" was really just another way of saying she didn't conform to the partners' stereotype of how a woman should look and act.

Common Questions

Q: An employee complained that her supervisor always gives lead projects to men. When I asked the supervisor about it, he told me that it's because he happens to be more comfortable working with the men in the department. He doesn't mean to discriminate; it's just a personality issue. Is this discrimination?

A: It could be. Discrimination doesn't have to be a series of calculated decisions intended to harm one group of people: It just means treating people in the same situation differently because of a protected characteristic. The supervisor's personal comfort level with the men who report to him doesn't justify giving them the lead assignments. It looks like his personal preference is clouding his professional judgment—and female employees are suffering as a result. Whether or not gender is playing any role in his decisions— that is, whether he is comfortable only around men generally or he just happens to be more comfortable with these particular fellows— this situation needs to change.

Dress Codes

In most cultures, including ours, men and women traditionally dress and appear distinct from one another. For example, it is customary for women to wear skirts, but not men. Courts have generally allowed dress codes or grooming standards that recognize these social differences, but not if such codes impose a greater burden on one gender or the other. For example, it is probably okay to have a rule that men can't wear their hair longer than collar length.

CAUTION
Dress codes can cause problems if they impose a burden on an employee based on membership in another protected class. For example, "no-beard" policies may be illegal as applied to African American males who suffer from pseudofolliculitis barbae, which causes a painful skin condition from shaving. So, your company may have to make an exception in such cases if it has a grooming standard.

Favoring a Paramour

Everyone is affected in an environment where the boss dates a subordinate. It can quickly and easily create feelings of distrust and discomfort and, worse, can put the company at legal risk.

As explained in Chapter 2, workplace relationships can lead to claims of sexual harassment, particularly if the relationship ends or one member of the relationship has less power at work than the other. These relationships can also lead to claims of discrimination where, for example, a supervisor gives her boyfriend better work assignments than she gives his peers. While a court may not find the existence of a relationship alone to be illegal discrimination against others (because everyone not in the relationship is equally affected, men and women alike), it's not a risk worth taking—and it's a bad business practice. No one wants to believe a relationship with a supervisor or manager is a prerequisite to professional success. If you allow this type of behavior to happen in your company, you will likely face high turnover and general feelings of dissatisfaction. For more information on handling workplace relationships, see Chapter 2.

Pregnancy Discrimination

Treating employees differently on the basis of pregnancy, childbirth, or medical conditions related to pregnancy or childbirth (including abortion) is also prohibited, sex-based discrimination. This doesn't mean the employee must be pregnant to be protected, however. For example, a federal court recently allowed a pregnancy-based lawsuit to proceed when an employee alleged she was fired because she was undergoing in vitro fertilization to try to become pregnant.

Your basic duty is to treat a pregnant employee just as you would any other employee who is in a similar position in his or her ability or inability to work. Put another way, you should treat pregnant employees as you would any other employee with a temporary disability. If you'd give an injured employee a flexible schedule to attend medical appointments, for example, do the same for pregnant employees.

 Common Questions

Q: I have a pregnant salesperson whose job requires her to travel a lot. She's had a lot of complications in the pregnancy and I am worried about whether it's safe for her to travel. I have an administrative position opening up—she won't make commissions anymore, but at least she'll be close to home and she won't have to take any unnecessary risks. Can I offer her the position?

A: You can offer her the position, but you can't require her to take it. Even though your intentions are good, forcing the employee to take the position would be discriminatory. Because the position you want her to take sounds like it pays less and is less prestigious, requiring her to take it would be demoting her because she's pregnant, a clear violation of the law. It's up to her and her medical care provider to decide whether she has to stop traveling.

Sexual Orientation Discrimination

Federal law doesn't explicitly prohibit discrimination based on sexual orientation. However, many states do offer this explicit protection. (See Appendix B for information on the law in your state.)

However, federal laws do prohibit discrimination based on sex stereotyping, as discussed above. So, treating people differently because they fail to live up to gender norms—for example, because a man acts effeminately or a woman acts macho—can be illegal sex stereotyping.

Gender Identity Discrimination

In recent years, many states and local governments have begun to include "gender identity" in their list of protected classes. Gender identity refers to one's self-identified gender, as opposed to one's anatomical gender at birth. (See the chart in Appendix B for the rule in your state.) An employee need not have undergone sex reassignment surgery to be protected by these laws.

To date, federal law does not explicitly protect employees from gender identity discrimination. However, as we've noted, employers can't discriminate based on stereotypes about how men and women should behave, and that could include stereotyping employees whose self-identified gender doesn't match their gender at birth.

Common Questions

Q: Our bookkeeper, Jim, just announced that he is undergoing a sex-change transition, wants to be called Jamie, and insists on being treated as female from now on. He's just started the medical transition and won't be finished for many months or longer. It's a big hassle to change all our records, figure out bathroom arrangements, and make sure Jim's coworkers and supervisor are handling this in a way that doesn't offend him. Can't we treat him like a man until he isn't one anymore?

A: Definitely not. Part of Jim/Jamie's transition is living as a woman, the gender with which she identifies. It's no more of a burden for your company to change Jamie's records than to add new employees or adjust records to reflect changes for other employees. Demanding that you be allowed to treat Jamie "like a man" could be considered gender stereotyping and may also violate your state law if it protects against gender identity discrimination.

Race Discrimination

Race discrimination occurs when an employer makes a job decision based on an employee's race or adopts a policy that appears neutral, but disproportionately affects members of a certain race. For example, in the Supreme Court case that first established the concept of "disparate impact," an employer required laborers to have a high school diploma. This disproportionately screened out Black employees. Even if the employer's intent wasn't to discriminate, the policy had this effect. An employer with a policy that has a disproportionate impact like this will have to show there is an important and legitimate work-related reason for it—here, that a high school diploma was necessary for the job of laborer.

Common Questions

Q: My employer, a garbage collection company, conducts background checks on all applicants, including getting credit information. Recently, the company rejected an applicant for a driver position after learning that he had bad credit (due to some late credit card payments). He's African American and was otherwise qualified for the job. I'm convinced his race had nothing to do with the rejection, but he filed a charge of discrimination with the state human rights commission. Are we at risk?

A: Maybe, because credit report information, while neutral on its face, could have a disproportionate negative impact on African American applicants, as the U.S. Supreme Court has recognized. And your company will have a hard time showing that an individual's credit report is necessary to being a garbage truck driver. Better to drop the practice and avoid the problem.

National Origin and Citizenship Status

An employer cannot discriminate on the basis of national origin (also sometimes called ancestry), either. National origin refers to the country in which someone was born, where his or her ancestors came from, or the nationality group to which he or she belongs. It does not have to refer to a country. Citizenship elsewhere is not in and of itself a protected status.

English-Only Rules

Some employers would like to require that everyone in the workplace speak English. Unless they're necessary for a job, however, these English-only rules are illegally discriminatory. If there is a business necessity for the rule—speaking only English to English-speaking customers, for example—and employees have advance notice of it, such a rule is usually allowed. But rules that are unnecessarily restrictive (not allowing employees on their break to speak their native language, for example) can cause problems.

 Common Questions

Q: An employee in our accounting department is excellent at what he does, but has a very thick accent that makes it difficult for people to understand him. This isn't usually a problem, except when he has to give a presentation at the monthly manager's meeting. Would it be discriminatory to demote him to a junior position that doesn't require the presentations?

A: In all likelihood, yes. Discriminating against someone because of an accent can be considered national origin discrimination.

That doesn't mean you can never take an adverse action against an employee because an accent affects his work. When an accent *materially* interferes with an employee's job performance, it isn't discriminatory to take appropriate action. But it doesn't seem that you would meet that standard here. The employee's accent doesn't interfere with his primary job tasks; it only interferes with his ability to communicate at a monthly meeting, and there might be other solutions that can overcome this. For example, consider asking the employee to bring handouts to the meetings or to prepare presentation materials that communicate the bulk of relevant information, so that others can read along as he speaks.

Besides the possible legal risks if you demote the employee, you risk losing a potentially dissatisfied high performer who might soon look for a job elsewhere. Replacing a competent employee could prove much more costly than trying to find a solution to the situation you're currently in.

Age-Based Discrimination

Employers can't discriminate against employees based on age. The ADEA protects employees age 40 and over from age-based discrimination. It is also illegal to discriminate against older workers in favor of younger employees who are themselves in the protected class—meaning it's illegal to hire a candidate who is 45 years old instead of a better qualified candidate who's 65—based on age.

Common Questions

Q: We recently promoted a younger employee into a more senior technical position that requires detailed knowledge of a computer application he learned in college. An older coworker has worked at the company for years and says he should have been offered training in the application; if he had been, he claims he would have been the best choice for the promotion. He says this is age-based discrimination. Is it?

A: It doesn't sound like it. The company cannot make decisions based on a person's age, but can make decisions based on a person's qualifications. Here, the younger applicant was more qualified. While there's certainly nothing to prevent you from offering specialized training to help a current employee promote, you're not legally required to do so (of course, you can't offer it only to younger workers). And there's nothing to prevent the older employee from seeking that training himself, to increase his career opportunities.

One part of the ADEA regulates benefits offered to older employees. The Older Workers Benefit Protection Act (OWBPA) prohibits employers from denying benefits to workers over 40. Because it costs more to provide certain benefits to older workers, the OWBPA does permit employers to reduce benefits based on age as long as the cost of providing the benefit to older workers is the same as the cost of providing the unreduced benefit to younger workers. However, this defense applies only to certain benefits and only in certain situations.

SEE AN EXPERT

The OWBPA also regulates the waiver and release of employment claims by older employees. A release that doesn't meet these requirements is not valid, and your company can't enforce it. Whenever your company wants to secure a release from any employee, consult with an employment attorney to make sure the release satisfies the OWBPA requirements.

Religious Discrimination

Title VII also protects employees from discrimination based on their religious beliefs. Discrimination based on religion occurs when an employer treats an employee differently, based on religion, or takes action that disproportionately affects employees of a particular religious faith. Discrimination against employees because they don't adhere to a particular, or any, religious faith is also illegal.

An employee's religious beliefs don't have to be associated with a mainstream religion, such as Islam or Catholicism. According to the EEOC, a belief is protected if it is "'religious' in the person's own scheme of things." So long as the belief is "sincere and meaningful," occupies a place in the believer's life "parallel to that filled by … God," and concerns ultimate issues of life, purpose, and death, it is irrelevant that it may not be affiliated with any particular religious group.

Common Questions

Q: An employee who describes himself as an evangelical Christian approaches coworkers on breaks to discuss his and their religious beliefs. A couple of employees told their supervisors they're offended. I know we're not supposed to interfere with his religious beliefs, but he's bothering other employees—what about their beliefs?

A: You aren't legally required to put up with conduct that offends employees or disrupts the workplace simply because the offending employee's conduct is part of a religious practice. But you do need to examine whether his religious practice can be accommodated in some way that doesn't impose a hardship on your company and its other employees. For example, you could propose that he advise his coworkers that they can come to him to discuss religion during breaks, away from their workspaces. This would permit him to engage in his religious practice but would also prevent him from confronting other employees about religion if it offends them.

Religious observances are defined broadly as well, and include, for example, attending worship services, praying, wearing religious clothing or symbols, displaying religious objects, adhering to certain dietary rules, proselytizing or other forms of religious expression, or refraining from certain activities.

Under Title VII, the employer has a duty to accommodate the employee's religious practices and observances, as long as doing so doesn't create an undue hardship. An undue hardship means an accommodation that imposes more than a "de minimis," or very slight, burden on the employer. For example, an employer might be required to relax a uniform requirement if doing so wouldn't affect the employee's safety and ability to do the job.

Common Questions

Q: One of my employees recently told me that her religion requires a vegan, not just vegetarian, diet. When the company orders food for working lunches, she wants a vegan option included. Do we have to comply with this request?

A: Whether you must provide such a meal depends on two things: (1) whether her diet is practiced as part of a sincerely held religious belief, and (2) whether her request for a vegan meal is reasonable and doesn't create an undue hardship for you. If you doubt that her beliefs are sincere or that they are truly religious in nature, you are allowed to ask her for further information that substantiates the practice. For example, if she had decided to become a vegan for health or ethical reasons, rather than because of her religion, you would not be required to accommodate her request.

The more common question most employers have is whether the request accommodation is reasonable. If it's going to create an undue hardship for the company, you do not have to agree to it. But the cost of an occasional single, vegan meal probably doesn't qualify. Your best bet is to provide the meal; it will protect you legally, and the employee will appreciate it.

The EEOC advises employers to "ordinarily assume that an employee's request for religious accommodation is based on a sincerely held religious belief." But, if an employee requests a religious accommodation that you have an objective basis for questioning, either as to its religious nature or the sincerity of a particular belief or practice, you may ask the employee for additional supporting information.

Lessons From the Real World: Refusal to Accept an Accommodation Can Create an Undue Hardship

A cashier's insistence on wearing facial jewelry for religious reasons imposed an undue hardship on her employer.

Three years after being hired by Costco, Kimberly Cloutier began wearing an eyebrow ring. The next year, Costco modified its dress code to prohibit all facial jewelry. Cloutier protested, claiming that her eyebrow piercing was part of her religious belief as a member of the Church of Body Modification, which requires that members display piercings at all times.

After firing Cloutier for refusing to comply with the dress code, Costco offered to let her return if she would cover the piercing with a Band-Aid while at work, an accommodation that Cloutier herself had earlier suggested. Cloutier refused.

The court noted that the accommodation offered by Costco was reasonable, which Cloutier had essentially conceded when she offered it originally herself. The court held that Costco had a legitimate interest in its public image and that exempting Cloutier from the dress code would have imposed an undue burden on the company.

Cloutier v. Costco Wholesale Corp. 390 F.3d 126 (1st Cir. 2004).

There is an exception to Title VII for religious entities, which may limit employment "connected with carrying on its activities" to members of its own faith. However, that doesn't give religious organizations free reign to discriminate on other bases, such as sex or race.

Discrimination Based on Disability

Under the Americans with Disabilities Act (ADA), an employer cannot discriminate against a qualified employee with a disability. A qualified worker is someone who is able to perform the job in question, with or without reasonable accommodation.

Person With a Disability

Under regulations promulgated by the EEOC, which enforces the ADA, an employee has a disability if he or she has a mental or physical impairment that "substantially limits a major life activity" (such as seeing, hearing, breathing, sleeping, reading, standing, sitting, walking, thinking, or learning). A major life activity also includes major bodily functions (such as immune, neurological, digestive, respiratory, eliminatory, and circulatory functions). A major life activity is substantially limited even if the limitation can be mitigated or corrected with medicine or devices (such as diabetes is by insulin treatments).

Employees are also protected if they have a history of such an impairment, or if the employer regards the worker—even incorrectly—as having a disability. So, for example, an employee diagnosed with epilepsy has a history of that impairment, even if the employee hasn't had an epileptic seizure at work. And, an employee who is openly gay and is treated differently by an employer who wrongly assumes that he is HIV positive faces discrimination because the employer regards him as having a disability.

Common Questions

Q: I recently interviewed a candidate for the traffic reporter job at our commercial radio station. The candidate told me that he'd recently had a "very close call" while on a heli-ski trip and, as a result of his stress from this scare, he is "disabled" from flying in helicopters. Our traffic reports are made live from our chopper as it flies over the freeways at rush hour. The candidate asked very insistently that we accommodate him by letting him report traffic from the studio or by hiring him into another reporter position. We don't have any other openings and traffic can't be reported from the studio. Could he make us hire him?

A: No. Flying in a helicopter is not a major life activity, and he's only limited from performing the particular job of traffic reporter. There are very few jobs that actually require an employee to fly in a helicopter—although yours sounds like one of them—so he's not prevented from working more broadly. Thus, his condition is not a disability under the ADA. Check with your company lawyer to see if state law has a broader definition of disability than the ADA.

Reasonable Accommodation

A reasonable accommodation is a measure that would enable an employee with a disability to do the job in question. Reasonable accommodations can include things like adjusting work hours, installing access ramps, providing special furniture or other work equipment, providing voice-activated software, or providing qualified readers. A requested accommodation is unreasonable if it imposes an undue hardship on the employer, as discussed below.

Common Questions

Q: Our company has a strict policy against employees eating at their desks. An employee who was recently diagnosed with Type 2 diabetes has asked that he be allowed to snack at his desk to keep his blood sugar stable. This seems like a reasonable request, but my boss is worried about other employees demanding to be allowed to eat at their desks. Will we have a problem if we bend the rules for this one employee?

A: No. You are not bending the rules; you are following the law. As long as the employee meets the definition of a qualified employee with a disability (and it sounds like he does), this is a reasonable accommodation. Unless they require a similar accommodation, other employees are not entitled to a waiver of your company's rule. As an alternative, you may prefer to give the employee permission to leave his desk to snack in private. And you shouldn't explain the reason for the different treatment to other employees; the information is confidential medical information you aren't allowed to reveal to people who don't need to know it.

Undue Hardship

An employer does not have to provide an accommodation if doing so would create an undue hardship. An undue hardship means significant difficulty, disruption, or expense to the employer.

Whether a needed accommodation is an undue hardship depends on several factors, including the cost of the accommodation, the employer's ability to absorb the cost, the impact of the accommodation on the work site, the size of the employer, and the type of business. For example, a change that might be reasonable and inexpensive for a large employer may be completely impossible for a small employer.

Genetic Discrimination

A new provision bars discrimination on the basis of an individual's genetic information. The Genetic Information Nondiscrimination Act (GINA) takes effect on November 21, 2009, and prohibits employment discrimination based on an individual's genetic tests, genetic tests of family members, or the manifestation of a disease or disorder in an individual's family members. GINA is not limited to discrimination based on the medical condition of blood relatives; it includes adoptive children and spouses.

When and How Discrimination Occurs

Discrimination has the potential to taint any stage of employment. This section discusses some of the key points in the employment relationship where discrimination commonly occurs. Chapters 3 and 4 cover some steps you can take at each juncture to prevent it.

Hiring

Discrimination can occur at the very earliest stages of the employment relationship—even before the relationship has officially begun. Claims brought by applicants alleging that they were discriminated against in the hiring process are relatively uncommon, perhaps because applicants typically don't know who else was in the running or even who else ultimately got the job. But, if you give an applicant reason to think that a protected characteristic played a role in your decision, through job postings, interview questions, or otherwise, you could run into some problems. Here are several ways employers, sometimes unknowingly, can create legal liability for themselves in the hiring process:

- **Advertisements.** Language in job descriptions, postings, and advertisements can violate the law. Usually, employers get into trouble by using words that are really codes for certain protected classes, or by including criteria that aren't necessary for the job but that screen people out disproportionately (for example, a height requirement for a bus driver, which could screen out women or Asian or Latino men but isn't really a requirement to do the job).

Common Questions

Q: I handle hiring for a national pop music publication. We need to hire a photographer. Our CEO has instructed me to post the job on a few websites, seeking, "fresh, new, budding talent." I'm a little uneasy about this wording, but he says he just wants to be sure we draw applicants who will "fit in" with the musicians and fans they'll be photographing. Should I push for a rewording?

A: Yes. The terms "fresh" and "new" look like euphemisms for "young," and your company cannot target younger employees, even indirectly. Instead, the ad should emphasize the skills you're looking for—it doesn't matter what age the person is, if he or she has those skills. (And perhaps you can gently remind the CEO that preeminent rock photographer Annie Leibowitz is hardly a "tween.")

- **Applications.** Employers can also cause problems by asking inappropriate questions in their job applications. Applications that ask about an employee's gender, age, disability, or other protected status may seem benign to you, but they raise red flags about whether you may be making hiring decisions based on these impermissible factors. For example, it's appropriate for an application to ask for confirmation that a person is 18 years of age or older, because employees who are not adults are subject to child labor restrictions. But "How old are you?" is not appropriate, because it means you have information that could allow you to make a decision about a person based on age.

- **Screening.** Applications should be screened based on the applicants' ability to do the job. It's important not to focus on protected class information to draw conclusions about an applicant's suitability for the job—even information voluntarily supplied by the applicant, such as membership in clubs or organizations on a résumé that suggest membership in a protected class.

- **Testing.** While job-related skills' testing is permissible, testing that doesn't serve a job-related function or that is required only of certain applicants raises suspicion. For example, if a company requires only applicants with foreign-sounding surnames to submit a writing sample or requires only applicants with obvious disabilities to show how they would perform the job's requirements, that would be discriminatory.

- **Interviewing.** It's easy to inadvertently ask an improper question that delves into an interviewee's protected status such as age, ancestry, or religious beliefs—even when you're talking to a candidate you like and want to hire. Questions like, "What year did you graduate from college?" or "Where are you from?" may seem like simple conversation starters, but they bring you into dangerous territory, exploring age or national origin, neither of which is probably relevant to the job. Keep interview questions job related. For example, instead of asking, "Do you have child care?" you can simply ask, "Are you available to work Monday through Friday, from 8 to 5?" The best practice here is to avoid asking questions if you are legally prohibited from considering the applicant's answer in your decision making.

Common Questions

Q: During an interview, a colleague nonchalantly asked the candidate what her necklace symbolized. The candidate replied that it was a gift from her mother, but evaded the question, and she seemed uncomfortable. I happen to know that it is a symbol for a Hindu deity.

The candidate isn't the most qualified person for the job, and we aren't planning to offer it to her. But in light of what my colleague said here, I'm a little worried about whether this creates an appearance of discrimination. What do you think?

A: This is a good example of a well-intentioned interviewer going a bit astray. The colleague probably didn't mean to go into off-limits territory, but that's what happened.

Even though you'd have preferred he not bring up the necklace, his error doesn't mean you have to hire the candidate if she isn't the most qualified person for the job. While she's unlikely to challenge your hiring decision, if she does and you have ample evidence that she wasn't selected because she's not the best candidate, you should be in the clear. It sounds like your colleague may need more direction about what kinds of topics are appropriate for interviews, however.

CD-ROM

Listen to sample "good" and "bad" interviews on the CD included in the back of the book.

Decisions During Employment

Many employment discrimination complaints arise out of decisions that occur during the course of employment. Unlike job applicants, who know little about the company, how it operates, and how its individual managers and supervisors behave, employees who have been with the company for some time have a basis for comparison. They can more easily recognize when they're being treated differently from their coworkers, and they may have more experience and facts to suggest that an improper motive may be at work.

Discrimination during employment can occur at many stages, such as:

- **Training and mentoring.** Opportunities to advance through training and mentoring should be available to all employees, and no one should be excluded or neglected because of race, gender, disability, or another protected trait. It's easier to recognize overt opportunities, like which employees are tapped for major training programs, than informal opportunities, like which employees are invited to socialize with key clients or assist on important projects, but you need to be aware of both.

- **Job assignments.** Even assignments that employers claim are designed to protect or help employees—for example, not allowing pregnant women to do physically arduous tasks— can be discriminatory, and are particularly problematic when they're tied to promotional opportunities.

- **Benefits and pay.** Pay disparities may be obvious from the beginning, or they may develop over time. Your suspicions should be raised any time two similar employees receive different compensation or benefits—for example, two employees who perform similarly get different raises or bonuses.

- **Performance evaluations.** Performance evaluations or appraisals are a good opportunity to communicate to employees how they're doing and what they can do to improve. However, if you treat employees differently or make any statements that suggest discrimination (noting that an employee who is sporadically unavailable for staff meetings due to a disability is not a team player, for example), you could run into trouble.

RESOURCE

For more information on conducting performance appraisals,
see *The Performance Appraisal Handbook,* by Amy DelPo (Nolo).

- **Promotions.** When it comes time to promote employees, decisions should be made based on job-related experience and performance only.

Common Questions

Q: An employee recently complained that his manager always takes a subordinate out to "mentoring" lunches—the manager's business receipts support this characterization—but none of the other employees in the department get the same treatment. The employee who gets asked out to lunch is the only woman in the group. There's a promotional opportunity coming up, and the employee who came to me wants to apply for it, but he feels like his coworker has an unfair advantage. How should I handle this?

A: He may be right. The manager's one-on-one mentoring of the only female may put everyone else at a disadvantage: They may not acquire the same skills or institutional knowledge, and that could further affect their promotional opportunities. You need to find out why the female employee is getting this special attention. Absent more information, it appears that the supervisor could be singling her out because she's female. Even if the supervisor's actions have nothing to do with gender, it's not a good managerial practice to play favorites like this.

- **Imposing discipline.** When imposing discipline, make sure it's done fairly—not just within the department, but within the company. Use your company's policies to establish appropriate levels of discipline, then apply these guidelines uniformly.

RESOURCE

Need help creating or implementing a discipline plan? Go to *The Progressive Discipline Handbook: Smart Strategies for Coaching Employees*, by Margie Mader-Clark and Lisa Guerin (Nolo).

Common Questions

Q: An employee claimed that his supervisor disciplined him for tardiness, while the friend he carpools with has had no such repercussions. This employee is Caucasian, and his friend in Asian. He believes this is race based.

I looked into it further and it appears he was written up according to company policy. There's no documentation that his friend, who works in a different department and has a different supervisor, was ever late. Should I stand by the discipline?

A: Before you can make this decision, you have more work to do. If the employee was disciplined according to company policy, the supervisor was doing what he was supposed to. But if another employee in the same circumstance wasn't disciplined, you need to find out why. Because they carpool together, you can assume that they arrive at work at the same time, as long as one of them doesn't routinely make an extra stop (for example, to get a latte or make a five-minute phone call home).

As long as they both actually start work at the same time, it sounds like the other employee's supervisor either doesn't know what time he arrives or isn't following company policy. As you can see, either one puts the company at legal risk. Even if neither supervisor is making a decision based on race, inconsistent enforcement of the rules leads to poor morale, hard feelings, and, as you've seen, suspicions of discrimination.

- **Change during tenure.** The potential for discrimination may also change during an employee's tenure, for example, if an employee becomes pregnant, develops a disability, ages, or adopts new religious beliefs.

> CAUTION
>
> **Customer bias is no excuse.** It is no defense to a discrimination claim for an employer to claim that its customers or clients insisted that only employees of a certain race, gender, or religion service them, or that only younger or fully able-bodied employees do. If your company is asked to make such discriminatory decisions by a client or customer, firmly refuse.

The End of Employment

The end of an employee's tenure is the most fraught transition in employment and the one most likely to lead to lawsuits, including allegations of discrimination. Claims may arise out of:

- **Termination, layoff, reorganization, or reduction in force.** Despite your best efforts, employees who are fired or otherwise involuntarily lose their jobs may question your motives. Even if your company has acted in strict compliance with the law, it may have to justify its decision.
- **Resignation.** If an employee is forced to resign because of discriminatory treatment (for example, to escape racial slurs or abuse), that may be viewed as a "constructive discharge"— basically, that the employee was forced to quit because any reasonable person in the situation would have. And even if an employee is not forced to resign, he or she may recover damages suffered during employment as a result of illegal discrimination (such as lost pay due to denial of promotion, or compensation for emotional distress).

TIP

Conduct exit interviews of all employees who leave the company, for any reason. Ask departing employees whether they feel that they were treated fairly by the company and if not, why not. Follow up any report of unfair treatment as you would a complaint of discrimination, by investigating the claims of the employee as discussed in Chapter 5. If an employee has responded that he or she felt fairly treated, this can be a useful piece of information with which to respond to a later claim of discrimination.

- **Providing a reference.** To avoid claims that you said something discriminatory or even defamatory when called by a prospective employer for a reference, you may want to recommend that your company provide only content-neutral information like the employee's title, rate of pay, and dates of employment.

Dos and Don'ts

Do:

- Know which antidiscrimination laws apply to your company.
- Treat employees consistently, fairly, and equally, regardless of their membership in a protected class.
- Provide reasonable accommodations when the law requires you to do so.
- Conduct exit interviews and investigate any reports of unfairness.
- Give out only neutral employment data to prospective employers.

Don't:

- Set job requirements that aren't tied to the needs of the position.
- Make decisions—even well-intentioned ones—based on an employee's membership in a protected class.
- Hold different employees to different standards or provide different working conditions to similarly situated employees unless it's justified by legitimate business demands.

What Is Harassment?

Which Laws Apply to Your Company? 44

What Is Harassment? 48

    Tangible Employment Action 49

    Hostile Work Environment 51

    Avoiding Liability 55

Who Is a Harasser? 58

    Supervisor Harassment 58

    Coworker Harassment 63

    Harassment by Nonemployees 63

Who Can Be Harassed? 64

What Is Not Harassment? 65

    Consensual Relationships 65

    Conduct That Is Not Related to Work 69

Like the word "discrimination," some people use the term "harassment" loosely, often to describe anything they perceive as unfair or overly critical, from a manager's insistence that all employees arrive at 9 a.m. on the dot to a company rule that prohibits employees from using the company postage meter for personal packages. Whether or not you consider rules like these to be sensible, they don't qualify as harassment.

Illegal harassment is a form of discrimination, and it occurs only when an employee is mistreated because the employee is a member of a protected class. Although sexual harassment is probably the most widely publicized form, employees may also be harassed on the basis of other characteristics, such as race or disability.

This chapter explains what constitutes illegal harassment, so you can recognize real problems when they come up and respond appropriately to employee concerns and complaints. It covers:

- which laws apply to your company
- how to identify illegal harassment
- who can be a harasser or a victim of harassment, and
- what doesn't qualify as illegal harassment.

Which Laws Apply to Your Company?

Because harassment is a form of discrimination, the same laws that prohibit discrimination—including Title VII of the Civil Rights Act of 1964 (Title VII), the Americans with Disabilities Act (ADA), the Age Discrimination in Employment Act (ADEA), and the Genetic Information Nondiscrimination Act (GINA), which takes effect on November 21, 2009—also prohibit harassment. (For more information on each of these laws, see Chapter 1.)

Most states also have laws that prohibit employment discrimination, including harassment. Some of these statutes expressly prohibit sexual harassment, separate from discrimination, and a few explicitly prohibit harassment based on other protected characteristics, such as sexual orientation.

If your company is subject to both state and federal law (as many are), it must follow both. This can be tricky, because state and federal laws aren't always exactly alike. Here are some of the most significant ways state laws often differ from federal law:

- **Size of covered employer.** As explained in Chapter 1, federal discrimination laws apply to employers with a lot of employees —15 under Title VII and the ADEA, and 20 under the ADA. But state laws may prohibit discrimination—and especially harassment—by smaller employers. For example, in California, even the smallest employers—those with only one employee—are subject to the state's harassment laws.

- **Protected classes.** Many states extend protections against discrimination and harassment to more protected categories than federal law. For example, state laws may prohibit discrimination or harassment based on marital status, sexual orientation, or gender identity. See Appendix B to find out what characteristics your state protects.

- **Amount of recovery.** Title VII limits how much an employee can collect from the employer after winning a lawsuit. The employee is entitled to all out-of-pocket losses (such as lost wages or medical bills), but the employee's award for compensatory damages (payments for future lost wages and damages that aren't purely monetary, such as pain and suffering) and punitive damages (meant to punish the employer) is subject to a limit of $50,000 to $300,000, depending on the size of the employer. Many state laws prohibiting discrimination and harassment don't have this limitation.

- **Training requirements.** Some states require employers to provide antiharassment training, and more are considering this type of requirement. As a practical matter, for reasons explained in "Avoiding Liability," below, many employers train managers and employees in avoiding and reporting harassment, even if training isn't legally required in their state.

- **Who is a "supervisor."** Federal law and some state laws hold employers liable for harassment by supervisors, high-level managerial employees, or officers regardless of whether the employer knew about the harassment. However, the definition of supervisor differs from state to state. Some states include anyone who has the authority to transfer, suspend, promote, demote, assign duties, impose discipline, or recommend such actions to the decision maker. As a result of this difference, your company might be legally liable for an employee's actions under state law, but not under federal law.

- **Individual employee liability.** Under the laws of some states (but not federal law), individual employees who engage in harassment may be *personally* liable for that harassment. This means the employee can be sued, and the employee's personal assets will be at stake in the lawsuit.
- **Protection for nonemployees.** Many states extend protection against harassment beyond employees and applicants to, for example, temporary employees and independent contractors.

Your company must follow every law that applies to it. And, if an employee sues the company, the employee may bring claims under both state and federal law. For example, if an employee in Colorado claims she was sexually harassed, she may be able to file claims under both federal and Colorado law.

SEE AN EXPERT

If your company has employees in more than one state, get some help to figure out your obligations. As noted above, employees are entitled not only to federal protections, but also to the protection of the laws in the state and locality where they work. You should consult a local attorney with experience in discrimination and harassment to make sure you comply with all applicable requirements.

Common Questions

Q: My company employs people in several states. I think we should have one company-wide harassment policy. Is this a good idea and, if so, what is the best way to go about it?

A: Even though federal law sets out the mandatory minimum level of protection against harassment for employees anywhere in the country, state laws are often more protective. For example, your company might do business in several states, only one of which prohibits discrimination based on sexual orientation.

In this situation, you have a couple of options. Some companies voluntarily commit to protecting employees from discrimination even if they aren't legally required to do so. For example, if gay men and lesbians are a large part of your company's customer base, it may make sense to adopt a policy that prohibits sexual orientation discrimination, even in states where this isn't a protected category. This will help your company attract and retain gay employees, market itself to its customers, and generally build a positive brand. If you do adopt a policy that isn't legally required, however, remember that you'll have to follow it. A court could very well find that your commitment in a handbook is an enforceable contract, giving employees the right to sue if they face sexual orientation discrimination.

If you want to adopt a single, company-wide policy without committing your company to anything beyond what the law requires, the best way to structure it is to make clear that your company prohibits harassment based on the protected classes recognized under federal law, as well as "any other category as provided by state or federal law or local ordinance." This assures employees that you will comply with the law, but maximizes your company's flexibility and ensures you don't forget to cover any category. And make sure that the supervisors in each state know the laws that apply there.

What Is Harassment?

Harassment is unwelcome conduct that creates an intimidating, hostile, or offensive work environment. But the conduct is illegal only if it is based on an employee's protected status—that is, on one of the characteristics protected by federal or state law. That means that not all harassing behavior breaks the law. It isn't illegal harassment to berate and belittle all your employees just because you're a mean-spirited person and don't like anyone, for example.

> CAUTION
>
> **Just because conduct doesn't meet the legal definition of harassment doesn't mean it's appropriate workplace behavior.** If an employee is being rude to coworkers or a manager belittles every employee on the team, you'll want to put a stop to it. Whether or not this behavior constitutes harassment, it's unprofessional and inappropriate, and should result in discipline.

Any conduct that meets the definition above is illegal harassment. However, courts have divided harassment into two categories, for which the employer has different levels of legal responsibility:

- **Supervisor harassment that results in a "tangible employment action."** When an employee suffers a tangible employment action at the hands of a supervisor—an actual adverse effect on the job or working conditions, like a firing, demotion, or undesirable transfer—the employer will always be liable for the harasser's conduct. This is true even if your company took steps to try and prevent or correct the behavior, and even if your company didn't know about the behavior (for example, because the employee never reported it). From an employer's perspective, this is the more serious and dangerous type of harassment. You can prevent future problems by taking immediate action as soon as you learn about the problem, but you'll still be held responsible for harassment that's already taken place.

- **Hostile work environment harassment.** If an employee is subject to a hostile work environment, but doesn't suffer a tangible job action like firing or demotion, the employer's liability depends on its response to the situation. If a company can show that it took reasonable steps to try to prevent and correct the behavior, and that the employee unreasonably failed to take advantage of internal company procedures to deal with the problem, it may be able to limit or avoid legal responsibility for the employee's complaints, as explained below.

Tangible Employment Action

An employee's job should never be conditioned on submitting to inappropriate workplace behavior but, unfortunately, it happens. And when a supervisor's unwelcome harassing conduct results in a tangible employment action, the employer can be "strictly liable" for the harasser's behavior. This means that the company is legally responsible for the supervisor's act, even if it was unaware of the situation or did everything within its power to prevent harassment. The logic here is that supervisors are agents of the employer and act on its behalf, so the supervisor's actions are seen as the actions of the company.

Problems often arise when a supervisor conditions some aspect of an employee's work—such as getting hired or promoted, getting chosen for plum assignments or opportunities, or just keeping a job—on submitting to the supervisor's sexual advances. (This has traditionally been called quid pro quo harassment.) The conditions don't even have to be explicit—sometimes they're just implied. For example, if a supervisor begins making sexual advances right before an employee is due for a promotion, the employee could infer that getting the promotion is linked to putting up with the sexual advances.

A tangible employment action is an actual, adverse job effect from the harassment. It includes firing, failing to promote, or any other decision that causes a significant change in the employee's job status. Threats to an employee's continued employment can also be a tangible employment action. And job or duty changes that result in a perceived demotion or less preferable shifts or hours can constitute a tangible employment action.

Sometimes, harassment makes an employee's working conditions so intolerable that any reasonable person would resign. In that situation, an employee can claim he or she was "constructively discharged." If an employee is constructively discharged due to harassment, then the forced resignation constitutes a tangible employment action just like a traditional firing. The idea behind constructive discharge is that it's unfair to require employees to put up with intolerable working conditions.

 Common Questions

Q: I work in human resources, and I recently saw a manager at my company giving a subordinate a neck massage while he read a document over her shoulder on her computer screen. When I told him in private it wasn't appropriate, he told me that if she isn't complaining, he doesn't think I should either. When I talked to the employee about it, she said she knows the manager likes to do it, it isn't a "big deal" to her, and she doesn't want to "make waves" because she is up for a promotion at her next review. Where, if anywhere, do I go from here?

A: You started down the right path. You need to stay on it, because it looks like the employee doesn't really welcome the conduct: She tolerates it because, based on the manager's position of authority, she believes it will affect her job prospects. This perception could lead to legal troubles for your company, which can be held strictly liable for the supervisor's behavior if the employee decides to sue. And, it's just not right to tolerate a situation where an employee feels she has to let her manager touch her.

An employer will be strictly liable for harassment only if the harasser is a supervisor. After all, the threat is real only if the employee believes that the person making it actually has the ability to carry it out. For more information on who qualifies as a supervisor, see "Supervisor Harassment," below.

Hostile Work Environment

The more common type of harassment, hostile work environment harassment, doesn't depend on whether the harasser is a supervisor or whether the harassment is based on sex. A hostile work environment is created when an employee is subject to unwelcome conduct that:

- is based on the employee's protected characteristic (such as race or age)
- is so severe or pervasive that it alters the terms and conditions of the victim's employment, and
- creates a hostile or abusive environment.

Unwelcome Conduct

Conduct is unwelcome if the employee doesn't invite or want it to happen. It can take many forms beyond touching or slurs. It may include cartoons, photos or other visual depictions, comments, jokes, nicknames, symbols, pranks, insults, or gestures. Pretty much any way that people communicate can be a medium for harassment.

Conduct can be unwelcome even if an employee voluntarily submits to it or puts up with it. An employee might not complain about conduct because he or she is concerned about not making trouble for the harasser or feels unsure how to handle the situation, for example. But merely putting up with conduct isn't the same as welcoming it.

Common Questions

Q: During a break in a meeting of the IT group I manage, Anna, one of my technicians, told an off-color joke about sorority girls. All of the other techs laughed, including Gerilyn, the only other woman. One of the men then told a slightly raunchier dirty joke and, again, everyone laughed. No one objected to the joking and, after a couple of minutes of banter, we resumed our meeting. Now Gerilyn has complained to me that she felt the jokes were inappropriate and offensive. But, Anna, a woman, started the whole thing, and Gerilyn laughed right along with everyone else. Her complaint seems bogus to me.

A: You shouldn't brush this off so quickly. Anna may have started the joking, but she isn't the one complaining (if she were, she'd have a hard time claiming that the next joke was unwelcome). However, Gerilyn didn't tell a joke, and laughing along in a group setting doesn't necessarily mean that she found the joking welcome and not offensive. People go along to get along in group settings, where peer pressure can be strong. Better take Gerilyn's complaint seriously and respond to it appropriately. And the next time you're in a group of subordinates telling dirty jokes, remember that it's much easier to put a stop to it at the time than to wonder whether anyone was really offended by it later.

Protected Status

Harassment is illegal only if it is based on the employee's protected status. Many hostile work environment claims are sex based, but that is not the only type of illegal harassment. Harassment may also be based on characteristics such as race, national origin, age, or disability.

Hostile conduct doesn't always explicitly refer to the employee's protected status. That means it isn't necessary for someone to make a direct connection between the conduct and the employee's gender or race, for example, for the conduct to be harassing. Stereotyping, visual images, or inappropriate jokes are just a few examples of behavior that can be based on a protected status, without specifically referring to a particular employee. For example, coworkers who tell racist jokes and post racist cartoons may create a hostile work environment for nonwhite employees, even if none of those employees are the target of the misconduct.

Also, conduct targeting employees in a protected category can still be harassment, even if the harasser "means well." For example, repeated comments to a female employee about her appearance, intended to be complimentary, can be harassing.

 Common Questions

Q: A female sales manager is much harder on female than male subordinates, often yelling at and berating them. She says she does this because women have a harder time in this business and need to be tougher to succeed. She had a strong female mentor and wants to give her female mentees the same "gift." I see her point, but I'm wondering if I still shouldn't step in.

A: You should step in. Her "gift" is going to keep on giving—in this case, giving her female reports ample fodder for a harassment lawsuit. Even though her motives may be understandable, it looks like she is singling women out for particularly negative and potentially harassing treatment, based on gender. She must treat men and women equally.

Keep in mind that coworkers who share the victim's protected status may also engage in hostile environment harassment. It doesn't matter whether harassers are in the same protected status as their targets. For example, women can harass women and African Americans can harass African Americans.

> **CAUTION**
>
> **Retaliation is illegal, too.** When an employee is retaliated against for making a complaint of harassment, that's also illegal. It doesn't matter if the conduct underlying the complaint is in fact illegal or if the employee is a member of a protected class, as long as the employee made the complaint in good faith. For more information on retaliation, see Chapter 7.

Severe or Pervasive

Not all "bad" behavior is illegal harassment, even if it is unwelcome and based on an employee's protected status. After all, most employers would be put out of business if they were held legally responsible each time an employee made an inappropriate joke or said something insensitive.

Instead, to be illegal, the conduct must be so severe or pervasive that it "alters the terms and conditions" of the victim's employment. What does that mean? A severe act is one that is extreme, such as a physical assault or the use of a particularly offensive term. One such act, on its own, can be serious enough to be harassment. Pervasive means multiple, continuous offensive acts. For example, if an employee is teased or taunted daily by her coworkers, that's pervasive. Generally, the more severe the behavior, the less pervasive it must be to meet the definition of harassment, and vice versa.

But whether conduct actually alters an employee's working conditions can be anyone's guess. After all, one person might think a teasing comment is no big deal; another might find it so distressing that she can't concentrate on her work. To account for these differing perspectives, the law requires the conduct be both objectively and subjectively severe or pervasive. Objective means that a reasonable person, in the victim's same position, considering all of the circumstances, would find that the conduct created a hostile work environment. Subjective means that this particular victim really did feel harassed.

Common Questions

Q: A female employee, Kerry, told me that Sterling, a coworker, had started hanging around her desk and asking her out. She declined and he backed off, but a few days ago, he put a love letter on her car. The letter expressed his feelings, but there was nothing sexual in it. From my point of view, Sterling seems pathetic and harmless, but Kerry is very upset. She told me she'd been attacked getting out of her car several years ago, and finding the note on the windshield reminded her of the assault. Though she feels Sterling's behavior is threatening, it seems to me that she's overly sensitive. Am I wrong?

A: Even though you don't think the situation is threatening, Kerry feels it is. You should consider her position as a female victim of an assault that occurred in similar circumstances. Is it reasonable for a woman in that position to be upset when she receives an unsolicited love letter on her car, after making it clear she wasn't interested romantically? From this position, Sterling's behavior could be seen as harassing. At any rate, this behavior is clearly bothering Kerry and it's not appropriate. She asked him to stop and he needs to do so.

Avoiding Liability

As explained above, an employer is legally responsible for a supervisor's harassment that results in a tangible employment action. A company is an entity, not a person; it can act only through the people who represent it. A supervisor's actions toward employees are considered to be the actions of the company, from a legal perspective.

In hostile work environment cases, however, your company isn't automatically liable. Even if an employee is subjected to illegal harassment, your company can avoid liability if:

- your company exercised reasonable care to prevent and correct the harassment, and
- the complaining employee unreasonably failed to take advantage of your company's antiharassment policies and procedures.

The purpose of this rule is to give the company a chance to correct the situation. An employer that doesn't take action, despite having an opportunity to do so, will be held legally responsible for harassment; an employer that never learns of the harassment may not be liable.

In hostile work environment cases, a company can avoid liability by showing that it tried to prevent or correct harassing behavior and the employee didn't take advantage of the company's antiharassment measures. In this situation, the company may have an "affirmative defense" to the employee's harassment claim: Even if the employee really was harassed and really suffered harm as a result, the company will not be held liable for it.

An employer may raise this defense, sometimes referred to as the *Ellerth/Faragher* standard after the two Supreme Court cases that first established it, only if all the following are true:

- The company had an effective policy banning harassment at the time the alleged harassment occurred. This means not only that the company had a policy, but that the company followed the policy. A company that routinely allows dirty jokes and lewd behavior at company events, for example, won't get any protection from its written policy.
- The policy included an effective procedure for employees to follow to report harassment. An effective procedure is one that results in appropriate action by the company, including an investigation; if the employee can show that the company didn't follow its own policy—for example, that complaints weren't taken seriously or that employees who complained of

harassment were subject to retaliation—the defense won't be available.

- The company thoroughly investigated the employee's complaint (if the employee made one).
- The company promptly remedied any harassment found (for example, by imposing discipline on the harasser).

 Common Questions

Q: My company has a written harassment policy that includes a procedure for reporting harassment to any managerial-level employee. One of our employees has filed a complaint of racial harassment with the EEOC, even though he never reported any harassment to me or any other supervisor or manager. The employee claims that he didn't read the policy and so didn't know about the complaint procedure. He also says he was too intimidated to report to his supervisor in any event. Are we in the clear on this?

A: It sounds like you have a good chance of mounting a successful defense. Did you have the employee sign an acknowledgment form when he received the policy? If so, it shows he knew or should have known about the policy and had the opportunity to follow it. And if the policy allowed him to report the problem to any supervisor or manager, his discomfort talking to his own supervisor doesn't explain his failure to complain to others.

Of course, your duty doesn't end there. Now that you know about the complaint, you should promptly investigate. You'll want to make sure the employee's reluctance to report the matter isn't a company-wide concern. That is, confirm that he didn't have a legitimate reason for not talking to *any* manager, not just his own. And then you'll need to figure out whether there's any basis for his claim.

This defense is one reason why it's so important to have an antiharassment policy (see Chapter 3), training program (see Chapter 4), and investigative procedure (see Chapter 5): These measures reflect your company's commitment to preventing and correcting harassment. Once your company has these protections in place, an employee has a responsibility under the *Ellerth/ Faragher* standard to use the procedures you've established to report harassment.

Your company will learn about possible problems more quickly if it has a good policy that encourages employees to report potential violations. This, in turn, gives your company the opportunity to deal with anticipated problems before they get out of hand. This not only protects your company's interests, but also promotes company employees' interest in a comfortable, harassment-free working environment.

Who Is a Harasser?

The law recognizes that companies can act only through their employees, contractors, and others they hire, and employers pay the price when these representatives commit harassment. As explained above, however, the extent of the employer's financial and legal responsibility depends on who's doing the harassing.

Supervisor Harassment

As explained above, when a supervisor takes some tangible action that affects an employee's job, the company is liable for the harassment even if it didn't know about it or tried to prevent or correct it. But the term supervisor is interpreted fairly broadly. For example, you may think a supervisor has to have a certain job title, level of responsibility, or pay. But a supervisor can include any manager, officer, or other employee or agent in a superior position to the employee, or anyone else who reasonably appears to be in a position to grant or deny, or influence the granting or denial of, job benefits to the employee. That includes anyone with the authority to hire, fire, set work schedules, or set pay rates. Some courts also include any employee who assigns work, supervises shifts, or directs employees. And, many states have defined the title supervisor even more broadly, to include, among other things, anyone with the authority to transfer, suspend, assign work to, discipline, or reward employees.

Even if the harasser doesn't actually have the authority of a supervisor, the company can still be held liable if it reasonably appears to the employee that the harasser has supervisory authority. For example, an employee may honestly believe that a coworker who's assigned to head a project can carry out a threat to have her removed from the team if she doesn't comply with his advances. Even if the coworker couldn't actually kick her off the project, he will qualify as a supervisor if the employee reasonably believes otherwise.

TIP
Review your company's organizational chart to confirm that authority matches job titles. For example, if an employee has the title "vice president" but doesn't really have the authority of an officer, your company may want to change the title to more accurately reflect the employee's authority and prevent confusion among fellow employees.

Lessons From the Real World

An employee's reasonable belief that she had to submit to her boss's advances supported her sexual harassment claim.

Holly D., a financially strapped single mother, worked as a Senior administrative secretary for Professor Stephen Wiggins at the California Institute of Technology. Holly alleged that Professor Wiggins made sexually provocative comments to her, stared at her breasts and buttocks, and displayed pornographic web sites to her. She asked him to stop and rebuffed his advances. Shortly thereafter, he gave her a negative performance evaluation.

Holly believed her job could be on the line if she did not submit to Professor Wiggins's advances. As a result, she alleged, she began a sexual relationship with him. Then, she sued the school and Professor Wiggins.

The trial court found for the school and the professor, but the appellate court reversed the ruling and gave Holly another chance to argue her claims. Holly could go forward with her harassment claim if she could show that a reasonable woman in her position would have "believed that her job depended on fulfilling Wiggins's demands."

Holly D. v. California Inst. of Technology, 339 F.3d 1158 (9th Cir. 2003).

A supervisor's empty threats don't constitute a tangible employment action. If a supervisor says he's going to fire an employee if she doesn't submit to his advances, but then doesn't fire her after she turns him down, the employer won't be held strictly liable. However, the supervisor may still have created a hostile work environment, as discussed above, and the company could be liable on that basis. And, if the employee submits to the conduct because she believes the threat and later alleges harassment, the employer will be on the hook even if the supervisor didn't actually intend to fire her.

Common Questions

Q: Our company hired a prominent local lawyer, Jerry Johnson, to work on a complicated merger agreement. Though he insisted on the title "vice president," he doesn't oversee any employees. A female employee in accounting was overheard telling a coworker that Vice President Johnson invited her to dinner a couple of times. She replied, "if he wasn't the VP, I'd have told him I'm not interested." I think this might be a problem, but I'm not sure how serious.

A: This could be very serious. Because Jerry Johnson is being held out as an officer of the company, regardless of his actual authority, an employee could reasonably infer from his title that he is in a supervisory position. If the female employee complained, a court could find the company strictly liable if the female employee submitted to his requests because she felt her job depended on it—that is, that she acted under the threat of a tangible employment action. You need to know more about what her comment meant. If she's really not interested, but feels compelled to accept because of his position of power in the company, that's a potential harassment problem.

Finally, supervisors are different from other employees in another important way: In some states, they can be found personally liable for harassing behavior. That means employees can sue them individually, in addition to suing the company, for their behavior.

Why Supervisors Get Sued

You might be wondering why an employee would ever sue an individual supervisor; after all, unless the supervisor chose to continue working after winning the lottery, the company is likely to have much more money ("deeper pockets," as lawyers say). There are two primary reasons why a supervisor might be dragged into court.

The first is emotional. Typically, the supervisor is the person who actually mistreated the employee, and the employee feels that the supervisor should be held responsible. Employees may want the supervisor to pay, whether in time, money, or stress. Some employees simply want to make sure that the supervisor understands exactly how much damage his or her actions caused, and requiring the supervisor to sit in the courtroom day after day certainly accomplishes this goal.

The second reason has to do with our federal system of government. An employee can sue under state law, federal law, or both, whether the employee brings the lawsuit in state or federal court. But in some states, the state judges—and juries—are perceived as more liberal than those in the federal system. So, employees who have a choice often sue in state court.

Employers can have these cases transferred to federal court, but only if the federal court has jurisdiction over the case. Federal courts don't have the authority to hear every type of case. In discrimination and harassment cases that include state law claims, a federal court can hear the case only if all of the named parties to the lawsuit are from different states (this is called diversity jurisdiction). If any two parties are from the same state, there's no diversity and the federal court can't take the case.

Back to our supervisor: The employee suing and the supervisor are almost always residents of the same state. So, by suing the supervisor, the employee avoids getting hauled into federal court, even if the company's headquarters or official offices are in another state (as is often the case for corporations, many of which incorporate in Delaware, regardless of where they do business). For more information on lawsuits against supervisors, see "If You Are Sued Personally," in Chapter 9.

Coworker Harassment

The law views hostile work environment harassment by the victim's peers or coworkers differently than it does tangible employment action harassment by a supervisor. In general, the best way for an employer to avoid liability for coworker harassment is to take all reasonable steps to prevent it and stop it as soon as the employer knows about it, whether through an employee complaint or otherwise. But don't just close your eyes and assume everything will be okay. Ignorance of harassment is no defense if an employer should have known about it because it was readily apparent in the workplace.

An employer should have known of harassment if it is aware of prior harassment by the same harasser, evidence of harassment is readily apparent (such as where there are pictures, graffiti, or other readily observable conduct at the job site), or supervisors or others with authority have seen sufficient evidence of harassment to trigger a duty to investigate. For example, if a supervisor overhears an inappropriate workplace remark and observed that an employee seemed upset by it, the company has a duty to investigate the situation, even if the employee doesn't make a formal complaint.

Harassment by Nonemployees

Even people who don't work for your company can create a hostile working environment for your company's employees. Your company has the same responsibility to protect employees from harassment, whether it's committed by employees or outsiders. If you have a client who makes inappropriate comments to female staff members, for example, you will have to put a stop to the behavior. Unfortunately, sometimes the only way to do this is to end the working relationship, because you do not have the same control over outsiders as you have over employees.

Who Can Be Harassed?

Just as many different people within your company can be harassers, many different people can be harassed, too. Behavior doesn't even have to be directed at a particular employee for it to be harassing: Any conduct that affects an employee's working environment could potentially be harassment. For example, if an employee personally witnesses offensive conduct aimed at another employee or group of employees, the witnessing employee may still suffer from a hostile environment. This is true even if the witnessing employee isn't a member of the protected class on which the harassment is based.

 Common Questions

Q: A lesbian employee recently reported to her supervisor that she witnessed a male coworker coming on to another female employee and using very lewd, inappropriate language. She said that the female employee didn't seem offended, but as a witness to the behavior, she was offended by it. Do we have to treat this as a harassment complaint?

A: You do, because the employee was offended by gender-based conduct. It's irrelevant that the employee was neither the target of the conduct nor heterosexual. Because she observed the inappropriate conduct, it can still create a hostile work environment.

What's more, you don't know for certain that the employee to whom the comments were made really didn't find them offensive. Although the employee who complained didn't think the target was offended, you should talk to the other employee to make sure. And, even if the other employee thought the conversation was harmless, you'll probably want to caution the lewd Lothario that he needs to observe professional standards of conduct at work.

Check Out Receipt

Beverly

Saturday, October 24, 2020 10:18:56 AM

Item: R0335726896
Title: RBG
Due: 10/31/2020

Item: R0424760480
Title: The essential guide to handling wor
kplace harassment & discrimination
Due: 11/14/2020

Item: R0424788331
Title: Your rights in the workplace
Due: 11/14/2020

Total items: 3

Thank You!

946

What Is Not Harassment?

It would be nice if all the complicated situations that lead to harassment claims could be completely banned from the workplace—but it's hard to do in practice. Let's face it—you don't want to create an oppressive work environment where people are afraid to have friendly conversations. And not everyone has the same idea of what's offensive.

Consensual Relationships

Get ready because you *will* encounter consensual relationships between coworkers in your company. The numbers speak for themselves: According to a survey by vault.com, 47% of professionals report that they have dated at least one coworker and, according to a survey by the American Management Association, 30% of all managers and executive-level employees report that they have dated at least one coworker.

A truly consensual relationship between employees who are not in a reporting relationship (for example, peers who are not in each other's chain of supervision) needn't concern you, as long as there are no workplace repercussions. But it's often not so tidy. Sometimes, dating employees bring their romance into the workplace with comments, gestures, or the like, which can affect employees who observe the behavior. Relationships that end badly may have repercussions at work, as well.

Some employers adopt antifraternization policies prohibiting all relationships between coworkers at any level. Barring coworker dating may seem like the easiest approach. But you must ask yourself this: If you have such a policy, how will you enforce it? In all likelihood, such prohibitions will just lead to secret relationships, reducing your ability to control how employees in those relationships behave. And employees may reasonably feel that such a prohibition infringes on their privacy.

In most cases, your best approach to coworker dating is not to prohibit it, but to make sure employees know that they still have to conduct themselves professionally at work. That means they understand appropriate workplace behavior—for example, that public displays of affection aren't acceptable, or that the company's email system is only to be used for work-related purposes. It's prudent to include a general requirement of professional workplace conduct in your company's personnel policies, with examples of violations (such as rude or disparaging comments, unprofessional conduct, public displays of affection, and so on).

 Common Questions

Q: Tony and Kamela work in different departments and report to different supervisors. They are dating and often spend breaks together, in one or the other's cubicle. Employees in neighboring cubicles have reported to me that they often overhear Tony and Kamela talking about their sex life. And others have told me that they've seen the two kiss at work. I've spoken to Tony and Kamela, who both assured me that their relationship is totally consensual. Am I out of the woods here?

A: No, because others are being affected by their conduct. You need to talk to Tony and Kamela and tell them in no uncertain terms that they need to cool the public displays of affection and discussions about their sex life in the office. Even if their conduct hasn't yet risen to the level of illegal sexual harassment, it is unprofessional and inappropriate in a place of business.

When Relationships End

Even the best relationships can turn sour when they end. Sometimes the blowback from a failed consensual relationship between coworkers creates an uncomfortable environment for one of the employees in the relationship, or for their coworkers if the animosity of the former couple spills over into their jobs.

One of the most difficult aspects of a failed relationship is the possibility that one person in the relationship will complain that the other has harassed or is harassing him or her. An employee may deny that the relationship was consensual or complain about being contacted by the former partner. Although these may seem like personal matters for the former couple to resolve, that's not all they are: The hard feelings that may be left behind after a workplace romance ends can lead to harassment claims if either partner is unwilling to let things go. This means you have to step in if one employee complains or if you notice personal behavior that's unprofessional (or worse).

Common Questions

Q: I just learned that two coworkers used to be romantically involved. Apparently, the relationship ended, but one of them had hard feelings. He has started to publically snub her at work, for example, by talking over her at meetings. She's complained about it. Is it harassment?

A: He may be creating a hostile environment by showing hostility toward her at work and by interfering with her ability to participate at work meetings. But, even if he isn't, he's creating a distraction and probably not just for the complaining employee. At the very least, you'll have to talk to him and tell him to behave professionally and leave the personal stuff at home. And if further investigation leads you to conclude the behavior is harassing, you'll have to follow your company's policy for handling it.

Relationships With Subordinates: Proceed With Caution

When a supervisor dates a subordinate, it creates a particularly delicate situation for an employer. The supervisor is in a position to affect tangible aspects of the subordinate's employment, and that leaves the door open for serious employer liability. And, of course, even if the supervisor doesn't misuse the position of authority, the relationship can create a sense or appearance of impropriety to other employees.

While it's hard to control or prevent coworkers from dating each other, it's much easier—and makes more sense—to prohibit supervisors from dating their subordinates. Courts around the country have upheld such policies in recognition of an employer's legitimate interest in preventing harassment. And your supervisory employees should understand that their position of authority comes with the responsibility to avoid even the appearance of impropriety. Given that they can be held personally liable for harassment in many states, they should be motivated to keep working relationships professional.

If you don't have such a policy and don't want to implement one, we nonetheless recommend that you act immediately when a supervisor and subordinate begin dating. The best approach is to remove the supervisor's authority over the employee, for example, by reassigning the employee to a different supervisor.

Relationships between supervisors and employees don't just affect the two parties involved—they also have an impact on others in the workplace. Even that can lead to legal trouble for the employer. Under some state laws, coworkers of an employee who is intimately involved with a supervisor can claim harassment based on the supervisor's favoritism toward his or her paramour. This happens when a coworker doesn't receive the same job benefits as the supervisor's boyfriend or girlfriend and claims it's based on sex. This is a form of harassment because it may appear to other employees that they have to be intimately involved with a supervisor to get ahead at your company. The EEOC has said that employers can also be held liable for discriminating against the coworkers in these circumstances.

Conduct That Is Not Related to Work

Conduct that occurs off the job and has no connection to work or the workplace won't subject the employer to legal liability. However, if there is any connection at all between an off-work event or location and the employment, the employer may be liable for harassment that occurs there.

Common Questions

Q: A group of account reps and their bosses went out to dinner to celebrate landing a major account. Apparently, a company VP and several employees left together and had an "after party" at a nearby dance club. Now one of the female employees says the VP fondled her during the dancing and grabbed her in a hallway and kissed her. She wants to file a formal sexual harassment complaint under the company policy. We didn't organize or sanction the after party; we didn't even know the team members had gone out until this complaint. Are we responsible?

A: Though it may seem unfair, you might be. Because the incident had some connection to the team's work, you will have to accept the complaint, investigate it, and treat it as you would any claim of employment harassment. Your company can argue that it should have no liability if the complaint goes to court, because it wasn't a company-sanctioned or associated event, but this is not a clear-cut case. The wise course is to investigate and respond promptly. Besides, if the VP did what the employee says he did, he needs to be reminded of the risks he creates for the company and himself.

Even where the alleged conduct doesn't occur at a company function, it may amount to harassment if the off-site encounter between the alleged harasser and the victim is work-related, such as a social get-together on a business trip. The same is true if off-duty conduct spills into the workplace—for example, if an employee brings to work an inappropriate and offensive photograph taken of a coworker in a social situation or posts the photo on his MySpace page and tells all of his coworkers to check it out.

 Lessons From the Real World

An employee's sexual assault by a coworker in a hotel room occurred in a "work environment."

Penny Ferris and Michael Young, both flight attendants for Delta Air Lines, worked a flight from New York to Rome and stayed overnight in a hotel there. While there, they shopped together, and later in the evening, Young invited Ferris to sample a bottle of the vintage wine that he had purchased. Ferris agreed. After one sip of wine in Young's room, Ferris felt dizzy and lost consciousness. She partially awoke to find Young sexually assaulting her; she told him to stop but then blacked out again.

When Ferris sued Delta for harassment, the company argued that the court should dismiss the case because the assault did not occur at work, on duty, or during work hours. However, the court disagreed and found that the assault had occurred in a "work environment."

Ferris v. Delta Air Lines, Inc., 277 F.3d 128 (2nd Cir. 2001).

Dos and Don'ts

Do:

- Know the protected classes in every state in which your company operates.
- Understand the difference between tangible employment action harassment and hostile work environment harassment.
- Consider whether conduct is harassing from the perspective of a reasonable person in the victim's position.
- Determine which employees are supervisors, as that term is defined under harassment law.
- Establish a policy to deal with consensual workplace relationships.

Don't:

- Assume that conduct is welcome just because an employee submits to or puts up with it.
- Hesitate to correct harassing behavior as soon as you know about it.
- Try to police employees' private lives; just be ready to step in if their personal relationships start to adversely affect the workplace.
- Automatically assume relationships (especially between superior and subordinate employees) are consensual.
- Take for granted that the company won't be liable for harassing behavior that happens off company premises.

Policies Prohibiting Harassment and Discrimination

Benefits of an Effective Policy..74

Elements of an Effective Policy.. 77

Complaint and Investigation Procedures...82

    The Complaint Process...83

    Investigation Procedures 86

Communicate the Policy to Employees...89

    Use Acknowledgment Forms...89

    Reinforce the Policy in Other Ways 90

    Lead by Example..91

Review the Policy Regularly..92

People sometimes do the wrong thing because they don't know that it's wrong—or because they believe they can get away with it. Wise employers make clear to employees that certain types of conduct cross the line and won't be tolerated. One of the most effective steps your company can take to prevent harassment and discrimination is to develop a good policy explaining what constitutes inappropriate behavior, how employees can report problems, and how the company will respond.

This chapter explains the benefits of a good policy. You'll learn what an effective policy should look like, with examples, so you can make sure your company's policy will be a powerful tool in preventing harassment and discrimination. And, because a policy works only if employees know about it, this chapter also explains how you can ensure that employees receive the policy and read it.

Benefits of an Effective Policy

Even the smallest companies should have a policy prohibiting harassment and discrimination, for a number of reasons. An effective policy helps employees understand appropriate behavior, gives them an avenue for raising concerns and complaints, and shows that the company takes those complaints seriously.

FORM

Don't have a policy? If your company doesn't have one, don't worry—you can use the information in this chapter, and the sample policy in Appendix C and on the CD-ROM, to develop one of your own. If you already have a policy, don't skip this chapter: Read on to make sure your policy gives your company all the legal protection possible.

A good policy ensures that employees are treated consistently and fairly, because it provides clear standards of conduct that everyone has to follow, as well as procedures for handling complaints and conducting investigations. Your policy should also tell managers how to handle complaints and incidents, so they don't waste time trying to figure out next steps or deducing what others in the company have done in the same situation. And, once all of your managers and employees understand what harassment and discrimination are, they are more likely both to keep an eye on their own behavior and to notice and report problems, which will go a long way toward helping your company maintain a positive working environment for everyone.

Another benefit of an effective policy is that it may provide your company with a valuable defense to lawsuits. As explained in Chapter 2, the company can defend itself in a hostile work environment lawsuit if it can show that it took reasonable care to prevent and promptly correct harassment. And one of the things a court will look at when determining whether your company took reasonable care is whether it had an effective policy in place at the time the alleged harassment took place.

Common Questions

Q: An employee called in today saying she is quitting because a coworker is sexually harassing her by making "daily comments" about her body. This employee never reported the harassment to her supervisor or to me, the HR manager, as our policy says she should. Now that the employee is leaving, do I need to worry about her bringing a lawsuit for this?

A: She might consider a lawsuit, but it sounds like your company should be on solid ground. If your policy was clear and given to the employee, she had an opportunity to report the harassment to you before it got so bad that she felt she had to quit. She had more than one avenue for making the complaint and did not use them. Even if the employee files a complaint with a government agency, you should have a legitimate defense.

Now that you know about the complaint, however, you should investigate. If her coworker really did harass her, you want to make sure he doesn't do it to someone else. And you want to apply your antiharassment policy consistently, which means you should discipline him according to company policy, even if the complaining employee no longer works for you.

While we're on that topic, if you conclude that the employee really was harassed and quit for that reason, you might want to ask her to reconsider, after assuring her that you have investigated her complaint and taken appropriate action against the wrongdoer. After all, even though she didn't follow the proper reporting procedures, reinstating her could be an appropriate way to remedy the harm done by the harassment—and to give her an opportunity to get past this misconduct and back on track.

In a discrimination lawsuit, an effective policy can show that the company made a good-faith effort to prevent discriminatory behavior from occurring. Under federal law, that good-faith effort means the company won't be held responsible for punitive damages—damages intended to punish the employer for bad behavior—even if it is found to be legally responsible for the discrimination. This is sometimes referred to as the *Kolstad* defense, after the U.S. Supreme Court case that first recognized it.

Elements of an Effective Policy

The exact language of your policy will depend on your company's culture and industry, but all good policies have a few elements in common. An effective policy should do all of the following:

- **Establish that the company is committed to preventing harassment and discrimination.** The fact that you have a policy shows this commitment, but you should also come right out and say it explicitly. A primary policy goal is to inform employees of the company's sincere intent to keep inappropriate behavior from occurring in the first place. So, start with a firm, clear statement that the company doesn't discriminate, and won't tolerate any harassment or discrimination (this is sometimes referred to as a zero tolerance policy).

Sample: Company Commitment

The Company is committed to providing a workplace free of discrimination and harassment for all employees and employment applicants. The Company has a policy of zero tolerance of discrimination and harassment, which means that we will not tolerate workplace discrimination or harassment of our employees by any coworker, company officer, manager, supervisor, or other person.

- **Explain who the policy covers.** Your company's policy should list all applicable protected categories—that is, the characteristics, such as race and gender, that may not legally be the bases for employment decisions. In addition to the categories protected by federal law, be sure to include categories protected under applicable state and local laws, such as marital status or receipt of government benefits. Rather than listing them all, you can add the statement "or any other category protected by federal, state, or local law." This statement maximizes flexibility—for example, if your state passes a law to protect a new category of people, or if your company operates in more than one state, your policy will still be valid and effective.

- **Inform employees of prohibited conduct.** In addition to saying that harassment and discrimination are illegal and won't be tolerated, your policy should give actual examples of prohibited behavior, such as slurs, insults, commentary, cartoons, pictorials, or symbols that denigrate any protected status or anyone in a protected category. This will help employees understand more fully the types of conduct you're trying to eliminate. The policy should make clear that these are just examples, however—you can't reasonably have a list that incorporates every potentially harassing or discriminatory behavior.

Sample: Prohibited Conduct

All discriminatory or harassing acts, behavior, and conduct are prohibited, including, but not limited to, comments, jokes, gestures, unwelcome physical contact, drawings, cartoons, videos, emails, name-calling, slurs, or use of derogatory terms. Prohibited sexual harassment includes all of these prohibited actions as well as other unwelcome sex-based conduct, such as unwanted sexual advances, requests for sexual favors, or sexually suggestive gestures, jokes, and propositions. These lists are intended as illustrations only. Conduct not listed may be considered discriminatory or harassing if it otherwise meets the definition above.

- **List the types of employment decisions that cannot be based on any protected status,** such as hiring, firing, layoffs, discipline, and granting or denying raises, promotions, leaves, work assignments, or transfers. Also make clear the list is not exhaustive and that discrimination in any aspect of employment will not be tolerated.

- **Set the company standard for how employees are to be treated.** A good policy clearly states that employees can expect a workplace free of harassment and discrimination, and that the employer will work to make sure this happens. It's also a good idea to include a general statement about standards of conduct, specifying that all employees are expected to act professionally and treat each other with respect at all times.

- **Advise employees of the repercussions of failing to meet the standard of behavior.** The policy should make clear that prohibited conduct will not be tolerated and can result in disciplinary action, up to and including termination. Reiterate that employees may also face discipline, possibly including termination, for failing to act professionally and respectfully, even if their conduct didn't amount to harassment or discrimination.

- **Include the company's employee complaint procedure.** As covered in more detail below, the policy should explain how employees may report violations, including a statement identifying for employees the managerial employees to whom they may report prohibited conduct, including the human resource manager, if any, and any other managers whom your company deems appropriate. Be sure to give employees more than one person to bring complaints to, in case that person is the one accused of misconduct. The policy should also make clear that the procedures will be applied consistently to all employees.

- **Describe the investigation process.** Give a general outline of the steps that the company will follow in response to reports of violations; this is covered below.

- **Assure confidentiality to the extent possible.** Inform employees that the company will disclose any complaints only to those who have a need to know and will otherwise keep the complaint and related information confidential. Caution, however, that complete confidentiality can't be guaranteed.
- **Make clear that retaliation is prohibited.** In a direct, firm statement, inform managers and employees that those who report possible violations will not be subject to retaliation, and that retaliatory conduct of any kind will not be tolerated.

Sample: Retaliation

The Company will not engage in or tolerate retaliation against any employee who makes a good-faith complaint or participates in an investigation, regardless of the outcome of the investigation. If any employee believes that he or she is being subjected to any kind of negative treatment because of making a complaint, assisting in a discrimination or harassment investigation, or filing an administrative charge or lawsuit alleging discrimination or harassment, the employee should report the conduct immediately to his or her immediate supervisor, or the Human Resources Director, any department head, or any Company officer.

Common Questions

Q: Our small start-up has grown to a staff of 30. The founders are very progressive and promote diversity and tolerance. We've never had an employee complaint and we have an open-door policy so employees can freely take concerns to their supervisors. Do we *still* need a written antiharassment and antidiscrimination policy?

A: Yes. A written policy ensures that all employees are held to the same standard of behavior, know what is expected of them, and know that they can expect the company's support if they feel harassed or discriminated against. Your current method of dealing with potential problems doesn't provide any standards: No one, including your supervisors, will know exactly what the company expects them to do if there is a complaint. This can lead to inconsistent (and therefore confusing) responses to complaints.

Just because you haven't heard a complaint doesn't mean there isn't one lurking. Employees may not even know how to make a complaint if they believe they may have experienced harassment or discrimination. Because you don't have a policy, employees may be unsure what to do in the face of a problem. Without clear guidance, they may opt to go straight to the state's fair employment agency without trying to resolve the problem internally. While normally employees can be expected to go through company procedure first, this isn't the case if there is no stated procedure.

Finally, it really doesn't matter that you think the company's founders support diversity and tolerance or that there have never been any reported problems. Neither of these facts will protect your company if it is sued. And, even if you're right, that doesn't mean that there won't be problems in the future, as new employees come on board and the founders move on to other endeavors.

Complaint and Investigation Procedures

Many companies have a policy stating simply that harassment and discrimination are prohibited, and nothing more. To make your policy effective, however, the company must enforce it by promptly responding to and investigating complaints. That's why your policy must describe the complaint process, explaining how employees may report possible violations, what the company will do in response to a complaint, and how the company will investigate.

Complaint and investigation procedures are the key to your company's "on the ground" response to harassment and discrimination. After all, you can't resolve problems until you know about them, through employee complaints or reports from managers who witness potentially inappropriate behavior. Your complaint procedure will encourage employees to come forward as soon as possible and tell managers exactly what to do if they receive a complaint or learn about misconduct.

You can't just take action on the basis of a complaint, however: You need to know all the facts before you can decide what to do. This is the purpose of the investigation procedures. It gives employees a general idea of what to expect when they make a complaint, and makes clear that your company intends to get to the bottom of every complaint.

Of course, once you put these procedures in your policy, you must follow them. If you don't, you may lose the opportunity to find out about problems early on, because employees will come to believe that you don't take complaints seriously. You'll also lose the opportunity to defend your company by claiming that an employee who files a lawsuit should have taken advantage of your internal complaint procedures. If you don't enforce your policy, a court will likely find that the employee's failure to use it was justified.

The Complaint Process

The complaint portion of your policy should describe:

- **Where to report violations.** As already explained, an effective policy absolutely must tell employees how and to whom they should report violations. Choose more than one person to receive complaints, so employees will have somewhere to go if they have a complaint about one of the designated complaint takers or they just aren't comfortable talking to him or her. Never require employees to report violations to their own supervisor or manager. In harassment and discrimination cases, the employee's direct supervisor is often the very person accused of wrongdoing. A good approach is to identify several individuals to whom employees can report possible violations to, including the human resources manager or department (if you have one).

Sample: Complaints and Reporting

Any employee who experiences or observes any incident that he or she believes may constitute discrimination or harassment should immediately report the incident to his or her direct supervisor, the Human Resources Director, any department head, or any Company officer.

Managers or supervisors who observe, learn of, or receive complaints of possible discrimination or harassment must promptly inform the Director of Human Resources.

Common Questions

Q: I'm the VP of my company, and I'm responsible for handling all of the HR issues. The only person above me in company hierarchy is the president. I'm drafting our complaint procedures and I need to decide where employees should go if they don't feel they can complain to me. The president told me she does not have time to deal with personnel issues (that's why she hired me, as she puts it). Who else can handle a complaint?

A: As you rightly note, the complaint procedure must give employees an option to report violations to someone else if they don't feel comfortable reporting to you. Even if the president isn't available to take complaints directly, any other company executive who reports directly to the president can take on this task. This prevents any appearance of impropriety, because you won't be in the chain of command.

However, the president needs to understand that she may eventually need to be involved in handling complaints, against you or others, in order to protect the company from legal liability.

- **Confidentiality concerns.** Your policy should make clear that complaints will be kept as confidential as possible. Often, it won't be possible for you to keep all of the information in the complaint, or the complaining employee's identity, secret. The accused employee should have the opportunity to respond to the allegations, which will require you to provide some details. In addition, you can't conduct meaningful witness interviews without revealing at least some of the information in the complaint.

Common Questions

Q: An employee reported that he saw his male boss grab and kiss a female coworker after she closed a major deal. According to the employee, the female coworker had a "creeped-out" expression on her face during the incident. The reporting employee doesn't have any problems with his boss, and he doesn't want to seem like a snitch, so he asked me not to reveal his identity. I plan to talk to both the boss and the woman he kissed. How can I avoid revealing the male employee's identity?

A: It's a good idea to respect confidentiality to the extent practical. Employees will feel more comfortable bringing problems like this one to your attention if they know you're not going to be sharing the details at the water cooler.

In a situation like the one you've described, it's perfectly reasonable to keep the employee's identity confidential—for now. You can simply tell both the boss and the coworker that someone reported seeing this inappropriate activity. Who saw it isn't important at this juncture; what is important is whether it occurred and how the alleged victim felt about it.

- **No retaliation.** Your policy should state that an employee will not be retaliated against for making a good-faith complaint— that is, a complaint that the employee genuinely believes is true, even if the employee turns out to be mistaken. In addition to showing your company's commitment to following the law, this assurance will bolster employee confidence in the process and their willingness to report violations.

Investigation Procedures

In addition to explaining the complaint process, your policy should briefly describe how your company will investigate complaints. You don't need to provide every detail of the process, because every complaint is different, and your company needs flexibility to respond to each particular situation. Instead, your purpose here is simply to tell employees what to expect after making a complaint, so they'll understand how the process works and see that the company takes complaints seriously. This part of the policy also tells other employees who might be involved in a complaint—such as potential witnesses or those accused of misconduct—what to expect in the investigation stage.

Though procedures may vary from company to company, effective procedures include several important elements:

- **A neutral investigator.** Your policy should state that the investigation will be conducted by an unbiased third party, someone who is not involved in the situation at hand. Many companies have human resources staff conduct investigations; some may train supervisors or managers to handle these tasks, while others hire consultants or outside lawyers to conduct investigations. Although the latter approach is more expensive, it may make employees feel more confident that the person doing the investigation really *is* neutral.

CAUTION

Don't plan on hiring the same attorney to investigate and defend against an employee complaint. If you hire a lawyer to investigate a complaint, consider hiring someone else if the case lands in court. Some courts have found that the work done by a lawyer acting as an investigator isn't protected by attorney–client confidentiality laws, which can lead to problems in the courtroom. Your company probably will want to reveal the results of the investigation, to show that you met your obligation to conduct a thorough, fair review. On the other hand, you probably don't want your lawyer to have to take the stand in the middle of trial to testify about the investigation. Make sure you know the rules in your state—or are willing to hire a different attorney to litigate the case—before hiring an attorney as an investigator.

- **Interviews and an investigative procedure.** Your policy should explain that the investigator may talk to the complaining employee, the accused employee, and any others who may have relevant information, such as witnesses. The policy should also state that these interviews will be conducted separately and privately. Likewise, you should briefly mention other steps you may take to investigate—for example, reviewing email messages or talking to clients or other outsiders.

- **Corrective action.** Your company also has to tell employees what will happen at the end of an investigation. For example, the policy should explain that appropriate disciplinary action will be taken if the investigation reveals that an employee violated company policy. Don't limit the type or extent of discipline that may be imposed; this could inhibit your company's ability to respond appropriately to each situation as it comes up. One good approach is to state that appropriate discipline, up to and including termination, will be imposed.

electronic confirmation form for employees to click to indicate that they have read and understood the policy.

> **FORM**
> **Need an acknowledgment form?** You'll find a sample acknowledgment form in Appendix C and on the CD-ROM at the back of this book.

Reinforce the Policy in Other Ways

We all know that employees sign forms (usually quite a few forms) when they're hired, often without reading every word. So you may want to do more to ensure that employees know about and understand the policy. You have several good opportunities to reiterate the policy's message:

- **Training.** If your company conducts regular diversity, anti-harassment, or other training for its employees, this is a prime opportunity to redistribute and discuss the company's policy. Training is covered in Chapter 4.

- **Performance evaluations.** Managers can remind employees of the policy during performance evaluation sessions and ask them to review it at least annually. A box on the written evaluation form can indicate that this was done and give the date.

- **Annual reminders.** Calendar an annual company-wide email or memo reminding everyone about the policy and send it every year at the same time. Make sure managers know that they should direct employees to the handbook or human resources department when issues or questions arise.

Lead by Example

A policy is just words on paper without actions to back it up. You are in a key position to show managers and employees how the words translate into reality in the workplace. In addition to always meeting the standard of professional, collegial behavior, keep an open door (and open eyes) so that you're aware of what's going on in the work environment. If you learn of potential violations or even of conduct that might start to move in that direction, step in early to address the situation before it escalates into a real problem. And always make yourself available to employees who have questions, concerns, or complaints.

 Common Questions

Q: Our company has an antiharassment and antidiscrimination policy that prohibits offensive conduct and requires employees to follow the Golden Rule. Jamie, who's responsible for HR matters at our company, overheard Mark say to his peer David, "You're just having a blonde moment." Other employees were working with them, including two women. David laughed in response. One of the female coworkers also laughed, but then said, "Hey Mark, that's sexist." Another male coworker piped up with "or maybe racist." Then the employees all laughed. Jamie figured it was just good-natured ribbing and shrugged it off. He didn't take any action or talk to any of the employees involved regarding the incident. Are we in the clear on this?

A: Not quite. Jamie should have spoken to all of the employees present individually to see how they felt about the remark because Mark's statement may violate the company's standard of behavior. It's not too late, however, so step in and talk to all present to make sure that no one was offended or uncomfortable. And, if any employee present responds that he or she was, follow up with Mark and instruct him not to engage in such banter in the future.

Review the Policy Regularly

Congress, legislatures, governmental agencies, city councils, and the courts make frequent changes to harassment and discrimination laws and regulations. Protected categories are added, new violations are recognized, and employer and employee obligations change as the law develops to address issues that arise in an increasingly diverse workforce.

As a result, your company's policies may become outdated and inadequate if you don't revise them to incorporate developments. Meet with your company's employment lawyer at least annually to go over the policy and make sure it's current. An outdated policy is almost as bad as no policy at all. It doesn't serve the purposes of setting standards for employees that comply with the law, informing employees of their rights and how to protect them, and protecting the company's interests. Worse, it can give the impression that your company makes only a superficial, half-hearted attempt to prevent harassment and discrimination—that it's all show and not a very good one at that!

Keeping your company's policy up to date is part of your commitment to create a harassment- and discrimination-free workplace.

Dos and Don'ts

Do:

- Make sure your company's written policy, especially the complaint and investigation components, comply with the law and are consistently applied.
- Distribute the policy to all employees, and make sure they acknowledge, in writing, that they have read and understood it.
- Ensure that human resources personnel, supervisors, and managers all follow the company policy for receiving and investigating employee complaints.
- Prevent harassment and discrimination by leading by example.
- Intervene early whenever you learn of possible harassment or discrimination and urge other managers to do the same.
- Maintain an "open door/open eyes" approach so you can learn of problems as soon as possible.

Don't:

- Hesitate to push for a strong policy. Your employer is relying on you to make sure the company is protected.
- Assume supervisors and employees are familiar with the company policy just because it's in writing and available to them.
- Forget to review the company policy regularly to make sure it complies with the law.

Training

Benefits of Training 96

Combined Training Session for Supervisors and Employees 100

Separate Sessions 101

    Supervisor Training 101

    Employee Training 105

How to Conduct Training 106

Who Conducts Training 107

Diversity Training 109

Most employers today know that creating an effective policy prohibiting harassment and discrimination isn't enough to protect them or their employees. Employees may not fully understand what's written on a piece of paper; they need more context to understand how issues play out in the real world.

That's where training comes in. You may have already been trained in this area, particularly if you work in one of the states that requires it. Even if you don't, however, your employer might choose to provide this type of training to help protect employees from inappropriate conduct and to reduce the likelihood of complaints and lawsuits.

Benefits of Training

Federal law generally doesn't require companies to train employees in harassment or discrimination prevention. In some cases, however, a company might be required to provide training as part of a settlement of an EEOC charge or a lawsuit. And, a few states require employers to provide at least certain employees with sexual harassment training—currently, California, Connecticut, and Maine.

State Training Requirements: California, Connecticut, and Maine

You can find a summary of each state's laws prohibiting harassment and discrimination, including training and other requirements, in Appendix B. Here is a quick rundown of the training provisions in the three states that currently require it:

- **California:** Employers with 50 or more employees must provide two hours of interactive (question and answer format) harassment training by "qualified" trainers (as defined in the law) every two years to all supervisors. Employees newly hired or promoted to supervisory positions must be trained within six months. Employers must retain records of trainings for at least two years. (Cal. Gov't. Code § 12950.1.)

- **Connecticut:** Employers with 50 or more employees must provide two hours of sexual harassment training to all supervisors. Employees newly hired or promoted to supervisory positions must be trained within six months. Retraining is encouraged (but not required) every three years. Qualifications of trainers are not specified. Employers are encouraged to retain records of trainings, but not required to do so. (Conn. Gen. Stat. Ann. § 46a-54(15)(B).)

- **Maine:** Employers with 15 or more employees must provide sexual harassment training to all new employees within one year of hire. No retraining is required. Qualifications of trainers are not specified. No records are required. (Me. Rev. Stat. Ann. tit. 26, § 807(3).)

Training offers a number of valuable benefits. It establishes standards of acceptable and appropriate behavior and tells employees how to proceed if they think they've experienced harassment or discrimination. It reinforces the message that the company is serious about preventing and correcting violations, which both communicates your company's commitment to employees and bolsters your company's ability to defend itself from lawsuits. If there has already been a workplace incident, training can help defuse the situation and alleviate stresses employees may be feeling.

Some employers resist training employees because it costs time and money, without an immediately apparent benefit to the business's bottom line. However, investing in training is a cost-effective preventive measure that protects both employers and employees from the greater damage (in terms of money, emotions, and productivity) that harassment or discrimination can inflict.

By training supervisors, an employer prepares its frontline responders to watch for, prevent, and address potential problems early and effectively. This will promote a work environment that's comfortable, functional, and compliant with the law. By training employees, an employer gives everyone the information they need to meet company standards of conduct and report any violations they observe to the appropriate managers. As discussed in Chapter 3, your company can take advantage of the legal defenses afforded by having an effective policy only if employees are informed of the rights and obligations the policy contains.

Common Questions

Q: My company operates in a state that doesn't require harassment training. Some members of the board of directors want us to institute it anyway, mostly as a PR device. I'm concerned that it may backfire by making it look like we have a problem when we don't, and also that it is an undue expenditure at a time when our budget is tight.

A: Because training can help the company defend itself in a lawsuit by showing that you took steps to prevent and correct illegal behavior, your company has a very good reason to conduct training even absent any existing problems. Also, training will help supervisors recognize and resolve problems and this, in turn, will help your company promote a healthy workplace and avoid lawsuits. Finally, training is more likely to enhance than hurt your company's image. It shows that the company is committed to preventing harassment and discrimination complaints—not just reacting to them.

Although it makes sense to train everyone, supervisors and employees should receive some of their training separately. Because the law confers more responsibility—and liability—on supervisors, and because supervisors are responsible for acting on your company's behalf, they will need more detailed information about what the company and the law expect of them in their managerial capacity. However, general information about harassment and discrimination can be conveyed in a joint training session for both supervisors and employees, with the two groups receiving additional training in separate sessions.

> TIP
>
> **Put your training program in writing.** If your company will require training, whether to comply with state law or on its own initiative, it's a good idea to put the training policy in writing. The policy should set out who is required to attend, how often training will be required, who will conduct the training, and what topics will be covered. This policy will help you ensure that your company's trainings are consistent over time, and will tell employees what to expect from the training program.

Combined Training Session for Supervisors and Employees

The content of training programs will vary depending on the law governing them (if any), who provides them, and what format they're presented in. Regardless of minor variations in content and style, however, a good training program must hit the highlights, which include:

- **The laws prohibiting harassment and discrimination.** Supervisors and employees alike need to understand which laws apply; these laws are the foundation of employee rights and employer responsibilities.
- **What harassment and discrimination are.** All supervisors and employees need to know what types of conduct are prohibited, so that they know what not to do and what kinds of behavior they should report.
- **Which characteristics are protected.** Your training should tell employees which traits (such as religion or disability) are protected under applicable federal, state, and perhaps local law.
- **When and how harassment and discrimination might occur at different states of employment.** The best training puts information in context, by providing examples of the ways that bias or inappropriate conduct might come up in the workplace.

- **Company policy.** Training gives you a great opportunity to go over the company's policy, which, ideally, will contain all of the topics covered in the policy (see Chapter 3), and to reiterate that violations will result in discipline, up to and including termination.

Separate Sessions

In addition to a combined training session covering the topics discussed above, supervisors and employees also need separate training. Supervisors and employees have different roles in the company regarding harassment and discrimination. Supervisors represent the company and act on its behalf. This means they should receive special training on what to do if they see misconduct, how their action (or failure to act) can expose both themselves and the company to legal liability, and what to do if they receive a complaint. Employees, by contrast, need to know how to make a complaint and how the company will respond.

Supervisor Training

Supervisors have a special role to play in preventing and addressing potential violations by other employees. They are the eyes and ears of the company, and many antiharassment and antidiscrimination policies direct employees to report violations to supervisors. And, supervisors may not only face personal liability for their own actions, but also create liability for the company. Supervisors need training tailored to these special responsibilities.

In addition, California and Connecticut require employers in those states to provide supervisors with sexual harassment training. The stringent requirements of the California training law, especially, call for close attention when designing a training program.

Even if it's not legally required, you should train managers and supervisors so they know how to deal with complaints and understand their responsibility to always act professionally and appropriately when dealing with employees.

Supervisor's Own Conduct

In addition to learning the types of conduct that can constitute harassment or discrimination, supervisors should be informed that their own actions can, in some situations, expose them to lawsuits by the victim. This risk of individual liability is unique to supervisory employees and gives them a powerful incentive to avoid inappropriate behavior.

An employer also has greater exposure to liability for the acts of its supervisors because the law views supervisory employees as acting on behalf of the company. This means that a company can be held liable for a supervisor's actions even if it doesn't know what the supervisor is up to. By contrast, an employer is typically liable for the conduct of a lower-level employee only if it is aware of that conduct and fails to do anything effective to stop it.

Supervisor training must explain these special liability risks, so supervisors can avoid creating problems for the company and themselves.

Common Questions

Q: One of our managers was accused of discriminating against an older worker. Part of the company's out-of-court settlement requires us to provide antidiscrimination training to this manager. The company is now considering requiring training for all managers, but I'm not sure this is a good idea. We are not legally required to provide training to anyone but the accused manager. Doesn't this make it look like we have a bigger problem than we really do?

A: When a workplace incident results in a complaint and a settlement, it's a good indication that some training is in order. After all, you want to make sure other managers don't repeat the same mistakes this manager did. Providing training can convert a costly settlement into a valuable teaching tool.

However, some delicacy may be called for here, particularly if the other managers know about the situation that inspired the training in the first place. If the accused manager senses resentment or judgment on the part of his peers, he may not fully participate in the training. Likewise, if the other managers are caught up in the "back story" of the alleged violation, they may not be able to focus. Separate trainings are an option to consider if you think a group session might prevent some employees—especially the accused employee—from fully engaging and grasping the material.

Prevention and Response

Supervisors are responsible for taking prompt action in the workplace to prevent harassment and discrimination and to address these types of misconduct if they occur. This is easier said than done, however, as the dynamics of real-life human interaction often make it hard for a supervisor to gracefully intervene before conduct gets out of hand. Training can provide supervisors with effective methods for intervening early and teach them the steps to follow in response to actual violations.

In general, the earlier a potential problem is caught and dealt with, the less damage done. In harassment and discrimination situations, this means your company wants to create sharp-eyed supervisors and managers who notice potential issues and step in to prevent them from escalating. This can be a delicate operation, because it calls for supervisors to step in before anyone has clearly done anything wrong. Effective training explains how supervisors can intervene without overreacting, including:

- **Leading by example:** By not telling off-color jokes, and by not responding favorably when employees do so, a supervisor sends a strong message that such conduct is not appropriate.

- **Changing the subject:** Heading off topics that could devolve into uncomfortable or inappropriate discussions is a time-tested way of avoiding problems.

- **Discouraging conduct:** A simple, terse word or two suggesting to an employee that he or she may be entering into an area that is off-limits may be enough to prevent a problem from developing.

- **Expressing disapproval:** If subtler methods won't work or a situation is more serious, a firm statement that the conduct or comment is not appropriate often does the trick.

If these methods don't work, supervisors should be instructed to escalate to a more formal response, starting with a complaint or report of the violation, followed by investigation and response, as explained in Part II of this book. This means supervisors should be trained in the company's complaint, investigation, and response procedures. The trainer should go over the steps set out in the company's policy and cover the supervisor's responsibilities at each step. For example, supervisors may be identified as company representatives to whom employees can bring complaints, as participants in the investigation of complaints, or in some other role. Give supervisors a full description of their role under your company's policy.

Employee Training

Employees need to know what types of conduct are prohibited and how to deal with violations they experience or observe. In contrast to supervisors, employees needn't, and shouldn't, be trained on investigating and responding to complaints, nor should they be trained on when the company or supervisors can be held liable for harassment and discrimination. Practically speaking, this is not the employee's concern—and being told how the company can escape legal responsibility for any misconduct they may suffer is likely to alienate or even anger employees. That's why employees need a separate training session.

Employees' Own Conduct

Although your combined training session will explain the types of conduct that violate company policy, you should separately emphasize to employees their responsibility to abide by the company policy and treat one another in a professional, respectful way at all times.

Reporting Violations

The other main area in which employees should receive training is how to report potential violations. An employer's policy is effective only if employees know how to use it. Your training program should refresh employees on the company complaint policy, reiterating the pertinent points:

- **Whom to report to.** Tell employees which managers and/or supervisors they can report violations to, if they aren't comfortable reporting to HR or their immediate supervisor. It's best to identify these individuals by title (for example, "any manager," if that is your company's policy), so that the reporting structure stays consistent as individual managers come and go.
- **How to report.** Let employees know that they can speak informally and confidentially, to the extent possible. But be

sure employees also know that the company has a duty to put a stop to inappropriate conduct, which may require the investigator to reveal some details of the complaint.

- **When to report.** Urge employees to immediately report any conduct that they believe might violate the company policy against harassment or discrimination. Even if the conduct doesn't actually rise to the level of a violation, they should err on the side of making a report.
- **No retaliation.** Emphasize that the company will not tolerate any retaliation against an employee who has reported a possible violation, even if the company finds that no violation occurred. Instruct employees to immediately report any act that they believe may be retaliatory.
- **Participation in investigation.** Remind employees that they have an obligation to cooperate with anyone who is investigating an employee complaint. Reiterate that confidentiality will be maintained to the extent possible and that the company will not allow retaliation for their participation.

How to Conduct Training

The most effective training isn't just a dry lecture that marches through each required topic. As with any presentation, it's important to engage attendees and keep their attention through the use of visuals (such as PowerPoint presentations, whiteboards, or blow-ups that set out key concepts); videos (a variety of commercially produced training videos are available, or you can create your own); scenarios presented by the trainer, followed by a guided discussion; and quizzes and exercises, which help the trainer assess how well employees are understanding the concepts.

California requires that sexual harassment training be "interactive," which means that attendees must have the chance to talk to the trainer about the concepts covered, ask questions, and answer hypothetical questions. The techniques described above are all interactive and, as such, fulfill that state's requirement. Even if interactive training is not legally required in your state, it helps ensure that the training session is interesting and productive.

Training can be conducted in a variety of ways that include:

- **In-person:** Traditional classroom training with the trainer and attendees all in the same room is a popular option. It allows for questions and answers and for lively discussions of the issues.
- **E-learning:** Computer-based training is a growing trend. Typically, the attendee logs in individually but can participate in some way (for example, by receiving instructions on how to contact a trainer who will answer questions or provide guidance or assistance within a reasonable time period). This is a popular choice because it allows employees to complete training on their own schedule.
- **Webinars:** Many companies now opt for a seminar that is transmitted via the Internet or company intranet in real time. Attendees are given an opportunity to participate in real time by either emailing questions or answers or by telephone conference.

No matter which training method your company uses, be sure to have each attendee sign a form confirming that they attended the full training. E-learning programs and webinars usually have a box for attendees to click beside their names to record their attendance.

Who Conducts Training

Many companies hire outside consultants or lawyers to run their trainings. You can also use in-house HR professionals. No matter whom you use, make sure the trainer is qualified to conduct an effective training. California, for example, requires that training be presented by individuals with knowledge and expertise (such as employment lawyers or HR experts) in harassment, discrimination, and retaliation prevention. (You can find California's regulation discussing trainer qualifications at www.fehc.ca.gov.) If your state requires training, and your company decides to hire an outside trainer, check the laws and regulations in your state for any required qualifications for trainers.

Beyond having the minimum qualifications and experience, the trainer needs to be right for your company and its employees. You or another manager may be the right choice, or your company's particular situation or needs may persuade you that an outside trainer is preferable. HR consultants, consultants who provide harassment and discrimination prevention training, and attorneys experienced in harassment and discrimination cases who've done prior trainings are all good candidates to conduct training.

TIP

Get referrals. Ask company employment lawyers, HR specialists, and other company HR professionals for recommendations of good trainers. You can also ask others in your professional network or membership organizations.

Once you've gotten some names, ask trainer candidates for references and find out if their other clients were pleased with their training. You can also ask other clients about the trainer's methods and style, to make sure the trainer's approach is right for your company. For example, if your company believes strongly in workplace democracy, you will need a trainer who can handle outspoken employees and vigorous debate and discussion. Trainer candidates should also give you a description of training techniques upon request.

Give the chosen trainer a summary of any recent complaints or issues at your company, any particular difficulties you anticipate that the trainer may confront, and the particular goals your company has in providing the training to employees. For example, if a company employee recently complained of sexual harassment, and the investigation revealed that sexual jokes and teasing were fairly widespread, you may want the trainer to carefully focus on sexual harassment, what constitutes a hostile work environment, and what types of comments and conversations violate the company's standards of appropriate workplace behavior.

 Common Questions

Q: My company just settled a religious discrimination lawsuit brought by a Sikh employee. We've retained a consultant to provide diversity training to our employees. We have other Sikh employees on staff besides the plaintiff in the lawsuit, and I'd like the trainer to address employee tolerance of that religion and culture. Is this advisable or even appropriate?

A: It makes sense to include religious tolerance and sensitivity in the training, given the recent lawsuit. However, the trainer needn't refer specifically to the Sikh religion or to any particular religion. In fact, he or she shouldn't do so, as that may embarrass the Sikh employees and make them feel singled out. A general discussion of religious tolerance will cover the necessary ground without spotlighting any particular employees.

Diversity Training

Many employers today conduct diversity training for all employees, in addition to harassment and discrimination training. Diversity training can foster sensitivity to, and tolerance of, differences among employees, and can build employee confidence in the company's commitment to a diverse and collegial working environment. Most importantly, it can remind employees of their role in helping to create and maintain that environment.

Diversity training can be especially useful in healing workplace dysfunction after a harassment or discrimination complaint, because it is forward looking. Diversity training reinforces the need for employees to respect the differences among them, rather than focusing on legal definitions and obligations. Although diversity training should refer to those definitions and obligations (and specifically to company policy), its main goal is to explore the motivation behind those legal imperatives: how to create a workplace where employees from different backgrounds can all be comfortable and productive.

One way to do this is by discussing scenarios drawn from cases or situations in the news. For example, an accusation of harassment or discrimination against a public figure can form a framework for part of the training.

EXAMPLE:

The coach of the New York Knicks was accused of sexual harassment. Among other allegations, a female employee said that the coach had frequently commented upon and complimented her appearance. She also said he put his arm around her shoulder on several occasions. She said that she told him she was uncomfortable with the conduct, but he continued, insisting that he was just being nice. This part of the real case could be used to highlight the fact that unwelcome conduct, even if it's intended to be flattering, can make the recipient uncomfortable and can lead to a charge of harassment.

Diversity training can accomplish two difficult goals: It can provide a way to talk about the challenges posed when employees of different genders, races, religions, ages, and abilities work together; and, it can give employees a broader, less personal perspective on such challenges. Some of the anecdotes in diversity training can focus on how these challenges are confronted and overcome in various settings. For example, the group could discuss experiences recounted by a female executive during her career in a male-dominated industry as drawn from her memoir.

⊘ CAUTION

Don't allow diversity training to devolve into a discussion of negative stereotypes or biased beliefs. Believe it or not, diversity training can provide fodder for a discrimination lawsuit—not to mention heated discussions and deeply hurt feelings—if participants are asked to discuss or reveal personal biases. It's appropriate to discuss some of the reasons why antidiscrimination laws exist—for example, that some groups in our society have been historically disadvantaged. Once participants begin sharing their own biases and beliefs, however, the discussion can quickly become uncomfortable or even hostile. Do you really want a company manager "confessing" that he believes women are too emotional to conduct hard-nosed business negotiations? Once that session ends and he denies a promotion to a female employee, you can bet you'll hear those words echoed back in a complaint.

A question and answer session can also be an effective tool during diversity training. A typical session starts with a scenario laid out by the trainer, who then asks employees questions about the conduct and/or response to the conduct in the scenario.

EXAMPLE:

Using the allegations of unwelcome comments and touching made by the female employee of the New York Knicks, the trainer then asks the employees at the diversity training the following questions:

How many times should an employee have to object to behavior before it's clear that the behavior is unwelcome?

Assuming that he was sincere, is it relevant that the coach thought he was being nice?

Should the employee have to do or say more than, "I'd rather you didn't do that" before the coach should have understood that he was making her uncomfortable?

Is it wise for someone in the coach's position to err on the side of caution and just not compliment a female employee's appearance?

The point of this kind of dialog is to spur employees to think about situations from one another's point of view and to understand that something they think is harmless—or even flattering—can cause insult, offense, or discomfort to another person. This will help employees increase their sensitivity to the differing perspectives of their coworkers and understand that everyone benefits when possible harassment or discrimination is reported and addressed.

In a perfect world, all employees would always show respect for their coworkers, regardless of any differences between them. Unfortunately, that ideal is probably some way off. Fortunately, perfection is not required by the law. The goal of training, and of all the measures we've discussed in this chapter, is to bolster employee confidence in your company and its policy; to prevent violations; and to make the workplace a professional, collegial, and respectful environment for all employees.

Dos and Don'ts

Do:

- Familiarize yourself with the training requirements, if any, of each state in which your company operates.
- Consider training all employees even if it's not required, to provide guidance to supervisors and employees, and to limit damages in case of a lawsuit.
- Provide training to supervisors and employees that is tailored to their different roles.
- Use scenarios, quizzes, and exercises to encourage attendee participation and to test their knowledge.
- Choose a training method that's effective and interactive.
- Choose a trainer who's qualified, experienced, and suits your company's needs.
- Consider diversity training, especially if your company has had some problems with discrimination or harassment.

Don't:

- Bypass the option of training in order to cut costs; it will pay for itself by preventing suits and limiting damages.
- Forget to have each attendee at training submit a form confirming attendance.
- Limit training to a dry lecture—it needs to be interactive.
- Neglect to distribute the company policy and refer to it frequently during training.
- Leave out a discussion of informal methods of intervention when training supervisors.

Part II: Dealing with Harassment and Discrimination Claims

5

Investigating Complaints

Receiving a Complaint.. 118

   Treat the Reporting Employee Respectfully... 119

   Get the Information You Need 121

Conducting an Investigation 124

   Preparing to Investigate... 125

   Interviewing Techniques.. 126

Concluding Your Investigation... 140

   Understanding Your Goal 141

   Reaching a Conclusion 141

   Crafting a Solution 145

   Communicating Your Findings... 146

Your initial response to a harassment or discrimination complaint may well determine whether the underlying issue is resolved successfully or ends up in court. Employees who file lawsuits often say something like: "If someone at the company had taken this problem seriously in the first place, I never would have sued." At the very least, a company's inaction or sloppy investigation convinces the reporting employee—and others—that the company doesn't take complaints seriously. Even worse, problems can escalate as the inappropriate behavior continues and the harm caused by discriminatory treatment mounts.

This chapter explains how to respond to a potential harassment or discrimination complaint effectively, from the moment you first hear about it. You'll learn:

- what to do when you receive a complaint
- how to interview the reporting employee, the accused employee, and other witnesses, and
- how to evaluate what you learn and decide what action to take once the investigation is complete.

Receiving a Complaint

You may find out about a potential problem in any number of ways—from the employee who feels harassed or discriminated against, from a coworker who sees or hears something fishy, from your own observations, or at worst, by receiving a complaint the employee files with a government fair employment agency. Or, you may find out about a problem indirectly, without any formal complaint. A current employee may report a potential violation during a performance evaluation, at an exit interview, or even anonymously.

No matter how you first become aware of a problem, your responsibility is the same—to investigate quickly, impartially, and thoroughly. Usually, your first step will be to talk to the reporting employee.

Treat the Reporting Employee Respectfully

Because employees often feel emotional about these situations, your job is a tough one. To be effective, you must respect the employee's emotions while working to get the information you need. You'll find that easiest to do if you follow these strategies:

- **Show that you take the complaint seriously.** Harassment and discrimination complaints are serious business. When you meet with an employee to discuss a complaint, you may be tempted to lighten the mood by engaging in small talk or avoiding the most pressing questions. You may worry that, if you're too serious, you could scare the employee off and not get the full story. But resist the temptation. Making light gives the impression that you don't take the complaint seriously. At worst, the employee might not share the full story with you or might hesitate to report further incidents.

Common Questions

Q: An African American employee complained to me that his Caucasian manager frequently makes race-based comments like, "I have a white guy's sense of rhythm" or "I bet you are really athletic, unlike me." I know the manager socially, and I know his heart is in the right place. But when I said as much to the employee, he accused me of "taking sides" and stalked out of my office. Should I let it be, or try to discuss it with the employee again?

A: You need to go back to the beginning. Your statement and belief that the manager's "heart was in the right place" told the reporting employee that you didn't think his complaint was serious, even if you believed it was true. You should ask the employee to meet with you again and make clear that you're ready to listen and objectively apply the company's policy on harassment and discrimination. If the employee is still reluctant to deal with you, have another qualified manager step in to handle the complaint.

- **Don't pass judgment.** When you receive a complaint, it's natural to want to draw some conclusions, especially if you know the employees involved. But don't—it prevents you from getting the full story. Instead, listen carefully and ask for all relevant facts. You shouldn't make any decisions about what happened until the investigation is fully completed.

Common Questions

Q: A hypersensitive employee (she even objected to the type of bottled water in the break room!) complained that her manager makes her uncomfortable by commenting on her appearance, saying things like "that looks nice" or "green is a great color for you." These sound like simple compliments and, in her usual way, she's making a big deal out of them. Do we really have to treat this as a harassment complaint?

A: As ridiculous as it may seem to you, yes. That the employee has a history of complaining—either about harassing behavior or water in the break room—doesn't tell you whether she is being harassed right now. You need to get the full story before you draw any conclusions. While the statements may seem harmless at first blush, you could find other facts that suggest there's more to the story.

- **Don't get caught up in emotions.** Employees who come to you to complain about harassment or discrimination may be dealing with a host of different emotions—and some may be occurring simultaneously. They may feel angry, hurt, humiliated, or even ashamed. But it's important not to let these emotions cloud your ability to hear the complaint objectively. Your job is to get the full story and draw a conclusion based on the facts.

TIP

You can treat the employee kindly without getting emotional.
You don't have to act like an unfeeling automaton when an employee
expresses strong emotions. Just maintain a professional, respectful
demeanor. If the employee is crying, for example, it's perfectly acceptable to
offer a tissue or glass of water. But don't cross the line: Too much sympathy
implies that you have already decided that the employee's accusations are
true, which compromises your neutrality in the investigation. You want
both the reporting employee and the accused employee to feel that they've
gotten a fair hearing. This makes it much more likely that they'll accept the
conclusions you draw and the steps you take to resolve the situation.

- **Be patient.** People in a charged emotional state often have
  difficulty articulating their thoughts. Be prepared to sit
  back calmly and give the employee time to explain what's
  happened.
- **Don't promise confidentiality or anonymity.** Many complaining
  employees do not want to be identified when you conduct
  an investigation, but that may not be possible. The accused
  employee deserves to hear the accusations and respond to
  them. For this reason, you shouldn't promise anyone you
  interview that you will keep information confidential. Instead,
  offer to keep things as confidential as possible, and assure the
  employee that you won't reveal information to people who do
  not need to know it.

Get the Information You Need

Even as you're careful about how you treat the employee, keep
in mind that your primary objective is to get the full story. You
can best do this by showing the employee you are a good listener.
Use active-listening strategies, such as repeating back what the
employee is saying, to make sure you are hearing correctly. If the
employee gets upset, acknowledge those emotions directly, by saying
something like, "You seem upset. Do you want to take a break?"

And keep your tone professional: The more business-like you are, the easier it will be for the employee to keep his or her emotions in check. That will help both of you stay focused on the task at hand.

Reiterate what the employee can expect, based on what's in your company policy. Even if he or she has read it, your confirmation that the policy will be followed provides reassurance and stability. Also, tell the employee that retaliation is prohibited, and ask the employee to come to you immediately if he or she faces any negative treatment as a result of the complaint or investigation.

Checklist: What to Say to a Reporting Employee

When you meet with a reporting employee, use this checklist to make sure you start your investigating on the right foot.

- ❑ Thank the employee for coming forward.
- ❑ Explain that you're going to initiate an investigation immediately.
- ❑ Remind the employee to bring further complaints to you and to let you know if the employee later remembers additional information.
- ❑ Tell the employee you're going to follow company policy, and provide a copy.
- ❑ Reiterate that retaliation is illegal.
- ❑ Confirm that you'll only share information on a need-to-know basis, but don't promise confidentiality.

Common Questions

Q: I happened to walk into the break room just in time to hear an employee heatedly telling his manager, "I can't believe you said that." As soon as I came in, the employee left. The manager quickly said, "We were just discussing last weekend's big game—he's mad his team lost." This could be a plausible explanation, and I didn't say anything at the time, but now I can imagine something much worse going on, too. Should I follow up?

A: You don't need to make a big deal of it, but you should, at a minimum, find out what the manager said that upset the employee. You can start by meeting individually with each of them and asking what happened. There's no need for anything extremely formal at this point, but it's a good idea to make sure you have the full story before you start drawing conclusions, good *or* bad.

Before you conclude your meeting, ask the employee what he or she thinks should be done to resolve the complaint. This allows the employee to express his or her perspective, and you can consider it later, when you'll have to come up with a solution. This is also your opportunity to address the employee's unreasonable expectations—for example, if the employee expects you to immediately fire the accused employee, you can explain why it's important for you to investigate before any disciplinary action is taken.

Of course, you'll need to make it clear that you cannot promise any particular response or outcome. After all, the employee may ask that you do nothing or that you do something that isn't consistent with company policy or your legal requirements. Your primary duty is to take all reasonable steps to end the illegal conduct and to prevent it from occurring again, not necessarily to please the complaining employee.

Common Questions

Q: I recently found our receptionist hiding out in the women's room. She explained that she was dodging one of the delivery men. She says he hangs over her desk to ogle her and makes suggestive sexual comments. When I told her I'd be contacting the delivery service, she said she didn't want to make a big deal of it. It's not really a problem to have someone else deal with the delivery man and this solution seems reasonable. Is this a workable approach?

A: No. Although the receptionist's approach may help her avoid the delivery man, it doesn't relieve your company of the obligation to deal with the situation. First, the receptionist shouldn't have to hide in the restroom during her work hours to avoid harassment. This doesn't do anything to address the harassment she's already suffered, doesn't prevent her from later claiming that you should have taken steps to protect her, could itself be considered degrading, and is a waste of her work time. Also, this delivery man may harass other employees. Now that you know about his behavior, you have to step in and address it.

One way to do this is to contact the delivery company directly and let them know that their employee is engaging in behavior that violates your company's policy. Then, ask that they send a different worker in his place. If they want your business, they'll comply. There is no need to even mention the receptionist in this exchange. Be sure to tell the receptionist that you've spoken to the delivery company, and ask her to report further incidents to you.

Conducting an Investigation

A thorough, prompt investigation is essential to the successful resolution of an employee complaint. It enables you to collect evidence while it's still fresh, before witnesses' recollections fade, documents get lost, or emails are deleted. It wards off speculation and gossip. And it inspires employee confidence in your company's policies and practices.

Although you may certainly hope your investigation will yield the absolute truth, it's often more complicated. You may have little evidence beyond "he said/she said" allegations, with no witnesses to corroborate either side's story. Even if you can't reach a solid conclusion, however, an investigation shows that the company did all it could to prevent and correct inappropriate behavior—which, as explained in Chapters 2 and 3, has the important legal consequence of either providing a defense to a hostile environment harassment case or avoiding punitive damages in a discrimination case. The law protects you as long as you investigate in good faith, even if you aren't ultimately able to draw a conclusion about what happened—and even if your conclusion turns out to be wrong.

Nevertheless, you should do everything you can during the investigation to get the full story. Sometimes, you'll have clear physical evidence—a series of emails or photos, for example—that will help you reach a conclusion. But more often, the majority of your evidence will come from the accounts of the reporting employee, the accused employee, and other witnesses. That means you'll have to find out what happened primarily through interviews.

Preparing to Investigate

Once you receive a complaint, you will want to jump in quickly to protect the company. But don't be too hasty. Spend some time creating an investigatory plan. The plan should cover:

- **Whom you need to interview.** This list may grow as your investigation proceeds, but start with anyone who may have relevant information. Then, decide the order in which you'll interview employees. For reasons explained below, after speaking with the reporting employee, it usually makes sense to interview the accused employee before moving on to other witnesses.

- **What you need to ask.** You don't need to write out every question, but you should take some notes to make sure you address the key issues with each witness. Create a rough outline of topics you need to cover. And, make sure you have clean copies of any documents, such as email messages or performance evaluations, you plan to show witnesses and ask them about.
- **Where you'll conduct interviews.** You want to respect the privacy of everyone involved and limit disruption—and gossip—in the workplace. Choose a location away from the witnesses' regular workspace, and make sure it's private, with a locking door.

Interviewing Techniques

No matter whom you're interviewing—the reporting employee, the accused employee, or a witness—you must approach each interview as an opportunity to get the most information possible, while protecting the company's interests and maintaining your neutrality.

Start With the Facts

To the employees you interview, the facts might not be the most important part of the story. Employees may be focused on how the behavior or treatment feels, how it feels to be accused of misconduct, what effect the problem is having on their work or home life, or how others in the company may respond.

While this is understandable, you need to know what actually happened. While being respectful of the employee's emotions, you must still get the information you need. It's easy to get sidetracked if you don't focus on the fundamentals. Gather information like a reporter, by asking:

- **Who?** You need to know who committed the alleged behavior or action, who witnessed it, whom the employee told about it, and whether anyone else might have relevant information.
- **What?** Get the details about what happened. Don't settle for "he harassed me" or "she's racist." Find out exactly what was done or said, in what context.
- **When?** You need to figure out how long the behavior has been going on and when any incident or alleged incident occurred. Be as specific as possible. If the employee isn't sure, you may have to provide some reference points ("Was it in the morning or afternoon?" "Was it before or after we closed the Jones account?") to try to narrow things down.
- **Where?** The location of alleged events can help you figure out what really happened. For example, if the reporting employee says that she was harassed in the break room at lunch time, there could be several witnesses to the incident. If no one heard or saw a thing, you may reasonably start to wonder about the reporting employee's story. If the activity occurred away from the workplace, you'll have to determine the company's responsibility for what went on. Make sure you find out where every alleged incident took place.
- **How?** Find out the means the accused employee used to instigate the harassment or discrimination—for example, through email, comments, or physical contact, or by altering the employee's work schedule, pay, or promotional opportunities.
- **Why?** You need to understand the context of the incident(s). Did the alleged violation occur suddenly or progress over time, such as joking that gradually became more and more offensive or the denial of a series of raises? You also need to know whether the employee believes the conduct was related to the employee's gender, race, or other protected characteristic, and the reasons for that belief.

Common Questions

Q: Our warehouse foreman is concerned that the night shift super-visor uses ethnic nicknames with his crew, a group of six guys, four of whom (plus the supervisor) are Latino. The examples he gave are in Spanish, but even translated, don't seem derogatory. Several of the crew members don't speak Spanish, and the foreman told me they just "blow it off because they don't know what he's saying anyway." No one has complained. How should I approach this? I don't want to put ideas in anyone's head.

A: You're right to investigate, but to avoid inciting anger or anxiety, you'll want to carefully word your inquiries. For example, you may ask the night shift employees, "Does anyone ever use nicknames in the warehouse?" If the answer is yes, you may follow up with questions about who does it, what terms are used, and how the employees feel about and respond to their use. These questions are likely to elicit some helpful answers, because you'll get confirmation that the alleged language was actually used, as well as get an idea about how employees feel about it.

Keep your questions open-ended instead of asking questions that require only a "yes" or "no" answer. And avoid leading comments or questions, such as "You must have been so upset!" or "That wasn't really offensive, was it?" These questions give the employee the impression that there is a "right" answer. You're less likely to get the employee's honest perspective if you approach things this way. Another way to avoid getting a biased viewpoint is to simply wait for the witness to respond, rather than providing a response when a witness is slow to speak. Sometimes witnesses need to gather their thoughts, or hope that they can avoid answering difficult questions by stalling for time.

CD-ROM
Want some help with interviewing the complaining employee?
Listen to a manager interview an employee reporting harassment on the CD-ROM included in the back of this book.

In addition to these questions, ask everyone you interview if they have any physical evidence related to the underlying problem, such as memos, payroll documents, pictures, emails, notes, letters, voice-mail, or text messages.

If the answers to your questions reveal new facts (and they often do), you may need to go back to earlier witnesses to ask more questions. You'll often have to go back to the reporting employee, because after interviewing others, you'll have a lot of new information to synthesize. It's a good idea to interview witnesses more than once as an investigation proceeds, so you can clear up (or nail down) inconsistencies and explore newly uncovered information.

Common Questions

Q: My company notified an employee on August 1 that it was eliminating her job. She complained to me of discrimination, because just a few days before the notification, she'd told her manager she was pregnant. The manager told me they'd made the decision a couple weeks before that, and had an email to his VP, dated July 15, definitively backing this up. But another employee in the department told me that the pregnant employee had informally started telling people about her pregnancy as early as the beginning of July and that "everyone knew about it." I don't know what to believe. What do I do next?

A: You definitely have more work to do here, because you need to find out when the manager actually knew about the employee's pregnancy. Although the manager can show you that he made the decision before the employee told him directly that she was pregnant, you haven't said whether he denies knowing the employee was pregnant before she told him.

To start, you'll need to go back to the employee and find out when she began telling others at work that she was pregnant, whom she told, and in what context. There's a big difference between, for example, telling one close friend in confidence and announcing her pregnancy at a team meeting. You'll also need to find out what the manager knew before July 15.

Provide Information

Your investigation is more than an opportunity to elicit facts—it's also an opportunity for you to assure the employee that you're going to conduct the investigation in compliance with company policy. This instills employee confidence in the process and also protects the company legally. To make sure you communicate this important message, start by giving everyone you interview another copy of the company's policy prohibiting harassment and discrimination and urge them to read it again. This helps ensure that employees understand their rights and responsibilities and what to expect from the investigation. (For more information on what should be in the policy, see Chapter 3.)

Make clear to everyone you interview, especially the reporting employee, that retaliation is prohibited and should be reported to you immediately. Explain that the company doesn't want any employee penalized or treated badly for participating in the investigation. (You'll find information on preventing and responding to retaliation in Chapter 7.)

As you conclude each interview, discuss what will happen next. There's no need to provide any specifics; you just want to let the employee know that you're going to investigate the complaint, and that you'll follow company policy and legal requirements. Make sure the employee knows to contact you about any further violations or additional information.

Third Parties at the Interview

Sometimes, an employee being interviewed will want to bring a third party along. Whether you should allow this depends, in part, on whom the employee wants to bring.

- **Union representative.** Union members have a right to have a union representative present if the interview could result in discipline.

- **A lawyer.** You don't have to allow an attorney to be present, but you can and may want to if you think it will put the witness at ease and encourage open communication. But don't allow the attorney to take over the process or limit your inquiries—your purpose is to find the truth (without invading the employee's privacy), not present a case in court. If you're worried that the interview may digress into a legal attack, you can have the company's lawyer present too. Just recognize that this may make things feel more formal and undermine your fact finding.

- **A spouse, coworker, or friend.** It's usually not a good idea to allow a personal friend or support person to be present, especially if you're dealing with the accused employee. Employees sometimes feel ashamed about their behavior and may not want to reveal it in front of someone they know. In some cases (for example, if an employee is accused of sexual harassment and brings his wife to the interview), the third party may have a significant personal investment in the outcome of the investigation and may interfere with your questioning. Also, having an outsider at the interview unnecessarily compromises the privacy of the people being discussed.

Separate the Reporting and Accused Employees

To reduce the risk of continuing problems and to show the reporting employee that you take the complaint seriously, you may want to separate the accused employee and the reporting employee as soon as you receive a complaint. Keeping the employees apart also makes it easier for you to conduct a thorough investigation, get each side's full perspective, and limit the potential for tension in the workplace. Given the pitched nature of harassment and discrimination allegations, separating the reporting and accused employees is generally a good idea if practical.

If an accused harasser is the victim's supervisor, you should definitely separate the two pending the investigation, to prevent the possibility of further harassment. It's also appropriate to separate employees if you're worried about the potential for violence or confrontation. This will depend on the situation. For example, if a coworker has allegedly directed a racial epithet at the reporting employee, emotions may be running so high that they have to be separated.

Separating employees doesn't always mean complete isolation, however. That level of distance may not always be possible or practical, especially in a smaller workplace. But at the very least, you'll want to instruct the parties not to speak to each other about the allegations, investigate quickly to minimize the discomfort, and keep them as far apart as you can.

Common Questions

Q: Recently, one of our salespeople, Glen, reported that a coworker, David, has made some "homophobic comments," like asking him to find a matching garment for a customer because he has good "color coordination skills." Glen thinks these comments are coded slurs about Glen's sexual orientation, wants a full investigation, and doesn't want to work the same shift as David. It's the holiday season (our busiest time of year), we're a small business and already stretched thin, and this is just impossible. I made sure that a supervisor was always present when they worked together and started to investigate, but midway through my investigation, Glen quit and has now filed a harassment charge with the state fair employment agency. Am I in trouble here?

A: You shouldn't be. You conducted an investigation in good faith and did all you could to separate the two without causing undue disruption to your operations. That's what the law requires of you. If it's truly not practical for you to separate the two entirely, the actions you took should be enough to protect the company.

If a supervisor is accused of harassment or discrimination, you should immediately consider whether it makes sense to have the employee who made the complaint report to someone else. This takes away the supervisor's opportunity to continue the alleged misconduct or engage in retaliation. You don't want a supervisor who's been accused of discrimination or harassment to be in a position to make any managerial decisions affecting the employee—about assignments, projects, discipline, raises, promotions, or layoffs, for example—until the allegations are resolved.

Of course, the degree of separation will also depend, in part, on the seriousness of the allegations. A physical assault is obviously much more serious than escalating joking between two friends, for example. In serious cases, you'll want to make sure the alleged harasser is far from the victim—perhaps even away from the workplace. The severity of the alleged conduct or the disruption to the workplace may call for placing the accused on paid leave. For example, if an employee accuses a coworker of sexual assault, you'll want to take the preventative step of keeping the accused employee away from the premises. If the company does not have an available place to move the accused employee, even temporarily, this might be the only logical solution.

But be careful: The law prohibits an employer from retaliating against an employee for complaining about harassment or discrimination. Transferring a reporting employee to a less desirable job or shift could be viewed as retaliatory, even if it's done to separate him or her from the accused employee. For this reason, if a transfer is necessary, it is best to move the accused employee, even if you haven't determined whether the complaint is valid. Recognizing that separating employees puts employers in a difficult position, courts have upheld the approach of moving the accused employee pending an investigation.

Common Questions

Q: A female assistant has accused the company CFO of grabbing her and fondling her breast in his office last night while the two were working late on an IPO scheduled to be announced next week. The CFO is the lead on the IPO, and the assistant has been working exclusively on it for months. I'm investigating her accusations and I know I should separate them, so I'm considering reassigning the assistant to another executive and another (probably lower-profile) project. The CFO really can't be taken off the IPO at this stage without harming its prospects for success. Is my plan okay?

A: Not necessarily. Reassigning the assistant to lower-profile work might be considered detrimental to her and/or her career and that could be considered retaliation. You don't say how many other executives your firm has in its financial group, so it's unclear whether the CFO really is indispensible to the IPO. If any other executive can step in and shepherd the IPO forward with the assistant's help, that's preferable. The CFO could advise his replacement outside the assistant's presence, if necessary, and could still be the "public face" of the firm for the IPO.

Special Considerations When Interviewing the Accused Employee

When you speak to the accused employee, you have several obligations. You have to find out what really happened, so you can take action to protect the company and the reporting employee. You also have to act fairly toward the accused employee, however. Accusations aren't facts: If the accused employee believes that you've already made up your mind and aren't interested in the real story, you could be facing a legal challenge to any discipline you later decide to impose. That's why it's so important to remain neutral and calm when you conduct your interviews.

Common Questions

Q: A disabled dispatcher for our elevator maintenance company reported that a shift supervisor has started calling her "the Crip." She said he pretends he's joking and he does use nicknames a lot when referring to other employees. After talking to the dispatcher, I called the supervisor in and asked him what the name Crip refers to. He stared at me, obviously angry, and said, "How should I know?" Then he said he wanted to talk to a lawyer before speaking with me any further on the subject. I'm not sure what to do next. Did I get off on the wrong track here?

A: You may have made a bit of a misstep because you opened your interview of the accused employee with, essentially, an accusation. Also, the way you worded your question gave him an out, because he could (and did) side-step it. Finally, the blunt question about the alleged slur immediately put him on the defensive and he clammed up. Try again with an open-ended, nonleading question, such as, "Do you ever call any of your coworkers by nicknames?"

It's usually best to interview the accused employee after you've spoken to the reporting employee but before you interview other witnesses. The accused employee is more likely to feel the process is fair if it doesn't look like you're building an attack arsenal. You also have a better opportunity to assess the employee's unrehearsed response if the employee first learns of the problem from you—not from a witness you've already interviewed in conjunction with the investigation.

Naturally, an employee accused of harassment or discrimination may be guarded during the interview. Start by assuring the employee that the investigation is a confidential process and that you won't reveal information to anyone unless it's necessary. Also make it clear that you haven't drawn any conclusions—that the purpose of the process is to get all the facts about what actually happened.

You'll have to provide enough information about the complaint so that the employee knows what you're asking about and can respond intelligently. For example, it's much more productive to ask, "What are the criteria you considered when deciding who should lead the Smith project?" than "Did you discriminate against Jane because of her gender?" You're looking for areas of agreement and disagreement between the reporting employee's and the accused employee's versions of events. In some cases, you may have concrete, documented actions to ask about, such as pay rates or promotion denials; in others, you may be dealing with complaints based on alleged statements, inferred intent, and general feelings. It will be your job to root out the details.

Common Questions

Q: After receiving a complaint of age discrimination from one of our employees who was recently demoted, I interviewed the accused manager. I explained, "You've been accused of making ageist statements." Right away, she got very defensive and told me that she'd joked about age with another female employee—not the employee who complained—who was "too sensitive about this stuff." Now that she's brought this up, should I speak with the other employee?

A: Yes. This is exactly why an investigation is so important: It can reveal facts you didn't know that can put the company at risk. Keep in mind that it's possible the other employee feels harassed too, and just hasn't reported it to you. And if the accused manager doesn't even remember making any inappropriate statements to the reporting employee, that may be a sign that she really doesn't understand appropriate workplace behavior.

As a side note, although you received a lot of important information that you wouldn't have if you hadn't started this investigation as you did, it's no surprise that your opening gambit made the employee defensive. To start with an accusation of bias, without any details or facts, generally leads the person you're interviewing to clam up or begin offering rationalizations, rather than answering questions fully. In this situation, the employee drew conclusions about what you meant by "ageist" statements and immediately started in on the justifications. Even though she revealed information you didn't already have, the tone of the interview was defensive. You could have avoided this by instead focusing on the who, what, when, where, and why facts at issue in the current complaint.

The employee may deny the allegations outright. Ask whether there are any documents or witnesses that may support the accused employee's version of events, then follow up to get that information.

Alternatively, the accused employee may attempt to justify, rationalize, or explain away the alleged conduct (for example, by saying "I was just joking around" or "He says the same things to me all the time"). You shouldn't argue with or cross-examine the employee. Just get the employee's side of the story, asking questions as necessary to get to the facts behind the employee's characterizations. For example, the employee who states, "he says the same things to me all the time," could then be asked to give examples, with information on when the incidents occurred, in what context, and who else was present. Then, you can follow up with additional interviews, if necessary.

> **CAUTION**
>
> **Don't give a supervisor any special deference.** As the investigator, you cannot allow your impartiality to be compromised by a supervisor's position of authority or tenure with the company. If the accused employee is higher than you in the chain of command—and especially if you report to him or her—you may have to bring in an outside investigator, to make sure the investigation is viewed as fair. If you hire an outsider to investigate, you'll need to follow the rules set out in the Fair Credit Reporting Act, including providing certain information to the accused employee. (For more, see *The Essential Guide to Federal Employment Laws*, by Lisa Guerin and Amy DelPo (Nolo).)

Concluding Your Investigation

Once you have gathered all the facts you can, you have to decide what you think really happened. This can be difficult: You may have five different stories from five different witnesses, and you'll have to determine whose version makes the most sense. In some situations, the evidence may conflict so much that you aren't able to draw any firm conclusions about the underlying facts.

Understanding Your Goal

Your primary goal isn't to determine whether the law was violated—
if worse comes to worst, a judge or jury decides that. But you can
and should try to determine whether the accused employee violated
your company's policy. You will want to base your disciplinary
decision on the options and requirements laid out for you in that
policy.

> CAUTION
> **If you're concerned that the law may have been violated,
> report it to company management.** Communicate this information to
> your boss, human resources, or company counsel. While your prompt
> disciplinary action may help your company avoid a lawsuit, you want to be
> fully prepared if there is one.

Again, your responsibility isn't to be the final arbiter of truth;
your responsibility is to conduct a fair and impartial investigation
and to reach a conclusion in good faith. As long as you do this, you
are legally protected, even if your conclusion ultimately turns out to
be wrong.

Reaching a Conclusion

After conducting a full investigation, you may conclude one of three
things:

- **Company policy was violated.** If you find an employee has
  violated your company's policy, your course of action is
  clear: You must immediately take steps to stop the behavior
  and prevent future violations. This might include discipline,
  training, or even firing the accused employee.
- **You can't determine whether company policy was violated.**
  Sometimes, the information you get will be too vague or
  contradicted by other evidence for you to determine whether
  the allegations are true. Don't succumb to the impulse to

reach a conclusion just for the sake of finality. Above all, you're seeking the truth insofar as it can be determined.

- **The accusations are false or the behavior occurred, but didn't violate company policy.** If you determine the behavior didn't occur, don't punish the reporting employee unless you are certain the complaint was intentionally false—and you have evidence to prove it. Otherwise, you're inviting a retaliation claim.

It can be frustrating to conduct a careful, thorough investigation, only to find that you can't reach a conclusion. Many harassment and discrimination cases are "he said, she said"—that is, you'll have nothing more than the conflicting statements of the reporting employee and the accused employee. You're not required to take one employee's word as true in these situations, especially if there are no witnesses, documents, or other evidence supporting either side. As long as you investigate fully and document your findings, you've done your job. If there are any further incidents, you can pull out your file and take a fresh look at the evidence.

Unless everyone you interviewed agreed on all the important facts, you will need to evaluate conflicting information. One way to do this is to develop a chart listing each significant fact, with columns to check for undisputed facts and disputed statements. In a third column, labeled "Contradictory Information," you can briefly note the person or document that contradicts the listed fact. You can scan this chart to determine which facts you can treat as true and which you'll have to evaluate to decide which version is more credible.

Sample Fact Chart

Fact	Undisputed	Disputed	Contradictory Information
Joe Adams called Seth Regan "grandpa"		✓	Seth Regan interview 10/10/xx Joe Adams interview 10/15/xx

If facts are disputed, you need to evaluate the two (or more) conflicting versions and assess the credibility of each. Which is more likely, sounds more like the truth, makes more sense? Here are some things to consider:

- **Plausibility.** Start by considering whose version makes more sense. For example, let's say an employee complains that a pornographic picture was taped to her computer monitor when she arrived at work in the morning. Several witnesses, all of whom arrive at work early on a regular basis, report that they saw the accused employee in her office, and that it was unusual for him to be at work so early. The accused employee says he was in the employee's office looking for a stapler, even though he has one on his desk, and that he just happened to arrive early that day. In this situation, the accused employee's account is not very plausible.

- **Specificity.** How much detail does each person provide? The more detailed the information, the more credible it is, in general. For example, one employee accuses another of making a racist comment in the company's parking lot. The reporting employee says, "I'm pretty sure it happened at around 3:00, because we were both there to meet the delivery truck on its afternoon stop. The truck was late, and Ned said something about how the driver was on "CP time." I didn't know what he meant; when I asked him, he said, "you know, colored people time; you guys are always late." Ned says he doesn't remember whether he was in the parking lot that day, but that he "wouldn't" make a racist comment. In this situation, the reporting employee's story is a lot more specific, in ways that support his claim.

- **The source.** If witnesses are the source of conflicting information, what is the demeanor of each during their interview? Do any of the witnesses have a possible motive for being other than totally honest? For example, a witness who just received a poor performance evaluation from a supervisor accused of wrongdoing might have a motive to make that supervisor look bad. Do the witnesses claim that they each personally observed the incident? Information about a first-hand observation is generally more credible than second-hand accounts.

If you've conducted the investigation and are having a tough time assessing the information you've gathered, have another manager or company HR professional take a look at it.

Common Questions

Q: Hanif, who is Pakistani, told me that a coworker, Chuck, called him a "camel jockey," and draped a dust cloth over Hanif's head as if it were a head scarf. Hanif said that when he yanked the dust cloth off, he accidentally struck Chuck in the eye. Chuck did indeed have a black eye and said he got it when he and Hanif were "horsing around," but said it "wasn't a big deal." He denied making comments about Hanif's ancestry and said they were friends. No one witnessed these events, and I don't know who's telling the truth. Where do I go from here?

A: This is a textbook "he said/he said": Hanif says Chuck made an offensive statement, Chuck denies it, and there's no other account that will help you sort this out. Your first step here may be to go back to both employees for more information. For example, it's possible that Chuck honestly didn't believe the comment he made is about ancestry.

If further exploration doesn't yield any new information, you should ask for help from an outside source. Have a human resources professional, your manager, or even company counsel review your investigatory file. With fresh eyes, they may help you see important details you didn't catch the first time around.

Once you've reached a conclusion, you must decide what action to take, if any. If you find that the accused employee has violated company policy, you'll want to impose a level of discipline consistent with the violation. Of course, the more serious or frequent the violations, the more serious the discipline should be in response.

Crafting a Solution

The best way to resolve a complaint depends on the facts of the underlying incident(s). Your goals in coming up with an appropriate resolution are to prevent and correct inappropriate behavior; and to restore the workplace to a professional, collegial environment. Taking quick, effective action to address misconduct not only puts a stop to the immediate problem, but also shows employees that the company takes their concerns seriously—and shows potential wrongdoers that violating company policy will result in discipline. The more quickly—and thoroughly—you address employee complaints, the more readily the work atmosphere will improve for everyone.

CAUTION
Supervisor harassment requires special attention. As explained in Chapter 2, the company faces a much higher liability risk when a supervisor harasses a subordinate. Because of this risk, supervisor harassment calls for a strong disciplinary response. In addition to taking away the supervisor's duty to manage the reporting employee, you should consider whether he or she should be in a position of authority at all. Because of the liability risks—and a supervisor's power to act for the company—you should allow a supervisor to continue in a managerial role only if you are very confident that he or she will behave appropriately going forward.

Communicating Your Findings

Once you've reached a conclusion, you must communicate the outcome to the reporting and the accused employees. Your approach will depend on whom you are talking to, as well as on the conclusion you reach.

Meeting With the Accused Employee

Your first meeting should be with the accused employee. Being accused of harassment or discrimination is doubtlessly a very stressful event. The accused employee should find out whether he or she will be disciplined from you, not through the office grapevine. And, if you decide that discipline is appropriate, you'll want to handle that before you talk to the reporting employee.

Be professional and respectful when meeting with the accused employee, even if your investigation revealed serious misconduct. Focus on your duty to enforce the company's policies and comply with the law. If you are unsure what level of discipline is appropriate, get some guidance from human resources or company decision makers first.

During the investigation, you should already have given the accused employee an opportunity to respond to the allegations directly. There's no need to reveal what particular witnesses said or all the reasons why you reached the conclusions you did. If you will impose discipline, simply explain that you conducted your investigation, you concluded, based on all of the available evidence, that the accused employee violated company policy, and you will have to impose disciplinary action.

 TIP

A good-faith investigation also protects you from defamation claims. Employees who feel they are wrongfully disciplined or terminated for harassment or discrimination may claim that you defamed them—that is, that you publicly spread information about them that wasn't true—or that their termination is wrongful or illegal. But as long as the employer has a reasonable belief, backed by a thorough investigation, that a violation occurred, courts have denied these claims.

 Lessons From the Real World

Employer's honest, good-faith belief that an employee engaged in sexual harassment defeats employee's wrongful termination claim.

Rollins Hudig Hall International, Inc., received an employee complaint that senior vice president Ralph Cotran had sexually harassed two female employees. Rollins conducted an extensive investigation, in which it interviewed more than 20 witnesses and obtained affidavits from the victims. Witnesses stated that Cotran had made obscene phone calls to female employees, exposed himself to them, and masturbated in front of them.

Rollins met with Cotran and reviewed the allegations with him. Cotran offered no explanations, but gave Rollins a list of additional witnesses to interview, which it did. One of the witnesses identified by Cotran said that she'd received a "strange" phone call at home from Rollins. Yet another told Rollins that Cotran had made obscene calls to her after a sexual relationship between them had ended. Based on all of this information, Rollins fired Cotran.

Cotran sued over his termination. After a trial in which Cotran offered evidence that he'd had consensual sexual relationships with the alleged victims, a jury found that Cotran had not engaged in sexual harassment and awarded him $1.7 million. Rollins appealed.

The California Supreme Court found that Rollins had good cause to terminate Cotran's employment. The company had an honest belief that he'd committed sexual harassment based on its investigation, which had included an opportunity for Cotran to respond to the accusations. The court also ruled that the question in such a case is not whether the accused employee actually engaged in the alleged conduct, but whether the employer had an honest belief, based on an adequate investigation, that he had.

Cotran v. Rollins Hudig Hall International, Inc., 17 Cal.4th 93 (1998).

Meeting With the Reporting Employee

When you meet with the reporting employee, you will need to walk a fine line. You must provide enough information to reassure the reporting employee that you took the complaint seriously, investigated it fully, and handled it effectively. At the same time, however, the reporting employee should not be privy to every detail of the investigation and the company's response. You must protect the confidentiality of the investigation and the privacy of the accused employee and any witnesses you interviewed.

To make sure the reporting employee understands your position, you may want to start the meeting off by stating that you aren't free to discuss all of the details your investigation uncovered or how the company decided to respond. Explain that, just as the reporting employee was entitled to confidentiality to the extent possible, so are the accused employee and any witnesses you spoke to.

Next, tell the reporting employee generally whom you talked to (for example, "I met individually with everyone who was at the meeting," or "I spoke to all of the employees you mentioned as possible witnesses to your conversation at lunch"), and whether your investigation turned up information that either supported or contradicted the reporting employee's complaint ("four of the employees remembered hearing him make the statement you described to me"). Be careful not to reveal information you shouldn't; this can be especially tough if the employee asks questions about who said what. For example, if the employee asks, "Who told you I raised my voice at the meeting?" you should tell the employee that you aren't free to reveal information like this, in order to protect the confidentiality of other employees.

Lessons From the Real World

Separation doesn't have to be total.

Philip Feiner told coworker Melody Swenson that he dreamed of her, watched her "ass moving," and wanted to take her alone into a room and kiss her. Though Swenson rejected Feiner's advances, he grabbed her wrist and tried to pull her to him. Swenson yanked her hand back, screamed at him to stop, and reported the comments and incident to her supervisor. The supervisor informed Feiner that he had harassed Swenson, instructed him to cease, and temporarily transferred him away from Swenson's immediate work area, although the separation did not eliminate all contact between the two.

Swenson sued the employer, alleging that it failed to take prompt, temporary steps in response to her complaint. The appellate court disagreed and reversed the jury verdict in her favor. The court noted that the employer had moved quickly to separate the two, and found that the separation was adequate even though not total because the employer did not have to "provide Swenson a Feiner-free workplace."

Swenson v. Potter, 271 F.3d 1184 (9th Cir. 2001).

You shouldn't give the reporting employee details about the discipline you will be imposing on the accused employee, if any. If the accused employee has been disciplined as a result of the investigation, you should say so, and tell the employee about any steps you've taken to prevent problems in the future. For example, if the employee complained of harassment by a supervisor, you can state that the supervisor has been disciplined and will no longer be responsible for managing the reporting employee. Let the reporting employee know that you appreciate his or her willingness to come forward, and encourage the employee to let you know immediately if there are any further problems or the employee faces any retaliation as a result of the complaint.

What to Say When Results Are Inconclusive

It's very hard to tell reporting employees that your results are inconclusive. They may feel they took a big risk in coming forward and feel hurt or angry that the company appears not to believe their claims. Make sure you don't compound the problem by denying it: Events may have occurred just as the reporting employee described, even if there wasn't evidence to support his or her claims.

When meeting with the reporting employee, make sure to:

- Thank the employee for coming forward.
- Explain that, after a full investigation, you were unable to substantiate the allegations.
- Make clear that you spoke with the accused employee and stressed the company's commitment to a harassment- and discrimination-free workplace.
- Encourage the employee to come forward if there are any future incidents.

TIP

Follow up to make sure corrective action is effective. Calendar a date shortly down the road to check in on any progress or changes. Make sure the accused employee has complied with any training requirements or other instructions (for example, to leave the reporting employee alone). Talk to the reporting employee to find out if he or she has experienced any further problems or retaliation.

Closure Letters

One option for communicating your findings to the reporting and accused employees is to give each a "closure letter." In this letter, you tell the employees that you conducted a full investigation of the reported conduct and state the outcome, as described above.

Conclude with a statement that the company will proceed consistently with its policy, taking whatever action, if any, is called for under the circumstances. Reiterate that the employees should contact you if they have any questions or to report any further incidents.

Dos and Don'ts

Do:
- Take complaints seriously and treat all employees involved with respect.
- Create a plan before you investigate.
- Ask who, what, where, when, how, and why questions to get details.
- Give every employee you interview a copy of the company's policy prohibiting discrimination and harassment.
- Separate the reporting employee and the accused employee as much as possible during the investigation.
- Take corrective action that complies with company policy and is reasonably calculated to stop the misconduct.
- Communicate your findings to the reporting employee and accused employee, without revealing unnecessary details.

Don't:
- Ask leading questions.
- Let your personal opinions cloud your objectivity.
- Reveal details about your investigation to people who don't need to know them.
- Hesitate to ask for management or human resources help when you're having trouble reaching a conclusion.

Documentation

What Your Documentation Should Look Like.. 155

What Documents You Should Have.. 158

Summary of the Complaint.. 158

Witness Statements 159

Interview Notes 162

Create a Timeline.. 164

Physical Evidence 166

Policy Distribution Log 168

The Final Report 168

Discipline Report.. 170

Document Management.. 171

How to Manage Documents 171

Where to Keep Documents 172

How Long to Keep Documents... 172

As you take complaints and investigate claims of harassment and discrimination, you must document as you go. Good documentation is an essential component of a thorough investigation. It helps you keep track of dates, documents you reviewed, whom you spoke to, and what everyone said, so you can put everything together and draw a conclusion. Keeping good records also helps you recognize gaps in information you may need to explore further. And it allows other decision makers to take the information you gathered and draw logical conclusions from it, too. This is helpful if, for example, you are responsible for conducting the investigation, but not for deciding what action the company should take afterwards.

A good paper trail also gives you valuable legal protection. It shows that you are actively trying to resolve the problem and demonstrates the facts you had at your disposal as you reached your conclusions and decided what action the company should take in response. These facts ultimately justify your decisions, showing others that you have followed company policy and complied with the law.

If you are unable to reach a conclusion about what happened, your documentation will play a very important role in protecting the company. Your records will demonstrate areas where there were conflicting facts that prevented you from figuring out who was telling the truth, which demonstrates that you investigated in good faith and tried to get to the bottom of things. And, if there are further incidents involving the same people, the company can evaluate them in light of the history recorded in your documents.

The best documentation is complete, detailed, and factual. You shouldn't write down every stray thought that crosses your mind during the investigation; your thoughts, feelings, or inclinations about what happened don't belong in your documentation. At the same time, however, your records should include all of the facts you considered in reaching your conclusions and the source of those facts (for example, a witness statement or email message). Be prepared for the worst-case scenario: If the company is ever sued, a clear record will help you recall what actually happened at the time and support the conclusions you reached. This chapter explains how to create documents that meet these objectives.

What Your Documentation Should Look Like

Your investigation file will contain different types of documents. Some of them were probably prepared for other purposes, but include information relevant to your investigation, such as email messages, performance evaluations, personnel records, and so on. Others are documents you prepare during the investigation, such as notes from interviews and memos regarding your findings.

You don't have much control over the content of the first type of documents: They've already been prepared before your investigation. The documents you create are a different story, however. All of these documents should serve as a useful, factual, and accurate representation of the information available at the time you conducted your investigation.

> CAUTION
>
> **Documents you create could be presented as evidence in court.** Unless you prepare the investigation and other documents for your company's attorneys or at their direction, the complaining employee can get copies of those documents after filing a lawsuit and perhaps even introduce them as evidence at trial. As long as you keep this possible audience in mind while drafting your documents, handing them over should help your company's case. The documents will show that you fulfilled your legal obligation to investigate the complaint and respond appropriately.

To create the most useful record of your work, make sure your documentation includes:

- **Dates.** Each document should include all relevant dates, including when it was created and when particular events described in the documents took place.

- **Source.** Your records should indicate where you learned particular facts or who gave you specific items, such as documents or photographs. This may be obvious on the face of the document—for example, you can write your own name on interview notes—but if it's not, make sure there is some additional notation that reflects its origins. This is particularly important if other names appear on the document. For example, you may have a printout of an email message containing a sexually explicit joke, sent by one employee to a group of coworkers. The document will probably show the names of the original sender and recipient, but it's also important to note where you got the printout: Did the sender give it to you? One of the listed recipients? Another employee to whom it was forwarded? Or did everyone deny the existence of the email message until you had the IT department comb the archives and dig it out?

- **Full names.** Names may become important years later, when witnesses no longer work at the company and you get another complaint or are involved in a lawsuit. It's much easier to find witnesses if you know their full names.

- **Complete sentences.** This makes it easy for anyone to read and understand your interview notes.

- **Facts.** Instead of drawing conclusions, explain the facts. For example, instead of saying an employee is upset, you might write, "When I asked her if she was upset by his question, she looked down and whispered, 'not really.' She then began to cry."

- **No legal conclusions.** Your job is not to determine whether behavior meets the legal definition of harassment or discrimination. In fact, putting a conclusion like that in your investigation file can do a lot of harm to your company in a lawsuit. Instead, you should decide whether the investigated conduct violates your company's policies; if you decide in the affirmative, that's the conclusion that should go in your records.

Common Questions

Q: I'm the head of Human Resources for my company. I received a complaint from a male employee, Scott, that his supervisor, Loretta, called him a "typical alpha male." Scott said this happened when he was in a product update meeting with Loretta and his coworker, Adrienne.

I interviewed Adrienne today and here are my notes: "Adrienne said she was in Scott's office when Loretta came in last Wednesday. I asked her if anything inappropriate happened in Scott's office at the time. She hesitated and then she said, no. I think she may not be credible because she could protecting Loretta; I've heard they're friends outside of work. This leads me to conclude that Loretta probably did make a sexist slur about Scott." Have I documented all of this properly?

A: Not even close. There are a number of flaws in your documentation (and your interview technique). First, you've drawn a conclusion rather than documenting the information you gathered. Your notes don't reflect that you even asked Adrienne if Loretta made the exact comment that Scott reported, but only that you asked if anything "inappropriate happened." You also don't indicate who told you that Loretta and Adrienne are friends outside of work or whether you asked Adrienne about that connection. Although this is a factor you may take into account when making your ultimate decisions, you have to nail it down—and decide how much weight to give it—before you can rely on it.

What's more, the document is undated, the writer is unidentified, you don't give the full names of the individuals to whom you refer, it contains an unsupported opinion (that Adrienne may not be credible), and a conclusion that doesn't logically follow from the facts you've related. A follow-up interview, documented by more complete notes, is necessary here, to start.

What Documents You Should Have

The documents you gather will depend on what you are investigating. For example, if an employee complains that she was denied a promotion because of her gender, you'll need to collect personnel records, internal application documents, and other information on those who were considered for the position, to evaluate everyone's qualifications.

In addition to the documents you collect, you will create several types of documents during your investigation. Your company may call these documents by different names than the ones we use below. That's okay—there's no requirement they take any particular form or have a specific title—as long as you're sure you're covering all the bases.

Summary of the Complaint

After interviewing the complaining employee, you should prepare a brief summary of the complaint. It should be a short, factual account of what the complaining employee told you.

Sample Complaint Summary

To: File
From: Leona Brown, Human Resources
Date: November 29, 20xx
Re: Tomiko Nishimura Complaint Summary

On November 29, 20xx, Tomiko Nishimura came into my office and she said that she believed her supervisor, Gordon Lewis, discriminated against her based on her race because he terminated her employment that day, and no other non-Asian employees were terminated.

The purpose of a summary is simply to provide a context for the other documents. It needn't be a detailed recitation of the employee's complaint—and it shouldn't be, as that will be found in the notes of the interview of that employee and in the witness statement, if the employee signs one. Just make sure your summary is a brief statement of what the employee actually complained of, not your opinion of it.

Witness Statements

Although much of the information you collect will be your own notes or summary documents, you may also receive written statements directly from the witnesses you interview. A witness's signed, written statement is perhaps the best type of document—his or her account of what happened, without any interpretation by a third party.

Witnesses may not volunteer to provide written statements, but you can always ask them to do so. However, not all witness statements will be written as you might like. Witnesses may forget to include important facts—for instance, the date of an alleged incident or the first and last names of everyone present—and they may include their own thoughts or opinions, which usually aren't relevant. A raw witness statement can even distract from the actual facts the witness could convey. For example, a statement such as "Tomiko was being really rude," tells you how the witness felt about Tomiko's behavior, but doesn't give you any idea about what Tomiko actually said or did and in what context. A better statement might say something like, "Tomiko raised her voice, then turned and walked away before Gordon had a chance to answer."

To get the right information in and keep the rest out, it often makes sense for you to draft the witness statement based on the facts the witness tells you during any interviews, quoting the witness verbatim on key points. The witness can then review it for accuracy and, if he or she agrees with it, sign it. This gives you an opportunity to make sure you understood the witness correctly and got all of the facts straight.

The witness may want to change something in your written statement. If you got something wrong, you should certainly change it to reflect the true facts. You can either correct the statement electronically before the witness signs it or cross out errors and write in your corrections on the original document. If the witness changes his or her story after the interview, however, you should have another conversation about it before getting a signed statement. Perhaps the witness is worried about retaliation or doesn't want to cause trouble. If the witness insists that the new version of events is the truth, you should allow him or her to sign a statement to that effect. However, you should draft a separate memo to the file describing the change; you may also need to do additional investigating to find out what's going on. Keep any draft statement that the witness marked up and note the date that you discussed it with the witness.

Common Questions

Q: I interviewed an employee who said he saw an incident that formed the basis of a discrimination complaint another employee made against their manager. After the interview, I prepared a statement and asked the witness to sign it. He took it to review and returned it the next day with some changes. The new version essentially denies that he directly observed the incident, even though he told me during his interview that he had. What to do?

A: You're going to have to have another conversation with the employee to find out the reason he changed his version of events. Tell the employee that the statement must accurately reflect what happened—that the company expects his honesty. Because he may feel apprehensive about making a statement that implicates his manager, you might want to also remind him that he can't be retaliated against for assisting in the investigation.

If the witness continues to insist that the revised version of events is accurate, keep the altered statement in the file and document the discrepancy. If you find other evidence that supports the complaining employee's version of events, you want to be able to show why you gave less credence to this witness's "new and improved" statement.

Don't argue with a witness who changes the "facts." Just ask about the change and make a note of the discussion and the changed version of events. And don't speculate in your notes about why you think the witness changed his or her story.

Common Questions

Q: I received the following written, signed statement from a witness I interviewed in connection with a sexual harassment complaint: "On January 5, 2010, I was in the lunchroom when Rebecca Cranston and Jorge Lopez came in. Rebecca bent over to get her lunch bag out of the refrigerator and Jorge said, 'nice view.' This was a disgusting comment. Rebecca stood up quickly and told Jorge she was 'sick of your jokes.' Then she left the room. She seemed really upset. Signed Lucas Owens, January 7, 2010." This is a good piece of evidence, isn't it?

A: It's not quite good enough because it's missing some key information and it contains some unnecessary and unhelpful material. The statement doesn't explain how the witness knew that Rebecca was upset. That is, it should present the facts that led to this opinion instead of just the opinion. It also doesn't indicate whether or not anyone else was present, which is an important fact, nor does it reveal why Lucas felt that Jorge's statement was disgusting (in other words, if it's because Jorge was clearly looking at Rebecca's posterior when he said it, the statement should relate that fact).

Interview Notes

As you conduct your interviews, you should take notes of the important facts. Start with the basics: the date, the witness's full name, and your name. Keep in mind that you might not work at the company forever—at some point in the future, the company may need to review the notes and will want to know all of these details.

The notes themselves should record the important questions you asked in the interview, how the witness responded, and any other information that was volunteered or seemed relevant. These notes are for you and the company—not for the witness. If you see a discrepancy in something the witness said, for example, you should note it here for follow-up questions.

Use a consistent format for your documentation from witness to witness and from investigation to investigation. This will help you make sure you include all of the necessary elements. Your company may have a standard form for this purpose; if not, you can do something like the Sample Interview Notes below—a simple memo to the file.

When possible, include direct quotes from the witness. Don't speculate about what the witness means or why he or she is saying it. If you want to record the witness's demeanor, focus on observable facts (such as, "she raised her voice when she said this," instead of "she was angry"). It may also make sense to document the next steps you plan to take to follow up on the information obtained.

Sample Interview Notes

To:	File
From:	Leona Brown, Human Resources
Date:	November 30, 20xx
Re:	Interview with Marnie Farrell

On January 7, 20xx, I met with Marnie Farrell to discuss an alleged incident between Rebecca Cranston and Jorge Lopez. According to Rebecca, Marnie was in the lunchroom on January 5, when the incident occurred (see memo to file, January 5, 20xx).

I asked Marnie if she was in the lunchroom on January 5 with Rebecca and Jorge. She said that she was. She told me that Lucas Owens and Bob Stevens were also there, but no one else was present.

I asked her if she saw Rebecca open the refrigerator and heard Jorge make a comment. She said, "I saw her open the door and I heard him say something but I don't know what because I was on my cell phone." When I asked her what happened after Jorge made the comment, Marnie said, "Rebecca slammed the refrigerator door and left the room. Jorge said, 'I'm just kidding; don't be mad,' but Rebecca didn't say anything, she just left."

Based on this interview, I will follow up and interview Bob Stevens and re-interview Lucas Owens.

This sample interview note contains all the necessary elements: the date of the interview; the full names of the interviewer, the interviewee, and all involved parties; a sufficiently detailed recitation of the substance of the interview; and no speculation.

Take notes as you're conducting each interview. It can be hard to get down every relevant fact and remain engaged in the interview, so you may find yourself taking shorter notes with abbreviations and codes only you can read. That's fine as long as you later translate them into full, coherent notes that others will be able to read and understand. It's best to do this immediately after each interview, when everything is still fresh in your mind. And make sure that if you quote the witness, the quote is accurate.

CAUTION

Use an intake form to interview the complaining employee. The form will give you a standard format for receiving complaints, thus ensuring you ask for all of the relevant information. This will help you conduct your investigation and make it less likely that you'll need to go back to the reporting employee for more details. You can find a sample intake form in Appendix C.

Create a Timeline

It's important to establish the chronological order of events relating to a complaint. As you get each employee's account of what happened, note when the events they describe occurred (or when the employee says they occurred). Rarely do all relevant events occur on the same day. Instead, there will often be a history or pattern of behavior or previous statements or acts that seem more relevant once a problem has escalated.

A detailed timeline of events will help you keep all the events and the witnesses' stories straight. You can create one after speaking to the reporting employee and add information as you speak to other employees.

Sample Timeline

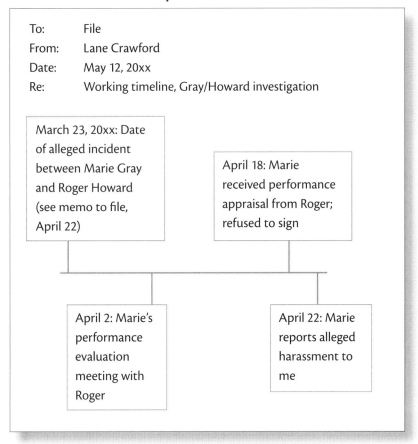

To: File
From: Lane Crawford
Date: May 12, 20xx
Re: Working timeline, Gray/Howard investigation

March 23, 20xx: Date of alleged incident between Marie Gray and Roger Howard (see memo to file, April 22)

April 18: Marie received performance appraisal from Roger; refused to sign

April 2: Marie's performance evaluation meeting with Roger

April 22: Marie reports alleged harassment to me

This sample timeline is helpful because it gives the dates and the events in a clear, chronological fashion. You may have to rework the timeline frequently as you gather more information that either changes the dates or order of events (for example, if you discover the performance meeting actually occurred on April 3, and Marie just got the date wrong) or that adds new events (for example, if Lane learned during a later interview that Marie had closed a major deal between the March 23 incident and her April 18 receipt of the performance appraisal).

If witnesses differ on their recollection of when an event occurred, put all of the dates in the timeline with a notation identifying who reported it, making clear that the chronology is in dispute. For example, if Marie and Roger insist that the performance evaluation meeting took place on different days, your timeline might say: "April 2: Marie claims she and Roger had a meeting to discuss her performance evaluation; Roger disputes (see email from Roger Howard, May 13, 20xx)." If you later receive information that definitively places an event on a particular date, note that on the timeline, too, with reference to the new information and its source.

Keep your timeline brief and to the point. Remember, you may have to use it as evidence and turn it over to the other side if there's a legal dispute later over the investigation, the events leading to it, or the company's response. Short entries will also help you make the best use of the timeline. Its purpose is to allow you to see the sequence of events and their relationship to each other, which will be easier if you keep your notes brief. Include only as much information as you need to trigger your memory, such as "alleged incident in kitchen" or "Ellen notified of promotion decision." The details of each event can be included elsewhere in your notes.

Physical Evidence

If you have photographs, cartoons, letters, email messages, or other items that are implicated in the reported incident, you should keep a copy in your file, along with a note that explains when, how, and from whom you received the item(s). If the originals are later destroyed or lost, there will still be a record of what you were considering when you evaluated the case.

Sample Evidence Note

On September 18, 20xx, I made a photocopy of a cartoon hanging on Mark Stuart's cubicle wall that Jeffrey Townsend had complained about (see Townsend complaint, 9/18/xx). The copy of the cartoon is attached to this note. I also instructed Mark to take the original cartoon home, at least until the investigation of Jeffrey's complaint is concluded.

At times, you may need to describe physical evidence that cannot be copied (such as online videos). Keep these notes in the investigation file and be sure to note the date and location when you examined the evidence.

Many companies have security software to track (and capture) employee Internet activity on company computers. If your company uses such software, it's possible to copy screen shots, Internet searches, keystrokes, or other data that may be relevant to an employee complaint. For example, if an employee reports that a coworker had pornographic material visible on his or her work computer screen, it may be possible to verify that the accused employee visited websites displaying offensive material, along with the dates and times of those site visits.

CAUTION

Advise employees of company monitoring in your handbook. Although employees have a limited right to privacy with respect to their conduct in the workplace, state laws differ about the degree of privacy they retain. Having a written policy informing employees that your company monitors them reduces employee expectations of privacy, which will help your company avoid legal problems. Disclosure is also in your company's interests: Fewer employees are likely to stray in cyberspace or use your company's email system to send inappropriate messages if they know that they may get caught.

Policy Distribution Log

During your investigation, keep a log of everyone to whom you've given a copy of the company's antiharassment and antidiscrimination policy. (Hint: Every employee you speak to during the course of your investigation should be on the list.) Be sure that you also put a signed form acknowledging receipt of the company policy in each employee's personnel file. The policy distribution log can be simple, with each employee's name and the date you gave him or her the policy, as well as a check box indicating that the employee returned a sign acknowledgment form with the date it was returned.

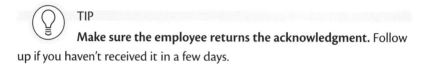

TIP

Make sure the employee returns the acknowledgment. Follow up if you haven't received it in a few days.

Sample Policy Distribution Log

Policy Distribution Log Scott Jansen/Lorenzo Doyle Investigation, October 15, 20xx			
Employee Name	Date Policy Received	Acknowledgment Received?	Date Acknowledgment Received
Scott Jansen	10/15/xx	✓	10/15/xx
Lorenzo Doyle	10/15/xx		
Adrienne Prather	10/15/xx	✓	10/16/xx

The Final Report

At the end of your investigation, you should write a summary report that puts your findings together. This is where you'll take the information you've collected from all of the sources and assemble it in one place, along with the conclusions you drew from all of the facts. You may wish to have a superior or Human Resources representative review the document, to make sure it includes all of the necessary information and supports your ultimate conclusion.

Sample Final Report

To: File
From: Nellie Ray
Date: July 30, 20xx
Re: Eli Dolan complaint

This report summarizes my investigation of Eli Dolan's complaint of discrimination by his supervisor, Katherine Ross.

On July 23, Eli reported that he had been denied a promotion to a position that recently opened up in his department and said he believed his supervisor, Katherine, selected someone else instead because of his ancestry. Eli is Israeli. Eli did not allege that Katherine had ever made any statements about his ancestry; he stated, "I just have a feeling it is because I am Israeli." I asked Eli if there were any other witnesses who might have relevant information and he stated that there were not. I also asked Eli if there were any other documents or information he would like me to consider and he said no. (See Intake Form, July 23, 20xx.)

I reviewed Eli's personnel file, which contained his two performance reviews and his application for the promotion. Each review rated Eli as "meets expectations" overall.

I met with Katherine on July 25 and asked her why Eli was not selected for the promotion. (See memo to file, July 25, 20xx.) Katherine said that she chose another candidate, Simone Cameron, because Simone is better qualified. She provided me with a copy of the job description. When I asked Katherine to list Simone's superior qualifications, she cited Simone's greater experience in the field, the fact that she held a similar position in her last job for several years, and that she has an advanced degree. Katherine also said that Eli doesn't have an advanced degree, nor has he held a similar position. Katherine said she would definitely consider Eli for promotion in the future and wouldn't hesitate to select him if he is the most qualified candidate, but he was not in this case. Katherine said that Eli's ancestry did not affect her decision in any way. I asked Katherine

Sample Final Report (cont'd)

if there were any witnesses who might have additional relevant information and she stated there were not.

After meeting with Katherine, I reviewed Simone's application and confirmed the information Katherine gave me. Simone did have the education and experience requirements listed on the job posting, while Eli did not.

As a result of the above information, I've concluded that no violation of company policy has occurred. I will meet with Eli to communicate the results of my investigation.

Discipline Report

If you decide to discipline the accused employee or anyone else based on your investigation, a brief report that discipline was imposed on that basis should also go in the complaint and investigation file. A copy should also go in the accused employee's personnel file, so that supervisors and managers will respond appropriately if he or she engages in similar violations in the future. The report should also state what discipline was imposed. It isn't necessary to include the reporting employee or victim's name in the discipline report. If there are conditions imposed on the accused employee or requirements that he or she must complete, list those, along with any due dates, and include a space to check once they have been satisfied or completed.

Sample Discipline Report

To: File
From: Alison Bruger
Date: March, 20xx

As a result of my conclusion that Marcus Green violated company policy during the holiday party (see Marcus Green Investigation Final Report, March 10, 20xx), Marcus must:

_____   complete a three-day suspension without pay from March 20 through March 23; and

_____   attend a harassment webinar on April 5.

Document Management

Preparing and collecting good records of the investigation doesn't do you much good if you can't find the documents you need, when you need them. And, if other managers or company lawyers need to review the documents, the papers need to be easy to locate and navigate. Here are some tips for creating an organized, coherent file on a complaint, the investigation, and any resulting disciplinary action or other company response.

How to Manage Documents

Keep all documents relating to a complaint and investigation in one file, separate from other employee files. This helps protect confidentiality, because the documents won't be accessible to people who shouldn't see them. It also helps prevent retaliatory behavior, because information that shouldn't affect other employment decisions won't be available to those making the decisions.

Within the file, organize the documents logically. The most common method is chronological order, with your investigatory notes first and leading up to your final report and disciplinary report, if applicable. If a witness refers to an item of physical evidence, such as a letter, cartoon, or email, attach a copy of that item to the interview notes for easy reference.

If the investigation turns up evidence that may deteriorate over time, such as handwritten notes or photographs, make back-up copies of that evidence for the file. Likewise, if the personal property of an employee or anyone else is possible evidence in the matter and you cannot take the item itself, make a copy or take a photograph of it. You may also need a photograph of physical evidence that cannot be copied (such as graffiti on a worksite wall). Keep the photocopies and photographs in the file along with a note that includes your name and the date and location on which you examined the item.

Where to Keep Documents

Keep the complaint and investigation documents in a secure and private place that employees and others without a need to know cannot access, such as a locked file cabinet. Some evidence, investigation notes, and reports may also be maintained in an electronic format. If so, be sure to protect them by saving them to a secure file that others cannot open, perhaps with password protection. And, if there are electronic documents as well as hard-copy documents, make sure they cross-reference each other.

Although it's essential to maintain these documents in a secure place, don't hide them. You may have trouble remembering where you put them, and others may need to look at them in the future. One way to make sure that documents don't get lost and are accessible to others with a legitimate need to see them is to share their location and any password with at least one other manager.

How Long to Keep Documents

Your company should keep the documents relating to a harassment or discrimination complaint and investigation for as long as it typically keeps financial and other sensitive documents. The EEOC requires employers to retain records related to potential violations for the period of the statute of limitations on the potential legal claim (at least one year after the incident) or until a matter filed with the agency is finally disposed of (via verdict, court order, or settlement), whichever is later. States may have their own retention requirements.

To be safe from a legal perspective, keep the complaint and investigation files and documents for at least five years. If the employees involved still work for you, you may want to extend this time period. This could be helpful if the investigation documents become relevant later—if, for example, there are more allegations against the accused employee.

Dos and Don'ts

Do:
- Include vital statistics in your documentation, including full names, dates, and other essential facts.
- Prepare witness statements and ask witnesses to review and sign them.
- Keep any draft statements that witnesses have marked up.
- Photocopy or photograph physical evidence to preserve a record of it.
- Protect the confidentiality of the complaint and investigations file.
- Organize documents in a logical fashion.

Don't:
- Insert personal opinions, impressions, or reactions into your documentation.
- Allow a witness to change his or her version of events without asking about the reasons for the change.
- Neglect to revise your timeline as your investigation proceeds.
- Draw legal conclusions.
- Inadvertently prevent others with a need to know from accessing your investigative files.

After the Investigation

Dealing With the Aftermath of a Complaint 176

    Controlling Gossip 177

    Handling Additional Complaints 179

    Communicating the Results of Your Investigation 183

Retaliation 184

    Preventing Retaliation 188

    Responding to Retaliation 190

Getting Others Involved 190

    Keep Management Informed 191

    Hiring a Lawyer 193

Once you've finished investigating a discrimination or harassment complaint, documented all of your findings, and taken (or recommended) any necessary disciplinary action, you might think your job is done. However, there may be some additional challenges to deal with, even after your investigation file is closed. A complaint can lead to a host of related problems, from office gossip to allegations of retaliation to new complaints by other employees.

Part of your job may be managing the additional challenges a complaint can bring to the workplace. The way you handle these issues can go a long way toward helping you maintain a positive work environment that's free of harassment and discrimination and helping you limit the company's liability in the unlikely event that an employee files a lawsuit.

This chapter explains how to:

- deal with the aftermath of a complaint
- handle new complaints as they arise
- avoid retaliation claims, and
- keep the company informed of your efforts.

Dealing With the Aftermath of a Complaint

Rarely will a complaint of harassment or discrimination completely escape the notice of other employees. Despite your best attempts to keep your investigation confidential, rumors often fly. Part of your job will be keeping these rumors in check. If you don't, employees may decide for themselves what's happened and why, regardless of the facts. They may misunderstand the company's role because they don't know what you've done to investigate and resolve the problem. And, all that time employees spend speculating, gossiping, or worrying about what happened and what it means is time they're not spending on work.

The solution isn't to publicize every detail of your investigation, however. You still have to keep the investigation and underlying issues confidential to protect the process and encourage employees to continue to come forward with complaints. Revealing things like who complained, what an accused employee was alleged to have done, or what discipline was imposed can also lead to legal problems if the employees involved believe that your comments have harmed their reputations. Your job is to provide enough information to assure employees that the situation has been handled appropriately, without giving too much away.

Controlling Gossip

One of the most common side effects of a workplace harassment or discrimination claim is an increase in office gossip. Even if all of the witnesses respect your requests for confidentiality, it's natural for coworkers to be curious if they see others heading to your office to be interviewed or learn that the accused employee has been put on paid leave, reassigned to another department, or even fired.

When dealing with the office rumor mill, your goal is to stop the gossip and redirect employees' attention back to their jobs. As soon as you learn that employees are spreading rumors about the complaint or the investigation, you are going to have to do what you can to limit or stop it. A good first step is to reiterate your company's policy on handling complaints. Take gossiping employees aside individually. If they were involved in your investigation in some way (for example, as witnesses), remind them that the process must be kept confidential. Use the opportunity to tell employees again that they should immediately come to you if they have concerns about new incidents or retaliation. Also ask supervisory staff to report gossip and rumors to you.

For employees who weren't involved in the investigation, you'll need to be a bit more circumspect. You might start by saying something more general, such as: "I've heard that you have some concerns about the company's antiharassment policy and investigations procedure. Do you have any questions or is there anything you'd like to discuss?" This may give you the opportunity to squelch speculation about a complaint, even if you're not able to provide detailed information about what really happened.

If an employee wants to know the details of a specific situation, tell the employee that the company takes violations of company policy very seriously. Anytime the company receives a complaint, it investigates immediately, as required by company policy. Explain that the company also respects the privacy of its employees and doesn't reveal information about investigations to those without a need to know. This means that you can't reveal any details of a particular complaint. Ask that the employee respect colleagues' privacy, too.

Sometimes, the gossip about a complaint may itself violate company policy against harassment or discrimination. For example, employees gossiping about a sexual harassment complaint may speculate in graphic detail about harassing conduct or joke inappropriately about the nature of the complaint. When you hear about situations like these, you need to intervene. In addition to responding as you ordinarily would when employees make inappropriate comments, tell the employees that they need to do their part to help maintain a collegial, professional environment. Emphasize that gossiping thwarts that goal and can itself violate company policy.

Common Questions

Q: A few months ago an employee complained that a coworker made a derogatory comment based on a racial stereotype. The accused employee admitted making the comment and apologized; in compliance with our company policy, he received a written warning and went to a diversity training class. The reporting employee was informed of the outcome and registered no further complaints. Now, though, another manager has told me that she's heard employee rumors that the accused employee was a "racist" and the company swept it under the rug. What do I do?

A: Following your company's policy was the right thing to do, and under the circumstances, it was reasonable to deal with a single discrete incident as you did—and to keep it confidential. But now you have more work to do. If the problem of employee gossip is too widespread to address it with individual employees, send out an email or memo with the company's antiharassment and antidiscrimination policies attached. You should also reiterate that employees are to bring any concerns about past or present discrimination to you promptly. Explain that you expect anyone who has further questions to discuss them with you privately—not with each other on company time.

Handling Additional Complaints

When one employee comes forward with a complaint of harassment or discrimination, it may give other employees the courage or confidence to report incidents themselves. While this may seem like a bad thing, at least it gives you a good opportunity to address systemic problems before they lead to legal liability. Multiple complaints should make you question whether there is an organizational problem that you need to correct before it gets worse.

When you are faced with additional complaints following an investigation, you should look for:

- **A pattern among the incidents.** A pattern—lots of discrimination complaints coming from a single department, repeated reports of inappropriate jokes being sent on company email, and so forth—is a red flag that a fundamental change may be needed. It may suggest that there's a common misconception about appropriate behavior within the organization, or that a supervisor or manager is failing to intervene or prevent discriminatory or harassing behavior. Understanding these patterns can help you make simple changes that have widespread effect. For example, if you have several reports that employees are viewing pornographic images on their computers, drafting or reiterating a company policy on appropriate use of its computer equipment—perhaps along with getting software that blocks access to inappropriate sites—could solve the problem.

- **A breakdown in the reporting structure.** Sometimes, receiving several complaints at once may indicate that previous violations weren't being reported or investigated correctly. For example, you may find that supervisors were dealing with complaints informally because it's less complicated, or because they didn't know they were supposed to report problems elsewhere.

- **A repeat offender.** You may have several complaints against the same person. If your separate investigations of each of the complaints reveal them to be true, your disciplinary response should take all of the events into account. In this situation, terminating the offender's employment may be necessary.

A systemic problem is going to require more work. You'll have to delve into the reasons for the repeat problems. You may need to circle back and interview people you talked to in the course of your previous investigations. You may also need to look for gaps in your company policy or discuss misunderstandings about the policy with the employees you talk to.

At the same time, your duty as a fact-finding investigator requires you to consider each complaint anew. Don't draw conclusions without taking a good, hard look at the facts in each case.

CAUTION

Make sure you report repeat patterns up the chain of command. A serious systemic flaw increases the potential for repeat problems and creates more legal exposure. Be sure company executives understand the problem and are ready to close the gap. If you discover a number of past incidents that have gone unreported or a major problem in one area of the company, this might be a good time to consider bringing in an employment lawyer to help you figure out how best to handle the situation.

If the problems you uncover stem from a single source, you'll have to figure out what to do about it. If there's a weakness in company policy that results in supervisors not reporting incidents, you may need to rewrite the policy to make reporting requirements more explicit and retrain supervisors. If you see a pattern of poor behavior, it may mean that employees don't realize they've stepped over the line, either because they don't understand appropriate workplace conduct or because their managers are letting them get away with it. In either situation, training, possible policy revisions, and consistent enforcement of the company's rules will help you get a handle on the problem.

If you're not sure how to resolve the problem, ask for help. Bring your concerns to your manager or to company officers and work together to formulate a plan that will turn things around.

TIP

Responding to a pattern of complaints protects your company. Judges and juries can be extremely unsympathetic to a company that has allowed problems to continue unchecked, especially if there's a repeat offender at work. Once you learn of systemic issues, you must take action to stop them—and your response should take into account the full scope of the problem. This will help you stay out of court, because you'll put a stop to the behavior going forward. And, if you do face a lawsuit, you'll be able to show that you did all you could to end the misconduct as soon as you learned about it.

 Common Questions

Q: We've recently had five harassment complaints in one department (way more than any other department), all against different employees. The complaints are all based on inappropriate comments or emails. I've investigated the complaints and found that all of them raise valid concerns. The responsible employees have been disciplined as company policy requires, but I'm wondering whether I should do more. I'm suspicious that something else is going on here, but I'm not sure what. What should I be looking for?

A: A collection of five complaints from one department is certainly troubling, but you don't really have enough information here to explain what's going on. You want to look for anything the company may be doing to communicate that the behavior is okay: Do the employees understand the rules? Start by speaking with the department supervisor. Has he or she received any complaints? If so, and you didn't know about them, it could be an indication that the problems have escalated precisely because nothing was ever done to deal with complaints in the first place. As a result, employees began to feel the inappropriate behavior was accepted or condoned by the company. Correct that problem by giving supervisors a refresher in the company complaint policy.

Look for patterns of behavior, as well. Are employees sending personal emails at work when they shouldn't be? If so, do they have any reason to believe that behavior is acceptable—for example, is the department supervisor aware of it, but either doing nothing to stop it or even participating? It may be that the whole department needs some training on what's permissible and what isn't.

Communicating the Results of Your Investigation

Usually, you will not need to tell employees that you've received, investigated, and resolved a complaint. And, to maintain confidentiality, you ordinarily shouldn't reveal this type of information. But there may be times—for example, if you fire someone after a high-profile incident—when you should address the decision publicly. After all, the unexplained "disappearance" of a coworker or supervisor can be disruptive and stressful for employees. If a number of employees knew about the incident, they may also be concerned about whether the company is doing all it can to prevent similar incidents in the future.

That you must address the situation publicly doesn't mean you should reveal all the facts, however. In most cases, it's best simply to explain that you conducted a thorough, unbiased investigation in accordance with company policy and came to a conclusion based on that investigation. Reiterate that the company is committed to a harassment- and discrimination-free workplace, and suggest that employees with questions or concerns come to you privately. In most cases, you needn't (and shouldn't) even mention names. If an employee has been terminated, however, you should say that he or she no longer works for the company. Employees will notice that the person is gone, and there's no point denying the obvious. Just don't give out any details or state the conclusions of your investigation. It's fine to say "John is no longer working here," but not to say, "We fired John after concluding that he discriminated against Andrea."

CAUTION

If physical safety is at issue, don't be so discreet. If you fire an employee because of a physical assault or threatened assault, you should tell employees that the attacker is barred from the workplace and that they should inform you immediately of any threats to safety. In such a case, it is more important to protect your employees' safety than the privacy of the accused individual. As long as you conducted an investigation and concluded that the threat was real, you should be on safe legal ground. You may also want to contact law enforcement authorities.

Common Questions

Q: We recently conducted an investigation of a male project manager who was accused by a subordinate of assigning jobs based on racial preferences. We couldn't substantiate the allegations. The project manager shares responsibility with another project manager, who heard about the incident and is demanding to know what's going on. She says that team members are asking her about it. How much should I tell her?

A: Not much, because there isn't any real need for her to know. Instead, explain to her—and encourage her to explain to employees —that the company was looking into an employee's concerns involving that manager, and that those concerns have been resolved. Tell her that the issue is confidential. If employees want to discuss this further, they can come to you. And if she has specific concerns, she should be encouraged to raise them with you as well.

Retaliation

Federal law and the laws of most states bar employers from retaliating against an employee who reports harassment or discrimination, or who participates or assists in an investigation, complaint, or lawsuit. These laws protect not only an employee who files a complaint, but also any witnesses you interview and any employee who opposes harassment or discrimination. Protection against retaliation ensures that other employees will not be deterred from reporting harassment and discrimination and that employees will participate fully in company efforts to investigate and remedy problems.

Lessons From the Real World

Witnesses who provide information during an internal investigation are protected from retaliation.

During an investigation into rumors of sexual harassment by a supervisor, a Human Resources officer for the Metropolitan Government of Nashville asked Vicky Crawford, a 30-year Metro employee, if she'd ever witnessed any inappropriate behavior. Crawford said she had and then recounted several harassing acts by the supervisor toward her. Nashville fired Crawford and two others who'd reported harassment, but didn't discipline the supervisor. Crawford filed a retaliation lawsuit.

Nashville argued that, because Crawford didn't file a complaint herself but instead reported the violations only in response to questioning, she wasn't protected from retaliation. The Supreme Court disagreed. It held that an employee "opposes" harassment by answering an employer's question, just as if she had reported the same information on her own initiative. To find otherwise would compromise the company's ability to investigate complaints and discourage employee participation in those investigations.

Crawford v. Metro. Gov't. of Nashville, 129 S.Ct. 846 (2009).

Despite these legal protections, retaliation still occurs. It can take the form of any action that has a negative impact on the employee, if that action is taken because of the employee's complaint or participation. While terminations or demotions are obvious adverse actions, transfers, reassignments, shift changes, pay changes, and benefits changes can be, too. In some cases, retaliation can even include actions taken outside of the work environment, such as a negative job reference or an unfounded criminal or civil charge against the employee.

Common Questions

Q: An employee complained six months ago that a coworker was harassing her. We found a violation of company policy, for which the coworker was disciplined. The employee who filed the original complaint recently told me that the harasser's friends at work are making her work life miserable. They barely acknowledge her and invite everyone in the department, except her, out to happy hour on Friday nights. If what she says is true, is that retaliation?

A: It depends on the situation. Social snubbing isn't retaliation. However, it's not an open and shut case. If the department supervisor uses happy hour as an opportunity to discuss how to staff projects, for example, the employee may be at a serious professional disadvantage by not being part of the discussion. Though there's no civility code, it's important that the employee's job opportunities aren't affected by the snub.

Also, you need to make sure that this truly is personal behavior—friends of the accused coworker acting out of friendship—rather than behavior by the company. If the department supervisor condones or approves the behavior, you need to step in. For example, if the coworker's friend talks over the employee in a department meeting, saying "No one wants to listen to a snitch," and the manager doesn't stop it, this is a larger problem. In that situation, it starts to look like the company is allowing the employee to be intimidated for making a complaint, which could well lead other employees to decide not to come forward with concerns.

If managers, supervisors, or company officers are aware of actions by coworkers that interfere with an employee's job, but fail to step in and stop the behavior, that may also be retaliation attributable to the employer. An employer that permits a reporting employee's peers to negatively affect his or her job is condoning that behavior.

Even though you must be conscious of negative reactions, not every adverse incident following a complaint will meet the legal definition of retaliation. The negative act must be significant enough to dissuade a reasonable employee from reporting or supporting a harassment or discrimination charge. As the Supreme Court puts it, "petty slights or minor annoyances" don't count.

Lessons From the Real World

Any action that might deter a reasonable employee from reporting harassment or discrimination can be retaliation.

Burlington Northern & Santa Fe Railway Co. hired Sheila White as a "track laborer" and assigned her to a forklift operator position. White reported that her supervisor, Bill Joiner, made inappropriate, sex-based remarks to her. Burlington suspended Joiner for 10 days and sent him to a sexual harassment training session. At the same time, Burlington also reassigned White to track labor duties, ostensibly because some of her coworkers had complained that the forklift position should go to a "more senior man." Although these duties were within White's job description and didn't affect her pay, they were more arduous, dirtier, and less desirable than her previous assignment.

White filed a lawsuit claiming that Burlington's reassignment of duties was retaliatory. The Supreme Court agreed, even though the reassignment didn't affect her pay or job level. The Court reasoned that the risk of being assigned to a less-desirable job could deter a reasonable employee from complaining about harassment.

Burlington Northern & Santa Fe Ry. v. White, 548 U.S. 53 (2006).

Preventing Retaliation

You can, and should, do all you can to prevent retaliation. Retaliation compromises your company's efforts to eradicate harassment and discrimination and allows problems to continue unresolved. It can also lead to significant legal exposure. The fundamental unfairness of punishing someone for coming forward to report mistreatment seems to resonate strongly with judges and juries, who are willing to award large damages in these cases.

Here are some steps you can take to help prevent retaliation:

- **Tell employees retaliation is prohibited.** Redistribute the company's written policy when you meet with or interview employees involved in an investigation. Encourage employees to report alleged retaliation.

- **Keep complaints confidential.** The fewer employees who know about the alleged complaint—particularly managers, supervisors, and those in positions of authority—the fewer opportunities there are for anyone to retaliate against the reporting employee or others involved in the investigation.

- **Take care when disciplining an employee involved in a complaint.** You are still permitted to discipline an employee for behavior unrelated to the complaint and should follow company policies consistently. But you'll want very good proof to support what you're doing.

Common Questions

Q: We were finalizing paperwork to terminate an employee for poor performance when she came in and complained that her boss was discriminating against her. We didn't find anything that suggested he'd violated company policy, and we want to go through with the termination, but are concerned about her claiming retaliation. Are we safe?

A: It sounds like it, but you'll want to be very careful. You must have solid evidence that your decision is based on her performance, not on her complaint. Your best evidence would be clear communications to the employee, prior to her making the complaint, that her performance was poor, and that you'd warned her of the likely consequences if it didn't improve. If you have other contemporaneous documents—for example, communications between her supervisor and human resources, discussing the plan to terminate employment prior to the complaint—those documents would also be helpful. To make sure you've dotted every "i" and crossed every "t," you may want to have your evidence reviewed by your attorney before proceeding with the termination.

Also, keep in mind that as long as she made her complaint in good faith, it doesn't ultimately matter that the complaint didn't pan out. You are still prohibited from retaliating against her. Even if you suspect she made the complaint to put you in this exact position—hesitant to discipline for a valid reason for fear of a retaliation complaint—you should not discipline her for it unless you can prove her complaint was made with this improper motive.

Finally, be aware that even if you do everything exactly right, there's no guarantee that the employee won't try to bring a lawsuit against you. Although you'll be in a good position to defend yourself, terminating employment close to receiving a complaint tends to make fair employment practices agencies and courts a little suspicious. You may have to defend the company's position, even if it's just.

Responding to Retaliation

Even the best efforts to prevent retaliation sometimes fail. If you learn that any employee involved in a harassment or discrimination charge or investigation may have been retaliated against, you must respond promptly to correct it. You goal should be to investigate the alleged retaliation just as thoroughly as the underlying complaint. While you're conducting the investigation, make sure the alleged retaliation stops. And, if your investigation reveals a violation of the company's antiretaliation policy, you need to restore the employee to the position he or she was in before the retaliatory conduct occurred. For example, if the employee was put on a less desirable shift, you should move her back to her preferred shift.

Getting Others Involved

As the person receiving or responding to a complaint, you play a major role beyond your job as investigative fact finder: You are the liaison between the reporting employee, the accused employee, and the company. You may have to report to company officers or directors about what's going on in the workforce, because these situations—and the way you handle them—significantly affect employee morale, may impact head count and staffing, and can create potential legal liability for the company. If you don't have the ultimate authority to make decisions and take disciplinary action for the company, someone else may need to take the information you gather and decide what to do with it.

> **TIP**
>
> **The company needs to track patterns, too.** Companies need to keep information about harassment and discrimination complaints in one place. Doing this helps identify patterns of behavior that need correction and makes it easier to find the information on past complaints, if necessary.

Keep Management Informed

No one likes to be the bearer of bad news, and a complaint of harassment or discrimination is certainly that. But the company—in the form of its officers, directors, or top management—needs to know what's going on, especially if the situation could lead to larger problems down the road.

Once you realize that the problem underlying a complaint is serious, bring in senior management. Don't wait until a problem has spiraled out of control. While you probably won't need to report every complaint you receive, you will want to notify higher ups when your investigation suggests that inappropriate behavior may have occurred.

You don't have to provide a thorough description of every last detail, and you don't need to draft a separate written report (beyond your documentation of the investigation, described in Chapter 6). Just be prepared to succinctly explain the root of the problem and to confirm that you've followed company policy in conducting your investigation. If you need help in deciding how to handle the problem, be sure to ask for it.

Investigating an Executive

Complaints can be lodged against anyone in the company, including high-ranking company executives or managers. In those cases, how do you avoid the awkwardness of handling a complaint against a member of upper management and reporting on it to his or her peers?

The best solution is to hire an outside investigator. An outside investigator won't face the same pressures you might to support a popular executive or find fault with an unpopular one. An outside investigator won't be—or appear to be—intimidated by the hierarchical disparity, either. Employees are more likely to see an outsider as truly neutral and, therefore, more likely to view the process and its outcome as fair.

For serious complaints, you may need to inform management of the problem when it first surfaces, then provide updates as you progress through the investigation. If you are pressed for a conclusion before you're prepared to give one, tell them that your investigation is continuing, or that the result is inconclusive. A hasty decision that's made before you know all the facts or one that's ultimately not supported by the investigation doesn't serve anyone's interests.

Common Questions

Q: I am investigating a harassment charge against one of the partners in the law firm where I'm the HR manager. The other partners are nervous about having this partner continue to supervise less senior attorneys, and they're really pushing me to tell them what I've found, but I haven't finished my investigation yet. How much information should I give?

A: Just tell them that your investigation is ongoing. You can't draw any conclusions because you're still investigating. You could find new information that will affect your conclusion and right now, your primary goal is still to act as fact finder. You'll lose credibility if you suddenly flip-flop midway. Moreover, you take the risk that your initial impressions will circle back to the partner in question, and that could compromise the credibility of your investigation if, for example, the partner puts pressure on witnesses to shore up his version of events.

Instead, explain why you're not ready to draw any conclusions yet. Emphasize the need to be fair and accurate: It's more important than being speedy.

Of course, you could have avoided this difficulty altogether if you'd hired an outside investigator. In situations involving an accused employee at the very top of the company ladder, it's almost always a better idea to bring in an outsider—and it avoids the politicking you find yourself caught in right now.

Hiring a Lawyer

Although you'll probably be able to handle most complaints on your own or with the help of an outside investigator (discussed above), there are instances that may call for getting a lawyer involved. If your company has an employment attorney or attorneys, it may be easy to ask questions or get legal input when you need it. Otherwise, you may want to consult an attorney knowledgeable about employment laws in your state.

CAUTION

You can hire a lawyer as an investigator, but don't plan on having the lawyer represent you in a lawsuit. It isn't uncommon for companies to hire employment lawyers to conduct investigations. Just keep in mind that if you do this, you'll need to hire a different lawyer to represent the company if sued. That's because you have to be able to disclose the results of your investigation in court in order to show that the company tried to resolve the problem. It's undesirable to have your lawyer take the stand to testify about this, so plan on hiring someone different for each role.

It usually makes sense to bring in an attorney if:

- **An employee has filed a charge with the EEOC or state fair employment practices agency.** If that's the case, your obligation will extend beyond conducting an investigation—you will have to respond to the employee's charge. Because this may be the first step toward a lawsuit, you need to make sure your response protects the company's interests. You may even be able to stop the charge from proceeding further with the right response. Agency charges are covered in Chapter 8.
- **The complaint is of physical assault or a serious threat of physical harm.** If you're concerned that employee safety may be at stake, you may want to pursue legal remedies to keep an accused employee off the premises and away from other employees. A lawyer can help you do this, quickly.

- **The accused employee is a supervisory employee and you find that a violation of company policy has occurred.** The company's responsibility for supervisory misconduct is significantly greater than for lower-level employee misconduct. A lawyer will help you protect the company as much as possible if a complaint against a supervisor turns out to be true.
- **The investigation was botched.** If the complaint and investigation process has been compromised in some way, an attorney can offer a legal perspective on how best to correct mistakes.

Dos and Don'ts

Do:

- Step in immediately to quash rumors and gossip about a complaint, an investigation, or an action taken.
- Examine systemic reasons for frequent or repeat complaints.
- Briefly explain the outcome of your investigation to employees who need to know.
- Separately and quickly investigate retaliation complaints.
- Keep company officers, directors, or other senior management apprised of serious problems and important developments.

Don't:

- Give details of the outcome to employees who are not directly involved in the complaint and investigation.
- Retaliate against an employee for making a complaint or participating in an investigation.
- Fail to keep management fully informed of the risks and possible liabilities in the course of an investigation.

Dealing With Government Agencies

The Role of Fair Employment Agencies 197

   The Equal Employment Opportunity Commission (EEOC) 198

   State Fair Employment Practices Agencies (FEPAs) 199

The Complaint Process 199

   The Employee's Complaint 200

   The Company's Response 202

   Agency Actions 208

Preparing for an Agency Investigation 209

Mediation 213

   The Mediation Process 214

   Attending Mediation 215

Your Role in Dealing With Investigative Agencies 217

   Prepare for the Worst 217

   Assisting the Company's Attorney 220

   Cooperating With Agency Investigators 221

   Preparing for Mediation 223

   Preventing Retaliation 224

E very employer hopes to resolve employment disputes internally, and the strategies provided in earlier chapters will help you achieve that goal. In rare situations, however, an employee may take a complaint outside the company. Perhaps an employee wasn't satisfied with the company's investigation or how it decided to resolve a problem. Or, the employee may not have made an internal complaint at all, choosing instead to go straight to a government agency or a lawyer for help.

Typically, your first indication that an employee has made a complaint outside the company comes in the mail, in the form of a notice that the employee (or, more often, former employee) has filed a harassment or discrimination complaint with a federal or state fair employment agency. Receiving a formal complaint can certainly be unnerving, and for good reason: It may mean that a government agency will investigate your company's handling of the situation, or even that the employee plans to file a lawsuit against your company. Once you understand how the process works, however, you'll see that there are steps you can take throughout to protect your company.

Once an employee gets a government agency involved, you'll have deadlines to meet and documents to prepare. Your company will have to respond to, and cooperate and communicate with, the agency. This chapter covers the agency's role in receiving, processing, and resolving complaints, so you know what to expect. It explains what you can do to make sure the process goes as smoothly as possible, including how to work collaboratively with a lawyer representing your company in agency proceedings. Although you may feel some anxiety after receiving an agency complaint, the information in this chapter will guide you through the process.

SEE AN EXPERT

If your company receives an agency complaint, consult with a lawyer. This chapter provides an overview of the agency process, but you shouldn't respond to an employee's complaint without some expert advice.

An agency complaint is often the precursor to a lawsuit, and the statements and arguments you make now may limit your company's options later. To best represent and protect your company, you should consult with a lawyer as soon as you receive an agency complaint. Even if you decide to write your own response and handle settlement discussions on your own, a lawyer can review your strategies and documents to make sure you're putting the company's best foot forward. A lawyer can also help you decide whether your company should try to settle a case—and for how much—or take its chances in court.

The Role of Fair Employment Agencies

Claims of workplace harassment and discrimination are handled differently than most other legal disputes. Usually, people who believe they were harmed by someone else's illegal conduct can go straight to court and file a lawsuit. When employees claim they've been harassed or discriminated against by their employers, however, they can't just file a lawsuit. Instead, they must first report their complaints to the Equal Employment Opportunity Commission (EEOC) or a state fair employment practices agency (FEPA).

What is the point of this requirement? These agencies were created to help look into and address violations of Title VII and laws prohibiting discrimination. Because they are devoted exclusively to workplace harassment and discrimination, the agencies can assess and handle these claims more effectively than courts that hear all types of cases. The administrative process is designed to:

- **Weed out claims that don't qualify.** The legal concepts of harassment and discrimination are a bit complicated and can easily be misunderstood by employees. By bringing their complaints to the EEOC or a FEPA, employees can gain a better understanding of what constitutes harassment or discrimination from a legal perspective—and what they'll have to prove to win a lawsuit. When employees get a better sense of their rights under the law from the agencies, they are more likely to abandon claims that don't meet the legal requirements and pursue only those that are well founded.

- **Focus resources on the most serious violations.** The complaint system enables the agencies to identify and pursue more serious violations of employee rights. Generally, agencies are more interested in cases involving a number of employees, extremely egregious behavior, or issues that are an enforcement priority. (For example, if a state governor ran on a platform of protecting low-wage workers, that state's FEPA may be especially interested in pursuing cases involving such employees.) If an agency wishes, it can prosecute complaints itself by filing its own lawsuit against the employer.

- **Resolve small problems before they get to court.** The EEOC or FEPA complaint puts the employer on notice that there is a problem and gives the employer and the employee an opportunity to resolve the problem before it goes any further. As explained below, agencies provide opportunities for mediation and for informal settlement discussions, which can help the parties come up with a workable solution on their own.

The Equal Employment Opportunity Commission (EEOC)

The EEOC is the federal agency charged with enforcement of federal laws prohibiting harassment and discrimination. It receives and processes complaints alleging violations of Title VII, as well as the Equal Pay Act, the Americans with Disabilities Act, the Age Discrimination in Employment Act, and the Genetic Information Nondiscrimination Act. An employee who believes your company has violated one of these laws can bring a complaint to the EEOC. But if federal law doesn't apply—for example, if your company is too small to be covered by these laws or the employee alleges that you are discriminating based on marital status, which isn't prohibited by federal law (but may be by state law)—the EEOC won't accept the complaint.

There are EEOC field offices in every state. If the EEOC accepts a complaint from one of your company's employees or ex-employees, the field office in your company's region will contact you, as discussed below.

State Fair Employment Practices Agencies (FEPAs)

Most states also have FEPAs that receive and process complaints alleging violations of the state's own laws prohibiting harassment and discrimination. Like the EEOC, the state FEPA contacts employers after an employee or ex-employee files a complaint. The process followed by state FEPAs is usually similar to that of the EEOC, but every state is a bit different. An experienced employment attorney can explain how your state agency operates. Differences might involve things like the deadlines for responding to the complaint, the extent of the agency's investigation or conciliation efforts, or the actions the agency is legally authorized to take once it completes its investigation.

Often, an employee who brings a complaint believes that the employer has violated both state and federal law—because, for example, both prohibit discrimination based on gender. In that case, the employee is typically required to bring a complaint to either the EEOC or the FEPA, not both. The agency receiving the complaint will file a duplicate complaint with the other agency, but only one agency (usually, the one that received the complaint) will process and investigate it. As an employer, this means you may be contacted by either the EEOC or a state FEPA regarding a complaint, but you will typically have to deal with only one agency.

The Complaint Process

An employee may file a complaint with the EEOC or FEPA in person, online, or by telephone. The agency must first decide whether to accept the complaint at all; it might not if, for example, the employee is complaining of something that isn't prohibited (such as sexual orientation discrimination in a state that doesn't protect employees from such discrimination) or there is some other basic problem with the complaint. If the agency accepts the complaint, it will follow a series of steps similar to those described below. Remember, if the complaint is filed with your state FEPA, the process may work a little bit differently.

The Employee's Complaint

If the EEOC or FEPA accepts a complaint against your company, it will notify your company in writing. As noted above, the agencies won't accept complaints that are not legally valid. If an agency rejects a complaint, it will typically send the employee a notice (called a "right to sue" letter), stating that the employee has met the requirement of first bringing claims to the agency for resolution and now has the right to file a lawsuit. (Lawsuits are discussed in Chapter 9.)

Common Questions

Q: We recently investigated an internal complaint of racial harassment and ended up firing the accused employee. We determined that he had teased several Chinese American employees about their accents and made fun of their appearance, even after they told him to stop. Now, the harasser has filed a lawsuit against our company! Doesn't he have to file an agency complaint first?

A: Not unless he's claiming that your company discriminated against him or harassed him. Sometimes, an employee who is fired for committing harassment or discrimination makes this type of claim, contending that he or she was disciplined more harshly than other employees. For example, let's say your company received a complaint that two supervisors—one white and one Latino—were engaging in sexual harassment. If your company gives a written warning to the white supervisor and fires the Latino supervisor, the fired employee might claim that your company discriminated in meting out the discipline.

If you're not facing that type of situation, the fired employee may be bringing claims of wrongful termination, breach of contract, or defamation, none of which have to be brought to an agency before the employee can file a lawsuit. Only claims of harassment and discrimination must be taken to an agency in the first instance.

Incidentally, some employees who claim to have been discriminated against or harassed bypass the agency, too, sometimes because they miss the deadline for bringing an agency complaint. If they sue for violation of the laws prohibiting harassment and discrimination, your company can move to dismiss their claims, because they should have been raised with the agency first. (See Chapter 9 for more on dismissing claims from a lawsuit.) However, the employee may choose to forego these claims altogether and bring a lawsuit for infliction of emotional distress or assault, for example. These other legal claims don't have to be filed with an agency before the employee may file a lawsuit, even if they arise from alleged harassment or discrimination.

A copy of the complaint will be sent to your company, along with instructions from the agency explaining how your company should respond (for example, the deadline for responding and the form your response should take). The claim will include only basic information: the name and address of the employee and employer; the basis of the complaint (for example, that the company discriminated against the employee on the basis of race); and a brief description of the allegations that support it.

The purpose of the claim is to tell you what the employee contends; it isn't an indication that the agency has adopted the employee's version of events. You'll have the opportunity to give the company's version in your response to the complaint.

The Company's Response

After receiving a complaint, the company gets the opportunity to answer the employee's allegations. Your written response is important: It sets out the facts supporting your company's side of the story.

CAUTION

Your company can be held to the statements in its written response. After the agency concludes its investigation, the complaining employee can obtain a copy of the agency file, including the company's written response. The complaining employee can argue in court that the company's statements to a government agency are binding or that any change in the employer's story shows that the explanation isn't credible. An employer's inconsistency in explaining its employment actions can be used as evidence that a discriminatory motive might be at work. Because your company's response can carry such legal weight, you may want to work with a lawyer, even if it's just to review the response you've drafted yourself.

You will have a limited amount of time, usually 30 days, to prepare your company's response and get it back to the agency. You should immediately pull together and review all of the materials from any investigation your company already conducted (if the employee reported the matter prior to filing the agency complaint). If your company didn't investigate, because the employee never complained internally or for some other reason, you should do so right away. Frequently, the agency complaint will give you some names of people allegedly involved in the matter, such as employees who may have committed or witnessed misconduct. Of course, you will want to speak to them if you haven't already, or follow up with them if the complaint includes new allegations.

Your response should address each of the employee's allegations in a separate paragraph. The purpose of your response is to use the facts available to you to show that the employee's claim isn't valid. Start with any dispute about the complainant's status (for example, if the person claims to be an employee but is actually an independent contractor). Then, address the employee's legal claims, which will be identified on the complaint form by category of discrimination. The employee will have checked a box or written a description of the type of discrimination he or she is claiming, such as age or sex. Beneath the identified categories of discrimination, there will be a brief statement explaining the claims. Your response should address each claim by providing any facts that refute the employee's facts— that is, facts that contradict or undermine what the employee says.

Sample Format for Company Response to Agency Complaint

The Parties

[Identify your company. Briefly describe its business. Give the number of employees in the location where the complaining employee worked.]

Example: ABC Interiors is a furniture showroom in Cincinnati, Ohio, with 18 employees.

[Identify the complaining employee and his or her job (or the job applied for). Note any issues with the employee's status (for example, that he or she was actually an independent contractor).]

Example: Jeremy Baker is a CPA with whom ABC contracted to provide accounting services for a few weeks each quarter. Jeremy Baker was not an employee of ABC and has his own office elsewhere in town.

The Company's Response to the Allegations

[Addressing each allegation in a separate paragraph, state the facts that support your company's decisions or actions. State the company's lawful reason for taking the challenged action. Note the number of employees in the complaining employee's protected category who are still with the company (for example, how many employees are over age 40, if the employee complains that he was fired because of his age). If the employee made an internal complaint, provide information on your investigation and findings. If the employee didn't make an internal complaint, make note of that fact.]

Example: ABC elected not to contract with Jeremy Baker last fall because of budgetary constraints. ABC assigned its accounting duties to the CFO, Margaret Ware, and her assistant, Jonas Young, both of whom were already employed by ABC. Mr. Baker's age was not a factor in ABC's decision not to contract with him. At present, ABC has seven employees age 40 or older.

Sample Format for Company Response to Agency Complaint (cont'd)

Company Policy

[Summarize and attach a copy of the company's antiharassment/ discrimination policy, including the investigation procedure. Firmly state that the company always abides by its own policy of zero tolerance of harassment or discrimination.]

Example: As noted in the attached ABC Personnel Policy, ABC does not engage in, nor will it tolerate, discrimination based on age or any other protected status.

Agency complaint forms can be quite terse and lack specifics. If you are not sure what something in the complaint means or need clarification to do a thorough investigation, contact the agency in writing to request additional information. Be as specific about what you need as possible (for example, "the complaint we received does not indicate what decisions the employee believes were made for discriminatory reasons" or "the complaint we received does not state who allegedly harassed the complaining employee"). The agency will then ask the complaining employee to supply more information. Once the agency receives that information, it will summarize the additional information in a letter to your company.

If you need more information, also ask for more time to respond to the complaint. Agencies typically will give employers additional time to respond to a complaint upon request. Ask sooner rather than later, however, so it doesn't look like you're just stalling. Confirm the new deadline in a letter to the agency.

Common Questions

Q: I just received an EEOC complaint of disability discrimination filed by a former employee. The complaint alleges that the employee has a disability and was denied accommodation, but no one involved in the complaint knew about the disability or recalls being approached for a reasonable accommodation. How do I respond?

A: Make a list of the information you will need to prepare a formal response. For example, it sounds like you'll need to know more about the employee's disability, when he requested accommodation, whom he asked to provide the accommodation, and what accommodation he requested. Send a letter to the agency, asking it to provide this additional material. In your letter, ask for more time to respond once the employee supplies the information you need. The agency will probably give you more time; if so, confirm the extension and your new deadline in writing.

TIP

Your questions may alert the agency to weaknesses in the employee's complaint. In the example above, an employee is claiming denial of accommodation but never told the company about his disability. If you ask the agency to get more information about the employee's alleged request for an accommodation, and the employee can't come up with the goods, the agency may dismiss the complaint or issue a finding that it lacks sufficient support. Had you not requested more information, the agency probably wouldn't know that the employee's complaint lacked merit.

A good way to prepare to draft a response to an agency complaint is to create a fact sheet that lists each of the allegations in the complaint and, in a separate column, lists facts that the company will use in response, along with a note of the source of the fact. Keep your fact sheet brief and, well, factual. As explained in Chapter 6, the documents you create may well become evidence in any resulting lawsuit, unless you prepare them for, or at the request of, a lawyer. Editorializing or noting issues that could be a problem for your company may come back to haunt you.

Sample Fact Sheet

Response to Dave Koi's agency complaint

Allegation	Response
1. Koi has a disability	1. Unknown to company (Human Resources, Supervisor)
2. Koi requested accommodation	2. No record of any request (Supervisor, Human Resources; personnel file)
3. Company refused accommodation	3. No request made (See 2)
4. Koi fired because of disability	4. Koi laid off in reorganization, along with 22 other employees; decisions based on seniority. (Re-organization memo from Human Resources to Koi, dated 2/23/09; Supervisor; selection committee (Todd Jones, Selena Ilosa, Mara Kwan)

Use this information to write out your narrative response, devoting a separate paragraph to each allegation. (This part of the response is sometimes also called a "position statement" or "statement of position.") If you are working with an attorney (for the reasons stated above, this is a good idea), he or she will probably write the statement for you, based on the information you provide, or review and revise the statement you draft. If the attorney writes the statement, make sure to read it over to verify that it is accurate.

The EEOC doesn't provide employers with a standard form for their responses, nor require you to follow a particular format. However, your state FEPA may have a specific form or require your response to meet certain requirements. If the complaint you receive doesn't indicate what your response should look like, contact the state agency to find out whether there are any rules you need to follow.

Agency Actions

Once your company submits its written response, the agency has a number of options. It may decide to pursue one or more of the following steps:

- **Conduct an investigation.** The agency will typically investigate the claim unless the employee has asked the agency to close the case. (As explained below, an employee may do this because he or she wants to file a lawsuit right away, without waiting for the agency to take action). An agency will not investigate if the complaint is invalid on its face. In this situation, the agency typically doesn't accept the complaint in the first place, so your company may never even find out about it.
- **Offer to mediate or settle.** If either or both parties express an interest in mediating or settling the dispute, the EEOC or FEPA may facilitate this through its own mediation process.
- **Issue a "right to sue" letter.** This is the most frequent response: The EEOC or FEPA will issue a letter to the employee, called a right to sue letter, which explains that the employee has the right to bring his or her lawsuit in court. As noted above, the employee has to file with the agency before bringing a lawsuit, and the right to sue letter shows that the employee has met this requirement. The issuance of a right to sue letter doesn't necessarily mean that the agency believes the complaint is valid. The agency can also issue this letter after its investigation, if it doesn't find a violation has occurred.

- **File an agency lawsuit.** If a violation may affect more than just the one complaining employee (because the employer is large, the illegal practice is widespread, or there may be grounds for a class action), the agency itself may file a lawsuit on behalf of the employee(s). This is a rare occurrence, but it can happen if the agency believes that the case has merit and will have a large impact.

The agency can also dismiss the complaint at any point in the process if it determines that further investigation wouldn't result in a finding that the law was violated. (As noted, it may even reject a complaint upon filing if, during the agency's initial interview, the complaining employee fails to provide sufficient evidence to support the allegations.) When an agency dismisses a complaint in this manner, it isn't necessarily the end of the road for the employee. Instead, the employee gets a right to sue letter, giving the employee the right to take the case to court. The complaining employee usually has 90 days to file suit after receiving a right to sue letter from the EEOC, although that time may be extended if the employee also has state law claims. States have their own, generally longer, time limits.

Preparing for an Agency Investigation

If the EEOC or FEPA decides to investigate an employee complaint, it will contact your company and ask for more information. Usually, this contact will come in the form of a written request after your company submits its written response. The agency likely will want to interview employees who may have information about the allegations. It also will request copies of company documents and possibly even visit the work site where the violation allegedly occurred. The agency will arrange interviews, document reviews, and onsite visits with your cooperation, to limit disruption.

Interviews are usually done by telephone. The agency often sets up a telephone conference with the person to be interviewed.

Typically, no one else is included in these phone interviews. Neither the complaining employee nor his or her attorney attends employee interviews, onsite visits, or document reviews.

Once you get a list of the employees whom the agency wants to interview, you should meet with each employee individually. During this meeting, explain that the EEOC (or FEPA) has received a complaint of harassment or discrimination against the company, and that the employee has been identified as someone who may have information related to the allegations. Tell the employee that he or she should answer the agency's questions truthfully, and that the employee will not suffer any repercussions for speaking to the agency. Explain that the interview is a normal part of the agency's procedures after receiving a complaint. You should also set a date and time for the interview, which you can pass along to the agency.

You may want to ask the employee if he or she has any information about the allegations other than what he or she provided during the company's investigation of the employee's internal complaint (if any information was provided previously). If so, ask the employee to share it with you so that you can look into the matter, in compliance with the company investigation policy.

If you are working with an attorney, he or she will help you prepare employees for their interviews, respond to the agency's requests for more information, and participate in its investigation. Your company has a legal duty to cooperate with the agency, but there's no reason not to do so in a way that puts your company in the best light—and protects your company's interests, if the dispute ends up in a courtroom. You may have questions about what documents you should make available, what information you should provide to the company's investigators, how to investigate a complaint internally while the agency's investigation is going on, and so on. Whether your company chooses to have an attorney represent it in dealing with the agency or simply consults with an attorney for behind-the-scenes advice, that relationship will be extremely valuable once you have government agency employees in your workplace.

Common Questions

Q: The EEOC contacted me to set up phone interviews with three of our salespeople. These employees travel a great deal, especially during this season, so it's hard to schedule the interviews. I offered to have each employee witness write a brief summary about the complaining employee's charges, but the EEOC investigator nixed that idea. Do we have to schedule these interviews? What if we refuse?

A: Bad idea. If you refuse, the EEOC will note that you did so and will likely find in the employee's favor because of lack of evidence from your company to refute the claims. A finding like this is not binding in court, but it's still important. It could embolden the employee and make it harder for your company to informally resolve the matter. The finding may also be presented as evidence in court if the employee sues.

At the conclusion of the investigation, the agency will make a finding. Among the options are:

- **The evidence doesn't establish that a legal violation occurred.** If this is the finding, the agency will notify the parties in writing, close the case, and give the complaining employee a right to sue letter.
- **The evidence establishes that a legal violation occurred.** In this situation, the agency will explain the finding in writing. The agency may then offer mediation or suggest terms for resolving the complaint. If the employer doesn't want to participate or the parties can't informally settle the dispute, the agency may decide to file a lawsuit on the employee's behalf. If not, it will issue the complaining employee a right to sue letter.
- **The evidence is inconclusive.** If the finding is inconclusive, the agency will inform the parties in writing and issue a right to sue letter.

The agency's findings are not binding in court if the employee later files a lawsuit. The judge or jury at trial will look at the evidence and decide whether or not the law was violated. However, the agency's finding is still important: A finding in the employer's favor may discourage an employee from pursuing a lawsuit (and discourage attorneys from taking the employee's case). A finding in the employee's favor may encourage the employee to sue or make it harder for the employer to resolve the matter informally, because the employee will believe he or she has a strong case. And, the finding may be introduced in court if the employee does sue.

 Common Questions

Q: I received a notice that the EEOC's investigation of an employee's age discrimination complaint didn't support the employee's allegations. Our lawyer said that we may not be in the clear, because the employee can still file a lawsuit. If there's no evidence of discrimination, how can he sue us?

A: An EEOC finding isn't like a verdict by a jury or a decision by a judge after a trial. An agency investigation is aimed at finding out whether the allegations justify filing a lawsuit. The process identifies cases that may be hard to prove or don't meet minimum legal standards, gives the parties an opportunity to settle before getting into the expensive process of a lawsuit, and helps employees and employers get a more realistic sense of the strength of their cases.

However, the agency's investigation doesn't have the legal effect of a trial. No matter what the agency finds, the employee is free to go forward. Even an employee who has a lousy case can file a lawsuit, although the case may be thrown out relatively early in the process if it's really groundless.

Common Questions (cont'd)

If the employee does decide to file a lawsuit and you have a full trial, both you and the employee will probably present a lot more evidence than was brought forth in the agency investigation. But take heart—the fact that the employee couldn't establish a violation at that point is good news for you, because it suggests the employee may not have the strongest case going forward, either. That means not only that your company may succeed in having the lawsuit dismissed early on, but also that the employee may have trouble finding a lawyer to take the case in the first place.

After the agency concludes its process, each side can request a copy of the agency's closed file on the matter. The file will contain correspondence with the parties, notes from witness interviews, and other materials related to the complaint and investigation. This information can be useful if the employee later files a lawsuit. You should request a copy of the agency file whenever an employee makes a complaint against your company. The information in it can be useful whether or not the employee ultimately files a lawsuit. It may alert you to gaps in your company's policies or practices or to ways that you can deal with the agency more effectively, if you ever find yourself in this position again.

Mediation

Rather than pursuing an investigation—or after doing so—the agency may offer you the opportunity to mediate the dispute. Mediation occurs only if both the complaining employee and the employer agree to it. If the agency hasn't yet investigated, it will put its investigation on hold while the mediation proceeds.

The Mediation Process

Mediation is an informal process aimed at reaching a settlement of the complaint through negotiations guided by a neutral third party trained to help parties resolve their disputes. The mediator doesn't decide what happens, but instead tries to help the parties come up with a solution that will work for everyone.

The discussions, offers, counter-offers, and everything else that occurs during mediation are confidential. If mediation is unsuccessful and the parties don't reach a settlement, the agency can resume its investigation. If a complaint is successfully mediated and settled, neither party may bring the matter to court unless the terms of the settlement are not honored.

If both parties are interested in mediation, the agency will send them a list of potential mediators. The parties can choose a name from this list or come up with their own mediator. A potential mediator may be unacceptable for a variety of reasons, such as a conflict of interest (say, because he or she previously represented one of the parties). Once both sides agree on a mediator, the mediation itself is scheduled for a date everyone can attend.

Before the mediation, the mediator may ask each side to provide him or her with a brief written statement of the facts and that side's position on the claims. If your company has retained a lawyer, he or she will prepare the statement. Your company's statement should refer to the evidence that supports its position, but you don't have to present the actual evidence to the mediator. It might make sense to include a particularly strong piece of evidence with your company's statement, but don't inundate the mediator with material. And, if you don't want the mediator to share the evidence with the other side, say so explicitly in writing and by marking the evidence "for mediator's eyes only."

Common Questions

Q: Our company is going to use the state human rights agency's mediation program to try to resolve a harassment complaint by an ex-employee. The company president stressed that when I attend this meeting, I am not to admit any liability. I'm a little nervous about how to follow his wishes or if I even can. What do you think?

A: You should be able to satisfy the president's demand, but you may not resolve your disagreement with the employee. The purpose of mediation is for the parties to reach an agreement about how to handle the dispute. Nothing about mediation requires the company to admit any wrongdoing. The company's position isn't uncommon: A nonadmission statement is frequently demanded by companies in settlement agreements.

Recognize, however, that sometimes employees are emotionally attached to their claims. They may feel an admission of guilt is fundamental to resolving the issue. If that's the case, and the company won't budge, you may find your attempts to mediate unsuccessful. If this becomes a problem during the mediation, you can always call the president to see if his position changes when the company has a chance to resolve the dispute.

Also, you may be able to negotiate for something less than an admission that's still valuable to the employee, such as a written apology, a positive job reference, removing certain materials from the employee's file (such as a poor job evaluation), and so on. In this way, you can acknowledge, in a roundabout way, that mistakes were made, without actually coming right out and admitting wrongdoing.

Attending Mediation

Even though mediation is fairly informal, especially compared to a trial, it can still be intimidating to attend as the company representative. If you're in this position, the attorney representing the company should accompany you, to help you weigh the strength of the employee's legal case and decide whether it makes sense to resolve it quickly. (For more on getting ready for the mediation, see "Preparing for Mediation," below.)

The mediation itself will probably take place in a conference room or several conference rooms, most likely at the EEOC or FEPA. You, the lawyer representing the company, the employee, and his or her lawyer (if there is one) will all sit at a table with the mediator, who will describe the process a little bit and probably ask each side if it wants to make an opening statement. Your attorney will usually make the statement, although he or she may ask you to speak about certain factual or other matters (which you'll cover in preparation meetings ahead of time, discussed further below). The statement is an opportunity for each side to make its case directly to the other party.

After each side makes its statement, the mediator often puts the parties in separate rooms. The mediator then goes between the rooms, talking to each side about its position and trying to find a way to address both parties' concerns. The mediator will communicate each side's offers and demands to the other side. You and the attorney representing the company will have time alone to discuss each offer made by the employee and how you wish to respond on the company's behalf. The proposed terms may include payment, requirements to conduct training, an apology—very few things are beyond consideration, though either the company or the employee may have some "sticking points" on which they refuse to budge. The mediator will try to help you work through these, too.

If you have settlement authority (meaning you have your company's say-so to approve a settlement agreement on the company's behalf without anyone else's approval), you can resolve the dispute as long as you and the employee agree. If you don't have settlement authority, your company will have to make someone who has such authority, such as a company officer, available during the mediation, either in person or by telephone. You will have the opportunity to consult that person about any offers and other settlement terms.

If the mediation isn't successful and you can't agree on a resolution, the agency will pick up where it left off. If it has not yet investigated, it can proceed with its investigation. If it has already investigated, it can give the employee a right to sue letter.

If the mediation is successful, either the mediator or one or both of the lawyers will write up the agreed resolution. Usually, there will be some back and forth between the parties on the exact wording of the document, with each side proposing changes, additions, or deletions. Once you come up with a final written settlement agreement, the employee and a company representative will sign it. The agency complaint will then be dismissed pursuant to the terms of the agreement.

Your Role in Dealing With Investigative Agencies

It can be stressful to act as the liaison between your company and the agency. You'll want to accurately represent the company's position and fully protect its interests, while also cooperating with the agency and trying to get the complaint resolved. Here are some tips that will make your job a bit easier.

Prepare for the Worst

No matter what direction an employee's complaint takes, it pays to be prepared. Whether you're responding to a complaint, attending a mediation, or responding to inquiries in an investigation, the more organized you are, the better prepared you will be to present the company's perspective. And, if you work with an attorney at any stage of the process, having everything in order will make it easier for you to hand the case off—and potentially less expensive, because the attorney won't have to spend billable hours digging for additional information.

Your responsibilities start when you first receive a complaint and respond to it. You will need to:

- **Get your files in order.** Chapter 6 described some of the important documents your files should contain. Make sure you have those handy, in an organized way. If other people in the company have important documents you need—for instance, if the employee's direct supervisor received and documented the initial complaint—make sure you also have those.

- **Review the files carefully.** Once you review the complaining employee's personnel file and any files related to complaints he or she made under the company policy, including the investigation file, you'll be in a position to prepare for attorney meetings, prepare the company's response, and cooperate in the agency investigation.

- **Create or update your chronology.** Chapter 6 explained the importance of creating a chronology of the incidents raised in the complaint. If you haven't already done so, create one now. If you have one, you may need to update it to include new or different information raised in the agency proceedings.

TIP

Documents created for company attorneys are privileged. If you create a chronology or other document to assist company attorneys or at their direction, the document is protected by the attorney–client privilege. This means that it doesn't have to be disclosed to the complaining employee, his or her lawyer, or anyone else. On the other hand, handing over documents to the company attorney doesn't convert them into privileged documents. For example, if you create a chronology for your own purposes, then later hire a lawyer to represent the company in dealing with the EEOC, your chronology doesn't become privileged simply because you give it to the lawyer. If, however, the attorney asked you to write out a list of steps you took in responding to an employee's complaint, that document would be privileged.

- **Use your chronology and fact sheet to outline your company's position.** The more complete a portrait of events you can paint, using the facts that you have evidence for, the more clearly you will see and be able to put forth your best arguments.
- **Prepare for meetings with the attorney representing the company.** Preparing for attorney meetings ahead of time can save a lot of time (and money, if the attorney bills by the hour). Make sure you understand the purpose of each meeting. Then, prepare written questions you have about the process, points you feel are important (for example, that the employee never complained of harassment), and lists of witnesses and documents. Give the attorney the fact sheet you've prepared and a copy of your chronology.
- **Organize your questions and information for the agency.** As explained above, get more information if you need it to respond to the complaint. Ask questions to alert the agency to areas of weakness in the employee's complaint. Have a list of such questions and of information supporting the company's position ready when you contact the agency to request more information.
- **Get your marching orders.** Discuss the complaint and the allegations with your manager and company officers, so you know the company's position and strategy for responding to the complaint. Find out what the company expects of you and wants to achieve during any mediation. Take detailed notes of these discussions to bring with you to meetings with company lawyers and to the mediation.
- **Be a model of calm professionalism.** An agency complaint is no cause for panic, so proceed methodically and coolly. This will reassure your superiors that you have things under control. It will also assuage the natural anxiety of any employee witnesses who may be contacted during the agency investigation.

Assisting the Company's Attorney

As we've discussed, your company should seek the advice of a knowledgeable employment attorney if it receives an agency complaint of harassment or discrimination. If you are the liaison between the company and its counsel, you'll have to be well organized, as described above. Share the investigation file with the attorney, as well as any thoughts, concerns, or theories you have about what's going on, based on your knowledge of the workplace and the employees involved. Remember, in most cases, the attorney will not have had the same access to the workplace you have—he or she will depend on you to share the company culture, practices, and attitudes, in addition to the facts of the actual case.

Your discussions with the attorney are confidential and protected by the attorney–client privilege. This means that neither of you will be required to disclose what you talked about in court. This is important because it gives you the opportunity to speak freely without worrying that it will somehow work against you. However, you can destroy this protection if you reveal your discussions to others, so keep things private. Your lawyer can explain how the attorney–client privilege works, if you have any questions.

As explained above, you should make sure you've read and understood the investigation file before you meet with the attorney. Also, be prepared to give the attorney copies of all documents that may be relevant to the complaining employee's allegations, including employee statements, investigation notes, and physical evidence, as well as any pertinent personnel documents. Find out if you need to schedule meetings between the attorney and any witnesses or other employees. If so, try to schedule all of them for the same day. This is most efficient for both you and the attorney, and will help keep costs down, because you'll use less of the attorney's time travelling to and from the work site, waiting around for witnesses to arrive at meetings, and so forth.

Cooperating With Agency Investigators

An agency investigator serves a very different function than your company's attorney. While the attorney is trying to protect your company, the agency investigator is interested only in determining whether the employee's claims are valid. You must cooperate with the investigation, but you should always keep in mind that the agency investigator is not "on your side." Your communications with the agency investigator are definitely not privileged, and whatever you or other company representatives say to the investigator will become part of the agency's file on the case. This means your statements will be available to the complaining employee and his or her attorney after the agency closes the matter.

Maintain your composure and professionalism in dealing with the agency and its investigators. You may feel the company has been unjustly accused of wrongdoing, but that's not something to discuss with agency representatives. Instead, focus on presenting the facts that will ultimately prove that your company did the right thing. Your calm, business-like response to the complaint and the investigation will reassure employees and lessen the impact that the investigation has on the workplace.

? Common Questions

Q: We're dealing with an EEOC charge of race discrimination that is likely to progress to a lawsuit. I'd like the EEOC to see our impeccable record: We have a very diverse workforce, regularly donate to organizations promoting diversity and equality, and have had almost no complaints of any kind in our ten years in operation. Would it be a good idea to prepare a presentation for the EEOC to promote this?

A: While your own attorney may find this information helpful, you should present it to the EEOC only if it's relevant to the specific issues raised in the complaint. The EEOC will be looking for information that responds directly to the employee's allegations. If the charge alleges that the company makes a regular practice of discrimination or that discrimination is tolerated, information about the corporate culture would be directly relevant to the charge and should be provided to the EEOC. Otherwise, it is likely not relevant at this stage. Talk it over with your attorney. And keep in mind that, although this type of information may not be useful during the EEOC investigation, it could be very helpful in a lawsuit or settlement discussion with the employee should you get to either stage, when you may be able to present it as evidence.

You should do what you can to cooperate with the investigation. However, don't provide information or documents without first discussing it with your company's lawyer, who can tell you what information must be provided to the agency and what information should be kept confidential (for example, because it is protected by attorney–client privilege) or is simply not relevant. Show agency representatives that you are cooperating in good faith by returning calls promptly, showing them courtesy and respect, helping coordinate necessary interviews, and providing relevant documents approved by your attorney.

Preparing for Mediation

If you are going to attend mediation as a company representative, you'll need to prepare ahead of time, likely with the help of the company's employment attorney. You'll probably meet at least once, when the attorney will explain the mediation process and talk about the relative strengths and weaknesses of the employee's claims. Be prepared to ask the attorney any questions about the mediation and your role in it, including when, if at all, you'll be expected to speak directly to the mediator. Also ask what documents or other materials the attorney wants you to bring to the mediation.

Talk to the appropriate company officers or managers to determine what the company's position is and what it expects of you at the mediation. As explained above, you (or another company representative whom you can reach during the mediation) must have authority to settle the dispute, but make sure you know the details. For example, the company may want a provision in the settlement agreement stating that the complaining employee will not apply for a job with the company in the future. Make detailed notes of this information to bring to the mediation, as it's easy to forget even key points and instructions in the heat of the negotiations.

Common Questions

Q: I've been selected to be the company representative at the EEOC mediation of a pregnancy discrimination complaint by an employee. In the EEOC complaint, the employee falsely accused me of making inappropriate statements about her pregnancy and of participating in her termination. I'm outraged to be maligned in this way and I'm ready to let her have it. How should I prepare?

A: It's normal to have a strong emotional response to the allegations against you, but you need to rethink your plan. The purpose of the mediation is to try and reach an agreement with the employee, not to get revenge or personal vindication. It is important to maintain your composure and professionalism at the mediation.

The best thing you can do is put together all the details ahead of time that show what really happened. When faced with these facts and supporting evidence, the employee will have a hard time proving her claims. This should enhance your company's bargaining position at the mediation.

Nonetheless, you can't focus on the employee admitting she is wrong. If you really don't think you can look past this and work on getting the best solution for the company, discuss it with your management and the company's lawyer. You may not be the best person to attend on the company's behalf.

Preventing Retaliation

As unpleasant as it is to receive a harassment or discrimination complaint from an agency, it's even worse to later receive a retaliation complaint based on the way the initial complaint was handled. When a current employee files an agency complaint, it can make things awkward in the workplace. However, you must make sure it doesn't result in retaliatory actions against the employee. (For a refresher on what constitutes retaliation, revisit Chapter 7.)

Retaliation against employees who participate as witnesses in an agency process is also prohibited. When you meet with employees identified as possible witnesses by the agency complaint or in connection with the agency investigation, tell them that they should be cooperative and professional during interviews with the agency. Reiterate that the company will not retaliate, and will not tolerate any retaliation, against them for participating in the agency process.

Dos and Don'ts

Do:
- Contact the EEOC or FEPA if you need more information to respond to the complaint.
- Make sure files and documents relating to the complaining employee and any internal complaints are in order.
- Maintain a calm, professional demeanor after receiving an agency complaint and throughout the agency process.
- Urge employees to be cooperative and professional if contacted during the agency investigation and reassure them that there will be no retaliation.

Don't:
- Hesitate to conduct an investigation of the allegations in the agency charge, if you haven't already done so.
- Let emotion govern your response to the agency complaint or interfere with your role in the agency process.
- Disclose terms of the settlement agreement reached at mediation.

Lawsuits

Why Employees Sue 229

    The Employee's Goals 229

    Monetary Remedies 231

    Nonmonetary Remedies..232

How Lawsuits Work 234

    The Employee Files a Complaint 235

    The Company Responds...237

    Discovery...239

    Pretrial Preparation...245

    Trial..248

Alternatives to Litigation...250

    Settlement...250

    Mediation 251

    Arbitration..251

Your Role in a Lawsuit 253

    Being an Effective Liaison 253

    Being an Effective Witness..258

If You Are Sued Personally...269

    Your Lawyer 269

    Your Role as a Defendant 272

    Limiting Your Exposure 273

A stranger comes into the office and asks for you by name. You greet her as she smiles and hands you a legal-sized envelope, saying, "You've been served." In the envelope is a complaint, along with other official paperwork, formally initiating a harassment or discrimination lawsuit against your company. Your stomach drops to the floor.

Getting hit with a lawsuit is every manager's worst nightmare. And while you may not be the one to whom the papers are actually handed (unless you are sued personally, as discussed below), you probably will be involved in defending the company, which may include defending the way you handled the employee's concerns from the start.

Of course, facing a lawsuit is a scary proposition. It can be even more anxiety provoking when the allegations include harassment or discrimination. Accusations like these may imply—or flat out state—that your company and its managers (perhaps including you) are prejudiced, boorish, or bigoted. The work you do to help with the lawsuit—and any work you did to address the employee's claims internally— may come under intense scrutiny. You may have to prepare documents to hand over or use as exhibits in court, face harsh questions from the employee's attorney, or even take the stand and testify in front of a jury.

The best way to prepare yourself is to understand the process and the role you will play. This chapter will unravel the mystery of litigation. It explains how lawsuits actually work, how cases are settled out of court, and how to work effectively with the company's lawyer to get the best result for the company. This chapter also covers the worst-case scenario: what to expect if you are sued, personally, by an employee.

Although you may be worried about what's to come, remember that you won't be alone—and you won't be unarmed. Your company's lawyer will take charge of the process, handling the legal filings and deadlines and working with you to present the company's facts in the best possible light. And, if you've followed the advice in earlier chapters, the hard work you've already done to prevent harassment and discrimination, investigate claims, resolve problems, and deal with any agency investigation will serve you well now. You'll have the documents and other evidence you need to show the judge and jury that your company handled the employee's situation appropriately.

TIP

Don't panic—it's a process. When an employee begins a lawsuit, you may feel an immediate sense of panic. Take a deep breath. Though things may feel urgent, the process of litigation involves a series of steps that take place over a long period of time. In other words, you'll have time to think, gather materials, and meet with the attorney representing the company before you even have to respond.

Why Employees Sue

Before considering the mechanics of an employment lawsuit, it helps to think about *why* you've arrived where you are. In other words, what does the employee want from the lawsuit and what is the employee likely to receive if he or she wins?

The Employee's Goals

Of course, employees may have a number of different motivations for suing. For many employees, a lawsuit is a last resort after efforts to resolve the problem within the company have gone nowhere. An employee may be frustrated with the company's failure to remedy an ongoing harassment problem or may finally decide to sue after seeing yet another promotion go to a younger employee. Some employees are motivated by a desire for revenge, vindication, or a simple apology. They may believe that they were not treated fairly and be unable to move forward in their lives until they get some confirmation of their feelings.

Understanding an employee's motivations, and the possible outcomes in court, may help you come up with a way to resolve the problem before heading down the protracted, expensive path to a trial where the details will be exposed to the world. In the long term, a settlement is always less expensive, time-consuming, and stressful than trial.

Common Questions

Q: My company has been sued by a former employee who lost his job in a layoff last year. We laid off 15 employees, all deemed by their managers to be the most expendable. Now, he claims that he was included in the layoff because of his national origin (he's originally from Iran). The employee says that his manager has made negative statements about the current government of Iran, which proves that the manager included him in the layoff for discriminatory reasons. I don't know what the manager said, but it seems to me that criticizing a country's government isn't discrimination—and I know that this employee had consistently poor performance reviews. The company wants to settle his claims, but I think we should fight it out in court. Why should we pay this guy when we didn't do anything wrong?

A: There are lots of reasons why cases settle, not all related to the strength of the other side's case. Even if there's no evidence of discrimination, the company might sensibly decide to pay some money to make the problem go away. Every day the case goes on, your company is paying attorney fees and spending time dealing with the employee's claims. Settling the case puts an end to these ongoing costs, as well as the uncertainty over how the lawsuit will progress.

Common Questions (cont'd)

Sometimes, a company wants to settle a case to avoid having to reveal unpleasant facts in discovery and in court. For example, even if this particular fellow doesn't have a good case, there may be some problems with the way the company handled the layoffs, or there may be some reason why the company doesn't want to have to reveal its current financial situation, which often comes out when the company's defense is that cost-cutting measures were necessary. Or there may be more to this case than meets the eye. The employee received poor performance reviews, but those reviews were written by someone accused of discrimination. Perhaps other employees have complained or there's some other evidence of discrimination that the company believes could tip the scales in the employee's favor.

Monetary Remedies

An employee who files a harassment or discrimination lawsuit may be seeking several different solutions. In most cases, the employee's complaint will ask for money damages to compensate for harm the employee suffered as a result of the alleged harassment or discrimination. For example, if the employee felt forced to quit because working conditions were intolerable (called "constructive discharge," as discussed in Chapter 2) and was unemployed for several months before accepting a job at lower pay, the employee might seek payment for the months of unemployment and the difference between his or her former and current salary. Or, an employee who began meeting with a therapist and taking antidepressants after being subjected to extreme harassment might seek reimbursement for these medical bills, as well as some compensation for pain and suffering.

Nonmonetary Remedies

While an employee usually requests money in a lawsuit, that may not be all the employee is seeking, or even what he or she cares most about. Most of us are very emotionally connected to our jobs. Employees considering litigation often feel that they were treated unfairly and want it set right. Here are some of the other things an employee may hope to get from filing a lawsuit:

- **An opportunity to be heard.** Particularly if the employee's problem wasn't properly or fully investigated the first time, or if the employee didn't feel the investigation was fair, the employee may want the company to hear what really happened and how the employee was harmed by it.

- **An apology.** Sometimes, an employee who feels wronged needs to hear the wrongdoer take responsibility and express some remorse. He or she may want an apology from the alleged harasser, the investigator, or even the company as a whole.

- **Reinstatement.** Frequently, employees do not want their jobs to end even after they've experienced workplace discrimination or harassment. They may want to go back to the way things were before the harassing or discriminatory conduct occurred. An employee who's been fired unfairly or forced to quit may want nothing more than to report for his or her old job on Monday morning.

- **A promotion, transfer, or job change.** An employee may feel either entitled to a previously denied promotion or a move to a different shift, position, or department or that such a change would make the workplace tolerable, particularly if the problem is caused by a supervisor or coworker.

- **Reasonable accommodation.** As discussed in Chapter 1, failing to accommodate an employee's disability may be a violation of the ADA or state disability discrimination laws. An employee may seek a court order requiring the employer to provide reasonable accommodation, so the employee can return to work.

- **A group- or company-wide action.** If the employee believes that he or she is one of a group of employees that has been treated unfairly, the employee might want the company to change the way it does business. For example, the employee may want the company to require diversity training, revise its promotion policies, or drop a discriminatory job requirement (such as a strength requirement for a job that doesn't involve much heavy lifting).

The employee's true objectives may not be obvious in the documents filed in the lawsuit. You may learn what else drives the employee during the litigation process, as you explore the possibility of settling the case out of court, discussed later in this chapter. While the company will ultimately decide whether to settle the case, having a sense of the employee's underlying motivations will help you come up with creative ways the company can meet them.

 Common Questions

Q: My company just got hit with a discrimination lawsuit filed by an ex-employee who's alleging six causes of action and seeking punitive damages. At our lawyer's suggestion, we held a meeting with the plaintiff and his lawyer to see if there was any way to resolve this quickly. At the meeting, the former employee looked right at me and said that he wanted the company to apologize to him for the shoddy treatment he suffered under his former boss (who, admittedly, is a difficult, demanding manager). I met privately with our lawyer, who urged me to offer an apology on behalf of the company. I'm suspicious and reluctant to walk into some kind of trap. Should I be wary?

A: Probably not, as long as you consider your words carefully. Apologizing to the plaintiff for having to work under a difficult boss is no admission of illegal conduct and may go a long way toward addressing at least some of the issues that led the plaintiff to file the lawsuit. And, it shows a willingness to negotiate. Your lawyer can then turn to the plaintiff and ask for the same in return, in the form of dropping some or all of the claims or making some other sort of settlement offer.

How Lawsuits Work

A lawsuit is made up of many different (and seemingly unrelated) steps, most of them occurring before the actual trial. There may be long stretches when you have little or no involvement in the case, while the attorney or attorneys representing the company take care of many legal maneuvers without your input. Then, there will be times when you'll have to devote your full attention to the case, helping the attorney(s) get the details and facts straight, providing documents and information, and preparing to testify. Often, your company's legal team will be working on very short deadlines, so you may need to act quickly and under pressure.

 CAUTION
You'll have a lot more to do if you've been sued personally.
Of course, if you are a defendant in the lawsuit, you will have more responsibilities and concerns. See "If You Are Sued Personally," below, for more information.

By understanding how civil lawsuits generally wind their way through the courts, you'll know what to expect and how to prepare for what's coming (and why everything seems to take so long). This section explains the typical steps in a lawsuit, from start to finish. The specifics of this process may differ somewhat from case to case and court to court, but the general stages of a lawsuit are similar everywhere.

One advantage to facing a harassment or discrimination lawsuit is that you'll usually have some advance warning—not only of the lawsuit itself, but also of the arguments the employee will make. As explained in Chapter 8, an employee who wants to file a discrimination or harassment lawsuit must first file a complaint with an agency, which will notify your company. You may even have had an opportunity to respond to the employee's claims and present evidence in an agency investigation. Although not all cases that go through the administrative process wind up in court, you can be fairly certain that an employee who goes to the trouble to file an administrative complaint is planning on following through with a lawsuit if the issue isn't resolved.

 CAUTION
This process will work differently if the company and employee have agreed to arbitrate. If that's the case, you can find out more in "Arbitration," below.

The Employee Files a Complaint

After following the procedure required by the EEOC or your state's fair employment practices agency, the employee, ex-employee, or applicant can begin a lawsuit by filing a document called a complaint. (The person who files the complaint is called the plaintiff.) The complaint will include a list of the plaintiff's causes of action—the allegedly illegal behavior the plaintiff believes the employer is responsible for (such as sexual harassment or race discrimination). The complaint will also include the facts that support each cause of action (in a sexual harassment case, for example, the complaint might state that a coworker created a hostile work environment by posting offensive cartoons). It also explains what the plaintiff is seeking, usually in general terms by referring to different kinds of money damages, like lost pay and punitive damages. Complaints frequently don't specify the precise amount of money the plaintiff is seeking in damages.

The plaintiff serves the complaint on the employer (now the defendant), usually by having it hand-delivered by a neutral third-party. Once that happens, the defendant has a set period of time to respond to the lawsuit, by filing a document with the court and serving it on the plaintiff.

Common Questions

Q: We just got served with a complaint filed by a former employee, who claims she was fired for reporting sexual harassment. She did make an internal complaint that her manager had touched her inappropriately, but our investigation was inconclusive. The manager denied touching her and there were no witnesses, so we moved him to a different department. A few months later, we discovered that she had been falsifying her time records for a few years, and we fired her for that. Now, she's filed a complaint that includes half a dozen causes of action, all based on the same incident! She's claiming sexual harassment, assault, wrongful termination, retaliation, defamation, and even breach of contract. Why are there so many different legal claims in her complaint?

A: It's fairly common for a complaint to include a handful of different claims based on the same underlying incidents. There are a lot of reasons why employees include a variety of legal claims when filing a lawsuit, some of them strategic and others having to do with damages. For example, an assault claim can be brought only against another person, not against the company. So this claim may have been included in order to name the manager as a defendant in the lawsuit, for the reasons explained in "If You Are Sued Personally," below.

You don't mention whether she's alleging harassment and retaliation in violation of federal or state law. If she's suing under federal law, there's a cap on the total amount of punitive and compensatory damages she can be awarded if she wins the case. The cap ranges from $50,000 to $300,000, depending on the size of the company. Because of this damages limit, employees suing under federal law often include "tort" claims: claims for personal injury, to which these caps don't apply. This may explain the defamation cause of action: Defamation is a common personal injury claim brought by plaintiffs in employment cases, often alleging that the reasons the employer gave for firing the plaintiff were false and damaged the plaintiff's reputation and prospects for getting a new job.

> ## (?) Common Questions (cont'd)
>
> Although the plaintiff has to prove different things to win each claim, the same fact may win each cause of action, for her or for your company. For example, if your company can prove that it fired her for a valid reason, that's a defense to most of her claims, which succeed only if she shouldn't have been fired. Similarly, if she can show that she was really fired in retaliation for making her sexual harassment claim, your company is likely to lose several times over.

The Company Responds

There are several different ways a defendant can respond to a complaint. (Remember, the process may vary slightly, depending on where the lawsuit is filed.) How to respond will be a strategic decision made by the attorney(s) representing the company, but you may need to provide some information to help with that decision.

Bear in mind that the company will have only a limited amount of time, often as few as 30 days, to file its response. If the company has not already hired a lawyer, it must do so immediately. If the company has hired an attorney, you need to contact the lawyer right away to make sure he or she knows that the complaint has been filed.

With the help of its attorneys, your company will respond to the complaint by filing one of the following documents:

- **An answer.** In this document, the company responds to each allegation in the plaintiff's complaint, either by admitting or denying them.
- **A motion to dismiss.** A motion is a request that the judge take a particular action in the case. A motion to dismiss, sometimes also called a demurrer, is a request that the court reject the plaintiff's complaint because, even if all of the allegations were true, the plaintiff wouldn't be entitled to relief. In other words,

even if everything the plaintiff claims actually happened, it wouldn't break the law.

- **A motion to strike.** A motion to strike is similar to a motion to dismiss, but it applies only to certain causes of action. For example, if the complaint's discrimination claim is legally sufficient but the harassment claim is not, the defendant might file a motion to strike just the harassment claim.

No matter which of these options your company chooses, the lawyer will let you know and will handle the necessary paperwork. If the company decides to file an answer, the case will then proceed to discovery, as described below. However, if the company files a motion to dismiss or a motion to strike, there will be a series of interim legal steps, with attorneys for both sides filing documents and perhaps even appearing in court to argue before the judge. For example, if your company files a motion to dismiss, the plaintiff will have the opportunity to explain why the complaint is legally sufficient and should not be dismissed. Eventually, usually after a hearing, a judge will decide whether the motion should be granted. If it is, the plaintiff may be given an opportunity to fix the problem by filing an amended complaint. You then start the same process over: The plaintiff files and serves the amended complaint, and the defendant can either answer or move to dismiss or strike. If the judge denies the motion, the company will probably have to file an answer.

This initial stage of the lawsuit won't require a lot of your time, because it's almost exclusively based on the words in the complaint and the legal standards that govern them. This gives you an opportunity to start organizing your files and documents in preparation for discovery, which, as explained, can be very time-consuming.

Common Questions

Q: Our company is defending a sexual harassment lawsuit, and the attorney just sent me the answer he's planning to file. I can't understand most of it, but it looks like he's denying every single fact in the complaint, including stuff that's obviously true. What's the point of this?

A: It's true that some attorneys can go a little overboard with the gamesmanship. But denying a fact in a complaint doesn't necessarily mean you're saying it didn't happen; instead, you're saying that the plaintiff is going to have to prove it. And there are often very good reasons for denying "facts" that appear to be true, typically because there's a legal argument buried in the way the fact is stated.

For example, the complaint in your case might say "John supervised Jane." Even if this appears to be correct, admitting it implies that John qualifies as a supervisor, for whose sexual harassment the company is automatically liable, under federal or state law. Similarly, admitting a fact like "XYZ is a parent corporation of ABC" could concede that XYZ should be liable for any damages award against ABC—or even that all of the employees of XYZ should be counted when calculating the size of the company, which determines whether the laws prohibiting discrimination and harassment apply and how large an award of damages can be, among other things. At this point in the lawsuit, it's often best to deny all of the allegations and keep your legal options open.

Discovery

If the complaint isn't resolved once the legal wranglings of the first stage are completed—a process that can take weeks or months—the case moves forward. The next step is for the parties to exchange relevant information and evidence through a process called discovery.

It may seem counterintuitive to share evidence with your opponent in the lawsuit, but the law requires you to exchange relevant information, documents, and other evidence. Each of you needs information that will be in the hands of the other, and the law is interested in getting at the truth. For example, if the plaintiff claims a coworker sent sexually suggestive emails to his or her personal email address, you'll want to see those emails, and you may have to rely on the plaintiff to provide them. Exchanging evidence also encourages settlement: Once each side has a good idea of the evidence the other side will present, it's easier for everyone to assess their likelihood of success and the strength of their arguments.

Practically speaking, the employer usually has a lot more relevant information than the plaintiff does. Like any business, your company probably keeps records throughout the employment relationship as a matter of course. For example, you might have a full personnel file, including signed documents, performance evaluations, disciplinary notices, information on compensation, and much more material related to the plaintiff's employment. You'll have even more records if the employee filed an internal complaint. It's very likely that you'll be asked to gather paperwork and other information—copies of emails, voicemails, photographs, and so on—by the attorney representing the company. You may also be able to help the attorney figure out what evidence to request from the plaintiff, which employees might serve as witnesses, and so on.

The parties exchange this information through a variety of methods, including:

- **Interrogatories.** These are written questions that each side asks about information related to the lawsuit, requiring written answers signed under oath. For example, an employer often asks the plaintiff to describe all of the damages the plaintiff claims to have suffered, list every incident of alleged harassment that occurred, or provide the names of all witnesses to any of the allegedly illegal behavior. Usually, the total number of questions each party can ask the other is limited by law.

- **Demands for document production.** These are written requests for documents, often including electronic documents and data, as well as any photographs, cartoons, emails, correspondence, diaries, and other types of written or recorded materials. For example, the plaintiff might ask your company to provide all records relating to your investigation of the plaintiff's internal complaint, or all documents relating to a particular promotion or layoff decision.

- **Requests for admissions.** In some cases, either party may ask the other to admit certain facts, so the party doesn't have to prove those facts in the lawsuit. For example, the plaintiff might ask the company to admit that it employed the plaintiff (rather than hiring the plaintiff as an independent contractor), so the plaintiff won't have to prove this fact at trial.

- **Physical inspection.** Either party may request to physically examine a location or piece of evidence that can't be handed over. For example, the plaintiff might request an opportunity to physically inspect and photograph the worksite to show that the plaintiff's work station and the entrance to the building were not modified in response to the plaintiff's request for a reasonable accommodation.

- **Physical or psychological examination.** In employment cases, companies sometimes ask that the plaintiff be examined by a psychiatric expert, if the plaintiff claims to have suffered emotional distress. The expert's role is to determine the validity and extent of the claimed distress.

- **Depositions.** In almost every lawsuit, each side wants to question people who may have relevant information. This usually happens through a process called a deposition, in which a witness answers questions under oath and a court reporter transcribes the testimony. If you investigated an internal complaint made by the plaintiff or played any other role in the events underlying the lawsuit, you may have your deposition taken in the case. You'll find more information in "Trial Testimony," below.

- **Subpoenas.** This is a court order that is served on a person, demanding that he or she show up to testify at deposition or trial, produce documents, or both. In most courts, a subpoena is used to require testimony or documents from someone who isn't a party to a lawsuit.

Common Questions

Q: I used to supervise an employee who was fired for poor performance, after plenty of warnings, coaching, and formal discipline. Now, he's filed a lawsuit claiming that he was really fired because of his race. His lawyer has filed a document request asking me to hand over my day planner. Our company lawyer explained that the lawyer probably wants to see any notes about the employee I made in the calendar, the dates of performance evaluations and meetings, etc. I guess I can see why the employee wants this, but the problem is that I use the same calendar for personal stuff, too. Does this employee really have the right to see all of my dates, doctor's appointments, and reminders about my kid's school conferences?

A: No, the employee doesn't have a right to see your personal information, but he does have a right to see everything on the calendar that might pertain to his claims against the company. This problem— documents that include both information that's relevant and information that's not—comes up fairly often in employment lawsuits.

The solution is to separate what's relevant and hand it over. First, the parties have to agree on what will be produced and what won't. If they can't agree, they'll have to file motions and fight it out in court, so the judge can issue an order explaining what information has to be provided. Then, someone—probably your company's attorney—will go through a copy of your calendar, blocking out (or as the lawyers say, "redacting") everything the plaintiff isn't entitled to see. The lawyer will then make a copy of the final product and give it to the plaintiff's attorney.

Unsurprisingly, discovery doesn't always go smoothly. Discovery works on a sort of honor system: It's largely up to each party to ask only for relevant information and to provide all relevant documents and information in response to discovery requests. Often, the parties don't agree on where the boundaries of relevance lie. For example, the plaintiff may ask for a record of all employee complaints against an employer, but the employer may feel that some aren't relevant to the lawsuit, that it would take an unreasonable amount of time to compile that much information (especially in a large company), or that some information in the complaints must be kept confidential to protect employee privacy. The parties may also need clarification of discovery requests. For example, if a question isn't clear, the answering party may have to ask for more information. If the parties can't work these issues out on their own, they may have to file motions requesting a judge to decide for them, sometimes followed by oral arguments. Again, this can take weeks or months.

 Common Questions

Q: My company is in the middle of a lawsuit filed by an unsuccessful job applicant who says we rejected her based on her age. During the interview process, the hiring supervisor sent me an email in which he referred to the applicant as a "cougar" (meaning an attractive, older woman). The supervisor meant it as a compliment and it was really just an off-hand remark—we didn't hire her because we found a candidate with much better qualifications. I deleted the email without responding. Now our attorney has asked me to gather all of the documents, including emails, related to the applicant, so we can respond to her document request. Our attorney doesn't know about the supervisor's email to me. Do I have to get a copy to the lawyer or can I pretend it never happened?

Common Questions (cont'd)

A: You'd better find it and turn it over to your lawyer. It may well come to light because the sender reveals it during his deposition, you're forced to talk about it when you are asked about communications regarding the applicant under oath, or someone else who saw or received a copy spills the beans.

Failing to produce the email will make it seem like you were hiding it. It won't seem like an off-hand remark if it looks like you tried to bury it because you were worried about its content. And, keep in mind, even if no one at your company reveals the email, the plaintiff's lawyer will probably want all emails and other electronic documents related to the applicant. There are technologies readily available that the lawyer can, and will, use to make sure everything is turned over.

The lawyers will be heavily involved in the discovery process as they try to work out these details. You should expect to be quite busy, too. The lawyers representing the company will want to talk to you about the information and documents you have that may have to be handed over. You should take these requests seriously, and err on the side of providing more information rather than less. It is not your responsibility to decide whether the other side gets the information—the attorneys will evaluate it and decide whether it must be disclosed under the law. They'd much rather have you provide too much than too little, so that they're not surprised by evidence they didn't know about later in the proceedings.

You may also have to help gather information from others, often by setting up meetings between the company attorney and employees who may have information about the allegations in the lawsuit. Even if you already interviewed these people (for example, in your original investigation of the incidents underlying the complaint), the attorney will no doubt want to interview them again. You will want to make sure they have a private place to conduct these discussions, such as a conference room.

You may be asked to sit in on meetings between the attorney and these potential witnesses. Just keep in mind that the purpose of the meetings is to allow the attorney to ask questions. If you think the attorney should ask about a particular incident or fact, discuss it privately with the attorney. You should not plan on offering your thoughts or opinions unless the attorney asks you to. Otherwise, it might look like you are telling the witness how to testify, which could undermine your own credibility, as well as that of the witness. Tell every employee the attorney interviews that the company's policy prohibiting retaliation extends to employees who testify or provide information in connection with a harassment or discrimination lawsuit, and ask them to come to you if they feel that they've suffered any negative consequences as a result of their participation in the case.

Pretrial Preparation

Once all the evidence is gathered and the discovery phase is finished (usually a specified number of days before the trial date), the company attorneys will begin preparing for trial in earnest. The attorneys will have to organize all of the physical evidence (such as documents) and witness testimony (from deposition transcripts and witness interviews). It usually also means a lot of meetings with company employees and, especially, with supervisors, managers, and human resource representatives who were involved in the incidents alleged in the complaint. The attorneys will also have to write their opening and closing arguments, prepare to select a jury (if there will be one), get ready to argue about what evidence should be admitted and kept out at trial, and handle dozens of other details.

During the weeks just before the trial begins, you, the attorneys, and anyone else present from the company will discuss how the attorneys plan to defend the company at trial. For example, the attorneys will tell you the names of the witnesses they intend to call and the order in which they intend to call them, the exhibits they'll introduce and in what form (for example, some may be electronically scanned or blown up to poster-size), and the overall anticipated trial schedule. Your feedback will be important as these decisions are made. And, you may have to prepare to testify yourself.

As a result, this is a phase in which you may have to devote a lot of time and energy to the lawsuit. Plan ahead: Ask the lawyer representing the company to tell you the trial date as soon as it is set, so you can put it on your calendar and make time in the weeks leading up to and during the trial to assist when requested.

TIP

Prepare a litigation calendar and tickler system for yourself. Ask the attorney to notify you of all hearings, depositions, and other important litigation dates that may require your assistance. Create a tickler system to alert you days or weeks in advance of critical dates (like depositions or the trial date) so you'll have time to prepare. (A sample litigation calendar can be found later in this chapter.)

A lot can happen in the pretrial stage. For instance, it isn't uncommon for the parties to settle the lawsuit just before trial. Each side will finally have all of the information that's relevant to the case, which may enable everyone to take a fresh look at the dispute and come up with a resolution. Once the discovery dust settles, the relative strengths and weaknesses of each side will be clearer, which often makes it easier for everyone to agree on a settlement figure.

Additionally, there may be more court hearings as the parties try to use the legal process to end or limit the case before trial. One common way for parties to do this is through a summary judgment motion. Summary judgment motions are very frequently filed by employers in harassment and discrimination lawsuits. Such motions are filed once all the evidence has been gathered and the parties and court can better see whether there is enough evidence to support the employee's claims. If all of the plaintiff's evidence, even if true, still doesn't add up to a valid legal claim, the defendant can try to have the whole case (or particularly weak causes of action) dismissed on summary judgment. Plaintiffs also occasionally file motions for summary judgment, in which they argue that the defendant's evidence fails to refute, or even supports, the plaintiff's claims.

 Common Questions

Q: Our company's lawyer wants to file a motion for summary judgment. We've asked her to give us a rough idea of the hours it will take, and her estimate seems astronomical! Is a motion for summary judgment really that time-consuming—and if so, is it worth the cost to file one?

A: Summary judgment motions eat up a lot of attorney time. To prepare a motion, the attorneys have to comb through all of the evidence—the documents, deposition transcripts, and so on—to show that the plaintiff doesn't have enough support for his or her claims. The attorney has to prepare a fairly long written legal argument, along with a separate document that lays out all of the facts supporting the argument, with citations to the exact place in the records where the fact can be found. Think "term paper," but with even more footnotes.

Whether a summary judgment is worth the cost depends on the strength of your company's arguments. If your company wins the motion, the plaintiff's case could be over. Even if your company wins only on certain claims, you could knock the legs out from under the case. For example, if your attorney gets all of the claims for personal injuries thrown out, the claims that remain for trial may offer only limited damages, and the plaintiff may be much more interested in settling the case. Talk to your company's lawyer about the likelihood of success on the motion. If the lawyer feels good about his or her prospects, it could well be worth the hefty price tag.

Trial

If the case doesn't settle, the next step is a trial. The trial is when the parties tell their stories, present their evidence, and argue their cases, either to a judge or jury. All the hard work you've done to help the company attorney gather evidence will be put to use here, as you get ready to go to court. No doubt you'll continue to work with the attorney at this point, helping to iron out details or gather evidence to present in the courtroom.

The plaintiff has what's called the burden of proof. This means that it's up to the plaintiff to show that the wrongs he or she alleges actually occurred; your company doesn't have to prove the opposite. Technically, the company could win the case without presenting any evidence or calling any witnesses, if the judge or jury thought that the plaintiff didn't prove that harassment or discrimination took place.

Of course, it doesn't work that way in reality. Your company didn't hire a lawyer just to fill a chair at the trial. Instead, the company's lawyer(s) will work hard to show that the company didn't violate the law. In a harassment case, this typically means showing that the incidents didn't occur or weren't as bad as the plaintiff claims, or that, even if they did occur, the company shouldn't be held liable. In a discrimination case, the company typically seeks to prove that it had legitimate, nondiscriminatory reasons for the actions the plaintiff is complaining about (for example, failing to hire or promote, or terminating employment).

The company will offer its own evidence to undermine the plaintiff's case. For example, if the plaintiff claims that the company failed to accommodate his disability, the company might offer evidence showing either that the plaintiff doesn't have a disability or didn't inform anyone at the company about it. The company may defend itself by proving that the employee was fired (or suffered another negative job action) for a reason that doesn't violate the law—for example, that a plaintiff who claims to have been fired because of her gender was actually fired for ongoing performance problems, which the company documented along the way.

A harassment or discrimination case may be tried before either a jury or a judge. Plaintiffs typically prefer a jury trial, if they have the option: Most jurors are employees rather than employers and may be more likely to sympathize with the plaintiff. In a jury trial, the judge presides over the action, rules on legal motions and objections (for example, that certain evidence shouldn't be admitted), and instructs the jury about the relevant legal principles. Once all the evidence has been presented, the jury goes into a private room, sorts through all of the facts, and applies the legal principles the judge gave to those facts to reach a verdict.

Sometimes, a judge decides the case without a jury. This means that the judge weighs all of the evidence and enters a verdict. In a trial before a judge sitting without a jury (sometimes called a bench trial), much depends on the leanings and predispositions of the judge who hears the case. Although judges are supposed to be impartial, any employment lawyer practicing in your area will have an opinion as to which local judges are considered to favor plaintiffs or defendants in employment cases.

Before any evidence is presented at trial, there will be several other preliminary steps. For example, the parties, with the judge's oversight, select a jury. And the parties will have to notify each other of the evidence they plan to put forth. In some cases, when one party objects to the other's evidence, they may file a motion to exclude it. Motions like these can delay the trial by days or weeks.

Once the trial is underway, it can last for a few hours or a few weeks. (Trials in employment cases rarely go longer than this, although there are occasional exceptions.) At trial, the plaintiff will usually present evidence first, and the defendant will have the opportunity to cross-examine the witnesses the plaintiff calls. You may be present for some or all of the trial. To prepare, you may be assisting the company attorney by gathering relevant information or documents to ask each witness about. The company may have its own witnesses to put on the stand, too. In fact, one of your important functions may be to serve as a witness, as explained below.

Alternatives to Litigation

After hearing about the arduous process of getting through a civil lawsuit, you'll probably be relieved to hear that most legal disputes don't end in a trial with a jury verdict. Instead, most cases are resolved before a full trial through settlement negotiations, mediation, or arbitration.

Settlement

A settlement is simply a private agreement between the parties that resolves a dispute. The parties (or more likely, their attorneys) often discuss settlement at various points after the lawsuit is filed. Even if earlier settlement discussions don't go anywhere, it's not uncommon for cases to settle "on the courthouse steps," on the eve of trial.

Sometimes, the court is involved in settlement efforts. For example, many judicial systems require the parties to attend a settlement conference, often with a different judge or a private lawyer in attendance to try to facilitate the negotiations. More often, parties work out a settlement agreement on their own.

In a harassment or discrimination case, a settlement usually involves the defendant paying some money in exchange for the plaintiff dropping the lawsuit and giving up the right to ever bring it again. In addition to—or instead of—money, the defendant may agree to take certain actions, such as promoting the employee, reinstating the employee to his or her former position, providing company-wide antiharassment training, and so on. The defendant may also want the plaintiff to do some things, such as agreeing not to reveal the terms of the settlement, not to disparage the company, or not to apply for a job at the company in the future.

Because settlements are relatively common, the company's attorney will probably raise the possibility with you before trial. This can happen at any stage in the lawsuit, and may happen more than once if the first effort to settle fails. Cases even settle after a jury verdict, to avoid spending time and resources on an appeal.

Mediation

Mediation of a lawsuit is quite similar to mediation of an agency complaint, described in Chapter 8. There are a couple of differences, however. One significant difference is that mediation during litigation will be done by a private mediator whom the parties select, rather than by one from a list proposed by the EEOC or FEPA. And, private mediation costs money, while mediations offered by an agency are usually free. Mediators, like arbitrators, are paid by the hour or day, and their fees can run to hundreds of dollars per hour.

Another difference is that the pressure to resolve a court case at mediation is higher than it is to resolve an agency complaint, both because a good deal of money is invested in the private mediation process and because the risks of failure to settle (that is, having to go to trial and possibly lose) are high for all concerned.

Arbitration

In an arbitration, the parties agree to have their dispute decided by one or more impartial third parties (the arbitrator(s)). Unlike a mediator, who tries to help the parties reach their own solution, an arbitrator decides the case much like a judge. And the parties must abide by the arbitrator's decision, unless they agree ahead of time that they will have the right to challenge the decision in court.

Arbitration is a private proceeding. Unlike a courtroom, where salaries are paid by the taxpayers, an arbitration proceeding is funded by the parties, who pay the arbitrator by the hour or day. The parties and their attorneys present their evidence to the arbitrator, much as they would at trial. There's no jury at an arbitration hearing, and the proceedings are a bit less formal. For example, the parties might sit around a conference table rather than standing to make arguments, and the usual rules about what evidence a party can present and how don't apply. Company representatives may be present at the arbitration and witnesses give testimony under oath.

Common Questions

Q: Our company requires new hires to sign arbitration agreements, stating that they must bring any legal claims against the company in an arbitration proceeding, not a lawsuit. An employee we fired has sued us anyway, and our company's lawyer says we have to file a motion to force the plaintiff to arbitrate the claims instead. Between the costs of filing and arguing this motion and the costs of arbitration, wouldn't we be better off just letting the plaintiff have her day in court?

A: Probably not. Arbitration offers companies a number of advantages over litigation. Arbitration is much faster than legal proceedings, and often pretrial procedures—such as discovery and motions—are limited. Also, arbitrators tend to be less swayed by emotional arguments (and less likely to make huge damages awards) than a jury would be, which often works in a company's favor in employment cases. All in all, arbitration is probably going to save your company money in the long run (which is undoubtedly why your company required employees to sign arbitration agreements in the first place). Keep in mind, though, your company won't have the option to appeal the arbitration decision as it would the results of a trial. Arbitration decisions are truly final and binding.

The less formal process makes the arbitration hearing shorter than a trial would be, so arbitration offers the benefit of speed. Unless the parties agree otherwise, the arbitrator's decision typically cannot be challenged or appealed (unlike a court judgment or trial verdict). This means that the dispute is decided, once and for all, quite a bit sooner than if it had been tried in court. The arbitrator's decision can be enforced by a court, however, if either party refuses to abide by it.

Your Role in a Lawsuit

As you read about all the stages of litigation and all the different ways employee complaints can be resolved, you may feel overwhelmed. But don't worry: The attorney representing the company will be there to walk you through these different stages, explaining the process as you go.

Although there will be plenty of ways you can offer assistance as the trial proceeds, the attorney will be responsible for the bulk of the work: making arguments to the judge, preparing paperwork for court, interviewing witnesses, and so on. Your two main roles during a harassment or discrimination lawsuit are:

- to act as the liaison between the company and its attorneys, and
- to be an effective witness on behalf of the company, showing publically that it met its legal obligations to prevent and correct harassment and discrimination.

Being an Effective Liaison

As explained above, the company's lawyer will need your help getting ready to defend the company in the lawsuit. Although the attorney knows the law, you know the facts: what actually happened, who was involved, and how the company handled it. You may also know the personalities of the various employees involved, including the plaintiff. And, you know the company's record-keeping procedures. All of this knowledge means you have an important role to play in assisting the company's lawyer.

When you first meet with the attorney after the lawsuit has been filed, remember that the attorney may not know much about the underlying events, especially if the attorney wasn't involved in making the company's case to the EEOC or state fair employment practices agency. That means you must be prepared to fill in the details. If you did the investigation and prepared the materials discussed in Chapters 5 and 6, this should not be hard to do. You can summarize the plaintiff's history with the company, the plaintiff's complaint, how you investigated, and what your investigation revealed. Share all of the documents and files that the company has concerning the plaintiff. While you may have to search for some of this anew, a lot of it will probably be material you compiled in the course of your investigation.

The attorney may ask you to prepare a brief, chronological narrative of events (similar to the timeline described in Chapter 6), which the attorney can use to quickly understand and organize the facts of the case. A list of pertinent documents is also tremendously useful. List each document and give the title or a brief description, the date it was prepared, the author, the recipient, and its location (for example, in a personnel file, database, or investigation file). List the documents in a logical order. Chronological order is a good method, but sometimes grouping documents chronologically within categories (for example, "personnel documents," "investigation documents," or "medical documents") is more sensible, especially if many documents were created in a short span of time. Remember to err on the side of providing too much information. Leave it to the attorneys to decide what is relevant.

 Common Questions

Q: Seven female mechanics who used to work for us have sued our company for sex discrimination in a single lawsuit. They each worked for us for a different amount of time, held a variety of positions, and complain about different supervisors and coworkers in the lawsuit. Three of them worked in the same shop, but the others worked at two of our other shops in town. Their records are located in different places, as are the witnesses they name. Our lawyer wants me to get all the relevant information to her about these plaintiffs. I don't know how to put it together in a way that will make sense for her. Ideas?

Common Questions (cont'd)

A: First, get all of their files. Do a separate chronology of the work history for each plaintiff. Include the events they each allege in the chronologies and note whether each event is disputed by the company or not. Then, create a document index for each plaintiff. That will get the basic information in order.

In a complex case like this, consider making a chart or other diagram that indicates any overlap in their histories, events, or allegations, as well as any evidence that's common to two or more of the plaintiffs. Try to get a "big picture" view of their work histories and their allegations. Fill in the details in a way that makes clear what is verified (or undisputed by your company) and what is disputed.

One of the first things your company's attorney will consider is whether to try to divide up the case—to force each plaintiff to bring her own lawsuit, rather than bringing all of the claims together. A divide and conquer strategy can be effective for a company because it requires much more attorney work for the plaintiffs, who may each need a separate lawyer. The damages and fees each case would generate might not be high enough to attract a good plaintiff's attorney. What's more, your company might have an easier time at trial answering the claims of one plaintiff, rather than a group of plaintiffs all making similar allegations. To convince the court to separate the lawsuits, your company's attorney will have to show that the claims are sufficiently different that they shouldn't be tried together. This is where your overlapping chronology comes in: The attorney can use it to determine how much the cases intersect and how likely a court would be to divide them.

If you prepare the chronology and document index or other documents specifically for the attorneys to review and use to defend the company in a lawsuit, those documents will be protected by the attorney–client privilege. That means you do not have to give them to the plaintiff, even if they are requested during discovery. This should encourage you to list every document and fact, good or bad, without having to fear that the plaintiff will see it and use it against you. With the chronology of events and the document index in hand, the company lawyers can then ask you for particular items they wish to review or employees they wish to interview.

Sample Document Index

Document	Date	Author	Recipient	Location
Offer letter	2/10/08	Jay Wilkerson	Todd Jackson	Personnel file
1st warning	8/21/09	Jay Wilkerson	Todd Jackson	Personnel file
Employee complaint	11/15/09	Todd Jackson	Bob Marshall	Investigation file

As liaison, you may also be involved in things like scheduling meetings between attorneys and potential witnesses, document reviews (when the plaintiff's attorney may be onsite to review relevant documents) or other physical inspections, and employee depositions. As explained above, it's a good idea to keep a litigation calendar: a separate calendar you keep just for the lawsuit, but with crucial dates entered into your regular office calendar. One reason to have a separate litigation calendar is that you can take a quick look at the whole schedule of dates and plan ahead. Often, you'll need days or weeks of lead time to meet a particular lawsuit deadline. For example, if you are helping answer interrogatories in discovery, it will take you some time to gather the necessary information, give it to the company's attorney, then review the attorney's final draft of the company's responses. This means you'll have to start your work at least a few weeks before the interrogatory responses are actually due.

By regularly reviewing the litigation calendar, you can note in your daily planner the dates when you'll need to start preparing for particular litigation events. This tickler system will help you plan ahead for periods of intense lawsuit work. That way, you won't be surprised on a Monday morning to find out that you have to show up at a deposition the next day.

Sample Litigation Calendar

Date	Event	Employee	Tickle Date	Location
05/07/10	Doc. Production Date	Bob Marshall	04/20/10	Office
06/15/10	Deposition Prep. Mtg	Jay Wilkerson	05/25/10	Lewis Graham office, 950 Main Street
06/25/10	Deposition	Jay Wilkerson	06/21/10	950 Main Street

In this sample, you would enter the dates on your daily planner, too. The tickler for Jay Wilkerson's deposition preparation meeting with attorneys will alert you, if you are the company liaison, to remind Jay about the meeting and make any other arrangements necessary (like setting up an office or conference room for the meeting or gathering documents that the attorneys have asked to have available).

Ask the attorney to notify you of upcoming court dates, and to keep you in the loop if anything changes (a fairly common occurrence). Don't hesitate to check in with the attorney every couple of weeks, to find out if there's anything new you should be aware of. As a company representative, you are the attorney's client, so don't be shy about asking for information. Most attorneys are happy to provide it, although they may occasionally need a gentle reminder.

Being an Effective Witness

In addition to being a liaison, you may have another important role: You may be a witness in the litigation itself. If you were involved in taking the complaint, investigating it, or managing the employee, the employee's attorney will almost certainly want to hear your version of events. And, your company's attorney may also want you to testify, to present the company's side of the story.

For many people, the thought of testifying in a courtroom under oath can be intimidating or scary. After all, testifying as a witness is different from simply being interviewed, say, by your employer's attorneys. When you testify, you take an oath to tell the truth, and you are questioned (usually by the other side's attorney) either in court or in a conference room with several people present. What you say is recorded by a court reporter, sometimes along with a video or audio recording.

Fortunately, it's highly unlikely that you'll be thrown into the fray without prior preparation. The attorney for the company will meet with you ahead of time to discuss the purpose of the questioning, answer any questions you might have, and explain how to handle yourself.

Still, even with that kind of preparation or training, it's a good idea to understand a few basic principles that will help you do your best as an effective witness on the company's behalf. Whether you are answering questions in a pretrial deposition or on the stand during trial, follow these tips to put your best foot forward:

- **Listen very carefully.** In a normal conversation, we often know (or think we know) what other people are going to ask or say before they finish speaking. But don't make this assumption when giving testimony. Your testimony will be accurate only if you know exactly what is being asked. And, if you don't allow the questioner to finish the question, you may end up giving him or her the answer to a different question entirely—one that he or she may not have thought to ask!
- **Ask for clarification.** If you're not sure what you're being asked, don't speculate. Politely ask the attorney to rephrase or clarify the question. Don't answer until you're sure you understand, even if you feel like the attorney is frustrated. The important thing is to be accurate.
- **Answer only what is asked.** Especially if you are answering questions from the plaintiff's attorney, you don't want to volunteer information. You have a duty to answer the questions asked, but don't blurt out everything you know. The best way to make sure your testimony is accurate and helpful to the company is to provide only the information requested, and nothing more. When your company's attorney questions you, he or she will make sure you have an opportunity to provide all of the information necessary to help your company make its case.

Common Questions

Q: I just had my deposition taken in a harassment lawsuit filed by an ex-employee. The employee's attorney asked me if I'd ever seen the employee's supervisor touch the employee. I answered that he never touched her in an inappropriate way and that he is a very professional person. I thought this would be helpful, but the attorney for the company spoke to me about it afterward and said I needed to only answer what was asked. What did I do wrong?

A: You were trying to be helpful, but providing extra information could be damaging. The employee's lawyer only asked if you'd ever seen the supervisor touch the employee. That calls for a "yes" or "no" answer, which is the only answer to give. Even though you wanted to give more of what you felt was helpful information, doing so can be dangerous. Many times, witnesses give the opposing party a whole new area of questioning. For example, here you concluded that the supervisor's touching had never been "inappropriate" and suggested that his "professional" behavior means he wouldn't do anything he shouldn't. This might lead the employee's attorney to ask about other touching (that is, touching that isn't "inappropriate") that you may have witnessed. Or, it could lead the attorney to explore whether your investigation was biased—that is, whether you let your personal opinion of the supervisor cloud your professional judgment about his actions. In the future, stick to the questions you are asked.

- **Don't explain if "yes," "no," or "I don't know" answers the question.** The urge to explain is a strong one. However, keep in mind that, if a question calls for a yes or no answer, that is all you should provide. Again, providing too much information can harm you by opening new areas for questioning or ambiguity.

- **Keep emotions in check.** It's common for a lawyer to try to rattle a witness. This tactic is used for a variety of reasons, including making the witness appear defensive and less credible or provoking the witness to blurt out more information than he or she otherwise would. Even if you feel insulted, offended, or angry, don't show it. And, don't let it cloud your ability to listen closely and answer only what is asked. If you start to get upset, take a deep breath and refocus on the exact words of the question. You can even ask to take a break, if you need a few minutes to compose yourself.

- **Always tell the truth, no matter how painful.** You may be asked to give information that you believe will hurt your company, your coworkers, or yourself. As hard as it may be to do, you must tell the truth when testifying. You are under oath and lying is perjury, which is a crime in most jurisdictions. Also, if the other side learns that you have lied under oath, it will destroy your credibility, causing the judge or jury to doubt the reliability of all of your testimony, even testimony that was truthful.

- **Be consistent.** If you contradict an earlier statement, be prepared to explain the discrepancy. Otherwise, the plaintiff's attorney will ask you the type of question no witness wants to answer: "Were you lying then, or are you lying now?"

Common Questions

Q: An employee has filed a discrimination lawsuit. My problem is that the employee did come to me and mention that he felt unfairly treated by his supervisor. After he described the situation, I could see that it was probably just a misunderstanding. I told him I'd talk to his supervisor, but I got buried in other work and forgot. Our lawyer said that the employee filed an agency complaint and requested an immediate right to sue, so the lawsuit was the first we heard of his claims. I'm afraid that if I have to testify and tell the truth about dropping the ball, it will hurt my company. And, the employee doesn't really know whether or not I looked into his situation. I'd like to just answer that I investigated and found no evidence of discrimination. Is that okay?

A: Not even close to okay. You would be lying under oath and could face some penalty for perjury if you're caught. And, you probably would be caught because, even though the employee doesn't know what you did or didn't do, other people do. You can safely bet that the employee's attorney is going to scour the evidence for information about your "investigation." Unless you're planning to create false documentation and coach other employees to lie for you, the attorney isn't going to find anything that supports your story. That would not only not help your employer, it would make the company look worse.

   Talk to the company lawyer about your concerns and let him or her figure out how to deal with the fall-out after you tell the truth during your testimony. Attorneys anticipate these problems and have ways to deal with them, but only if you don't compound the problem by lying.

There are two different situations in which you may be testifying: at a deposition and at trial. As explained above, a deposition occurs during the discovery phase, when you are asked questions outside the courtroom, usually by the plaintiff's attorney. The deposition testimony is transcribed and can then be used as evidence in pretrial motions and in some cases, at the trial. You may also testify at the trial itself. Because these situations are a little different, you should prepare for, and handle, each of them a little differently.

Deposition Testimony

A deposition is a question-and-answer session outside of court, usually in a conference room at the offices of the lawyer who's taking the deposition. In spite of the relatively informal setting, deposition testimony is given under oath, has the same effect as testimony in court, and can be used at trial (often by the other side's attorney reading the testimony aloud to show that the witness has changed his or her story).

It's very important that you are well prepared for your deposition. You want to make sure that you don't say anything that will conflict with statements you've made in the past or will make in the future, at trial.

TIP

Ask the attorney representing the company for any materials you can review about general deposition procedure. Some law firms have videos or other informative products for witnesses to review before a deposition. You can also check out *Nolo's Deposition Handbook*, by Paul Bergman and Albert Moore. Keep in mind, though, that the plaintiff's lawyer can demand to see anything you reviewed in preparation for a deposition.

You won't be alone during the deposition—the attorney representing the company will be with you. He or she will meet with you beforehand as well, to help you prepare. You'll cover the most important topics that are likely to come up during the deposition, so the attorney can hear how you plan to answer and can help explain or explore the effects of that answer—for example, to prepare you for more intense questioning by the plaintiff's attorney on a specific issue.

At the deposition itself, you will probably sit at a table with the company's attorney sitting next to you. (If you are being sued individually, as explained below, it may be your own attorney sitting next to you.) Across the table will be the employee's attorney, who will ask you questions; the employee may be there as well. A court reporter also will be at the table, taking down everything you say, and there may be someone present with a video camera too. Do not get distracted by the crowd or the recording equipment; just focus on the questions themselves.

If you follow the tips described above, you will do the best you can to represent the company. And don't worry—the attorney for the company won't just be sitting there. He or she will be making sure that the questions asked are proper. In some cases, the attorney may object to certain questions before you answer. This is a clue to wait before answering. When an attorney objects in court, the judge can immediately rule on, or decide, the objection—that is, whether the question is proper (and therefore, you have to answer it) or not. For example, a judge may decide that you don't have to answer a question because it isn't relevant. Because the judge isn't present to make these rulings at a deposition, the attorney must register the objection on the record (that is, the court reporter must write it down). It is important that you give the attorney an opportunity to do this, because it may affect the company's right to have the evidence excluded at trial.

In some cases, the company's attorney will instruct you not to answer particular questions. Very heated exchanges can occur between the lawyers for each side during a deposition. The attorneys may raise their voices or disagree about something you don't understand. Don't worry about this. Just stay focused on answering the questions asked of you, unless otherwise directed by the attorney representing the company. If you start to get upset and feel it's interfering with your testimony, ask for a break between questions. Then you can step out and cool off, or talk to the attorney representing the company about what's happening.

Although the attorney representing the company will go over the entire process with you ahead of time, it's a good idea for you to review relevant documents and get ready even before that, so you can ask any questions you have and assuage your fears or concerns about the process. Write down the issues you'd like to discuss with the attorney before the deposition. Although you may have the opportunity to talk privately during the deposition, you may be too confused or flustered to remember what you wanted to ask. And if you leave the room for private consultation, the plaintiff's attorney may try to prevent you from doing so and suggest that it looks like you are getting coached by the company lawyer, which can hurt your credibility.

 CAUTION
Don't reveal privileged communications at deposition.
As a witness for the company, your communications with the attorney representing the company about the case are protected by the attorney–client privilege. This means you shouldn't talk about them in the deposition. If you have any concerns about these communications, discuss them with the company's attorney ahead of time, and don't answer a question on the subject unless you're certain you're not disclosing something confidential.

As mentioned above, a court reporter will be taking down everything that's said at the deposition, in shorthand. A few days or weeks after the deposition, the court reporter will provide the attorneys for each party with a written copy of the transcript of the deposition: a full record of all of the questions, answers, objections, arguments, and discussions on the record. (Any whispered discussion between you and the company attorney, or conversations you have outside the deposition room aren't recorded.)

The company attorney will probably ask you to review the written transcript of your deposition to make sure all of your answers are accurate. You can make changes to your deposition testimony, but if you do, the other side's attorney can comment on the changes at trial. The attorney may try to make it look like you were not completely truthful either at the deposition or in your changes to the transcript. However, if there are any errors in the recorded answers or the court reporter made a mistake, be sure to point them out to the attorney representing the company, who will decide how to handle them.

Trial Testimony

As virtually everyone knows, thanks to TV and the movies, when you testify at trial, you do so on the witness stand, beside the judge and in front of the jury. Like deposition testimony, trial testimony is given under oath and recorded by a court reporter. However, the much more formal courtroom setting, the judge's oversight role, and the interruptions of objections, argument, and rulings by the judge can make the procedure more anxiety provoking than a deposition. And you can't correct the record of your trial testimony, nor take breaks to calm down. Preparation is even more important.

? Common Questions

Q: I investigated an employee's discrimination complaint, and now the employee has sued. I have to give a deposition and probably testify at trial, and I'm terrified. I've never been comfortable with public speaking, and now I'm going to be cross-examined in front of a judge and jury! Every time I think about it, I start to panic. What can I do?

A: First off, realize that you're not alone. Most people are afraid of speaking in front of others, and having to testify at trial provokes anxiety even in the most fearless among us. Tell the company's attorney about your fears and ask what you should do. One option that may help is to have the attorney videotape you during a couple of practice sessions, so you can see how you sound and what you can do to improve. The more confident you are about how well you are going to do, the more comfortable you'll be.

If you're a party to the lawsuit or are the designated company representative, you will be at trial every day, sitting beside your attorney. If you're simply called as a witness, you'll probably be at trial only on the day when you testify, although you may still play a very active behind-the-scenes role in assisting company lawyers, as discussed above.

The company attorneys will prepare you to testify in court, often by pretending to be the plaintiff's attorney and asking the questions you are likely to face, so you can rehearse your answers. The attorneys will also review with you any documents that you're likely to be asked about. They'll go over how you should present yourself, and how to listen carefully not only to the questioner but also to the judge if he or she speaks. And, they'll tell you to stop answering and listen if either attorney makes an objection, being sure to wait until both attorneys and the judge have finished speaking. When objections are made at trial, the judge will usually signal when you can answer the question.

A courtroom is a lot like a stage—and when you're in the witness box, you're the lead actor! All eyes are on you. This can be extremely unnerving. It's important to get as comfortable as you can with the idea of answering questions in public. (Again, ask the company lawyers if they have any resources to which they can direct you to help you get more comfortable. Some people find that watching movies with trial scenes is helpful.)

> **TIP**
>
> **Sit in on a trial.** If at all possible, go to your local courthouse sometime before you have to testify and sit in the audience of a trial during witness cross-examination. It doesn't matter what type of case you observe; the idea is to get more comfortable with the setting and the roles of the witness and other trial participants.

Your prior deposition testimony may come into play during court testimony, because the plaintiff's attorney will ask a lot of the same questions and pounce on any deviation in your trial testimony from your deposition testimony. So, it's important to review the written transcript of your deposition as you prepare to testify at trial. Of course, if your deposition was videotaped, you will have to sit through a replay of the particular question and answer that the questioning attorney wants to highlight. This can be excruciating (few of us enjoy seeing our images on screen!), but focus on the question and answer and on the next question, and you'll get through the awkward moment just fine.

As with deposition testimony and other stages of litigation, the company's attorney will guide you through the process and prepare you for your role. If you have questions or feel unprepared, be sure to ask for help.

If You Are Sued Personally

A plaintiff may name you individually as a defendant in his or her lawsuit. This may happen if the plaintiff alleges that you personally harassed him or her, or that you engaged in other conduct for which you can be sued individually (for example, that you defamed the plaintiff by lying to prospective employers about the reasons why he was fired).

As distressing as it is to be called as a witness in a case against your employer, it's considerably more troubling to be named as a defendant to a harassment or discrimination lawsuit along with your employer. Not only are you being personally accused of misconduct, but your personal assets may be at risk if the plaintiff wins. This means you have a lot at stake, and you will have to work even harder to make sure you're prepared. But don't panic. As explained below, you will be represented by a lawyer—in most cases, the same lawyer who represents the company or your own lawyer who is paid by the company.

Your Lawyer

If you are named as a defendant in a lawsuit, the first order of business is to make sure you have a lawyer. If the company has also been sued (as is almost always the case), the company attorney will often represent you too, at least at the outset. The attorney will explain that he or she can represent you both as long as there is no conflict of interest between you and the employer. A conflict of interest means that your interests are sufficiently different—and opposed—that the lawyer cannot represent you both at the same time.

You will likely have the option of either agreeing to the dual representation (with the understanding that the attorney will notify you if a conflict arises) or hiring your own lawyer. Many individual supervisors and managers choose joint representation, probably because the company will often foot the entire bill for the attorney's fee.

If you go this route, problems may arise if you and the company have different interests. This may come to light during the course of the lawsuit. For example, if the company comes to believe that that you actually harassed an employee, it may no longer want to fight the employee's claim. Instead, it may want to settle for a small sum of money and move on, while you may want a full trial to "vindicate" your name. If there is a conflict like this, the same attorney cannot represent you both. The attorney will likely continue representing the company, his or her original client, and leave you to find your own lawyer.

Sometimes, an individual manager is named as a defendant purely for legal or strategic reasons. For example, by naming an individual as a defendant, a plaintiff can avoid having his or her case transferred from state to federal court in certain cases where that otherwise would be allowed. (See "Why Supervisors Get Sued," in Chapter 2, for more information.) But even if you are plainly not the real target of the lawsuit, your personal assets are still at risk. It's important to take the claims against you seriously and make sure that the attorney representing you protects your interests. Even if there's no conflict of interest between you and the company at the beginning of a lawsuit, keep an eye out for conflicts that might emerge as the case proceeds.

TIP

Get a "second opinion" as to potential conflicts of interest. Although you may have no reason to doubt the judgment and ethics of the attorney representing the company, it's a good idea to consult with another lawyer privately and make sure there's no conflict of interest. Do this both at the outset of the lawsuit and at any later time when you think your interests may conflict with the company's.

? Common Questions

Q: My company and I personally have been sued by a job applicant who was interviewed and rejected by the hiring committee. While I was a member of the committee, the rejection decision was made by all of us together. I attended the deposition of another member of the hiring committee and he testified that I made the final decision to reject the applicant. This is not true and my deposition is coming up. Obviously, I'll tell the truth, but that's going to create problems for my company, isn't it?

A: It might, but there is a more immediate problem. You need to see an attorney who isn't affiliated with your company to find out whether you need your own lawyer in the lawsuit. The committee member's testimony conflicts with yours in a way that puts the blame on you for the hiring decision. The company may simply be caught in the middle of the dispute between you and the other committee member, or the company may be trying to focus liability for any harm from the rejection decision on you. If the latter is the case, the company's attorney clearly cannot represent your interests and the interests of the company at the same time.

Make an appointment with an employment lawyer right away to talk about the problem. If you can't schedule an appointment before your deposition, ask that the deposition be delayed until you are able to speak with an attorney.

If you need your own attorney, your company might be willing —or legally required—to pay your separate attorney's fees. Some states require employers to indemnify employees: to pay all costs associated with doing their jobs. In these states, employers may have to foot the bill for an employee's lawyer and/or the cost of a damages award against the employee, as long as the lawsuit stems from the employee's official duties. If the employee is accused of behavior that falls outside the scope of his or her job (such as sexually assaulting an employee), however, the employee wouldn't be entitled to indemnification. When you speak to a lawyer to find out if there are any conflict of interest problems, ask whether the company might be required to pay for your lawyer.

The company may elect to pay your lawyer even if it isn't required to do so. For example, the company may simply want to help you out financially, it may do so under the terms of an insurance policy that pays for such fees, or it may do so to keep you on the team and make sure that you present the company in a positive light. This latter motive highlights the potential problem with allowing the company to pay your lawyer: An employer may want to exercise subtle (or not so subtle) control over you or your attorney by pulling the purse strings to compel you support their case. Discuss the pros and cons of an arrangement like this with your own lawyer before agreeing to it.

Your Role as a Defendant

As long as there is no conflict of interest, you will work with the attorney representing the company in much the same way as you would if you were a witness in the suit, at least up to the point of trial. However, you need to stay on the look-out for possible conflicts of interest and seek outside advice if you're concerned that you aren't being adequately represented.

The plaintiff may be willing to settle his or her claims against you and proceed to trial only against the company. In that event, you likely take on the role of company liaison and witness, as discussed, above.

If you're still a defendant when the trial starts, however, your role shifts significantly. As a witness and liaison, you only have to show up on the day that you are scheduled to testify and help company lawyers with trial preparations as necessary. As a party, you must attend every day of trial and sit at the defendants' table in front of the judge's bench. Although your active role during the trial is still restricted to testifying and helping behind the scenes, you have to sit there, in full view of the judge and jury, throughout the trial. This means you'll have to pay attention to your appearance and demeanor. Maintain your composure no matter what goes on around you. This can be quite difficult, because you may hear accusatory, harsh, and even dishonest things said about you, to which you cannot respond or react.

A harassment or discrimination trial can last days and even weeks. Having to sit silently and passively for such a long stretch can be exhausting, even without the added stress of being personally attacked and at risk as a defendant.

 TIP

Attend the depositions of the plaintiff's witnesses and read the transcripts. As a party to a lawsuit, you have the right to attend the depositions of witnesses. Although you may not want to attend all of them, sit in on those of witnesses whom you know will testify about you or your actions. And, read the depositions of all witnesses before trial, so you're not surprised by what they say in court.

Limiting Your Exposure

Individual defendants are often dismissed from the lawsuit before trial. Compared to the company, individual managers are usually not viewed as having deep pockets filled with assets and resources to pay a large judgment. Throughout the litigation, your attorney will likely try to get you out of the lawsuit by filing motions, such as a motion to dismiss or a motion for summary judgment, as discussed above. Ask the attorneys about making such a motion as early as possible. Typically, a motion for summary judgment is not made until after some or all of the discovery is done in a lawsuit, but there may be enough evidence early on to prove that you can't be sued personally for your actions.

If you're jointly represented along with your employer, this is another potential source of conflict: You will naturally want to get out of the lawsuit as soon as possible, while the attorney might prefer to wait until he or she can make all of the defense arguments at once. In this instance, you should see another lawyer to assess the situation.

Settling Individual Claims

Plaintiffs often settle their claims alleged against individual defendants. In part, this is because individuals typically do not have the resources and assets to pay large verdicts. But dismissing an individual defendant may also make the plaintiff's case stronger. Juries may sympathize more with an individual defendant, but be more likely to award large damages against a faceless business. Dropping an individual defendant also helps the plaintiff focus on the strongest claims; because individuals are often sued for tactical reasons (rather than because they acted particularly badly), claims against them aren't likely to be the best in the bunch.

Talk to your lawyer (whether you're jointly or individually represented) about engaging in settlement talks with the plaintiff early and often throughout the litigation. If you're jointly represented and the attorney resists these requests, this may signal a conflict of interest. You should consider consulting an attorney unaffiliated with the company to make sure your interests are protected.

If you can't get out of the case, ask your company whether a damages award against you might be covered by insurance. Some employers offer insurance coverage for damage awards against company officers, directors, and other employees for actions they take in the course of their jobs. Early in the litigation, ask whether such coverage is available for you. If there is no such insurance available, talk to an outside lawyer about other possible arrangements that you could negotiate with the company to protect you in the event of an unfavorable judgment. For example, it may be possible to get the company to agree to pay for some or all of a damages award against you.

Dos and Don'ts

Do:
- Prepare a chronology of events and document index for the initial meeting with lawyers.
- Create a litigation calendar and consult it often.
- Prepare questions for lawyers prior to testifying at deposition or in court.
- Sit in on and review the transcripts of the depositions of other witnesses.
- If you're named as a defendant in the lawsuit, consult with an unaffiliated lawyer to make sure that the company's interests don't conflict with yours.

Don't:
- Panic—a cool head works better!
- Hesitate to ask the lawyers questions about what to expect at all stages of a lawsuit.
- Try to help your company or yourself by hiding the truth.
- Be bashful about reminding company lawyers to keep you in the loop on dates and scheduling.
- Let your emotions get the best of you at your deposition or in court.
- Answer unless you know what's being asked when testifying.
- Ignore potential conflicts of interest if you're named as a defendant: You have a lot at stake, and you must act quickly to protect yourself.

How to Use the CD-ROM

Installing the Files Onto Your Computer..279

   Where Are the Files Installed?..279

Using the Word Processing Files to Create Documents....................280

   Opening a File...280

   Editing Your Document 281

   Printing Out the Document 282

   Saving Your Document..282

Listening to the Audio Files..282

   Playing the Audio Files Without Installing..282

   Listening to Audio Files You've Installed on Your Computer 283

Files on the CD-ROM 284

The CD-ROM included with this book can be used with Windows computers. It installs files that use software programs that need to be on your computer already. It is not a standalone software program.

In accordance with U.S. copyright laws, the CD-ROM and its files are for your personal use only.

Please read this appendix and the "Readme.htm" file included on the CD-ROM for instructions on using the CD-ROM. For a list of files and their file names, see the end of this appendix.

Note to Macintosh users: This CD-ROM and its files should also work on Macintosh computers. Please note, however, that Nolo cannot provide technical support for non-Windows users.

Note to eBook users: You can access the CD-ROM files mentioned here from the bookmarked section of the eBook, located on the left-hand side.

How to View the README File

To view the "Readme.htm" file, insert the Forms CD-ROM into your computer's CD-ROM drive and follow these instructions:

Windows XP and Vista
1. On your PC's desktop, double-click the **My Computer** icon.
2. Double-click the icon for the CD-ROM drive into which the CD-ROM was inserted.
3. Double-click the file "Readme.htm."

Macintosh
1. On your Mac desktop, double-click the icon for the CD-ROM that you inserted.
2. Double-click the file "Readme.htm."

Installing the Files Onto Your Computer

To work with the files on the CD-ROM, you first need to install them onto your hard disk. Here's how.

Windows XP and Vista

Follow the CD-ROM's instructions that appear on the screen.
    If nothing happens when you insert the CD-ROM, then:
    1. Double-click the **My Computer** icon.
    2. Double-click the icon for the CD-ROM drive into which the CD-ROM was inserted.
    3. Double-click the file "Welcome.exe."

Macintosh

If the **Workplace Issues CD** window is not open, double-click the **Workplace Issues CD** icon. Then:
    1. Select the **Workplace Issues Resources** folder icon.
    2. Drag and drop the folder icon onto your computer.

Where Are the Files Installed?

Windows

By default, all the files are installed to the **Workplace Issues Resources** folder in the **Program Files** folder of your computer. A folder called **Workplace Issues Resources** is added to the **Programs** folder of the **Start** menu.

    MP3 files are installed by default to a folder named **Audio** in the **Program Files**.

Macintosh

RTF files are located in the **Forms** folder within the **Workplace Issues Resources** folder. MP3 files are located in the **Audio** folder within the **Workplace Issues Resources** folder.

Using the Word Processing Files to Create Documents

The CD-ROM includes word processing files that you can open, complete, print, and save with your word processing program. All word processing files come in rich text format and have the extension ".rtf." For example, the file for the Intake Form discussed in Chapter 5 is on the file "IntakeForm.rtf." RTF files can be read by most recent word processing programs including MS *Word*, Windows *WordPad*, and recent versions of *WordPerfect*.

The following are general instructions. Because each word processor uses different commands to open, format, save, and print documents, refer to your word processor's help file for specific instructions.

Do not call Nolo's technical support if you have questions on how to use your word processor or your computer.

Opening a File

You can open word processing files in any of the three following ways:

1. Windows users can open a file by selecting its "shortcut."
   i. Click the Windows **Start** button.
   ii. Open the **Programs** folder.
   iii. Open the **Workplace Issues Resources** folder.
   iv. Open the **Forms** folder.
   v. Click the shortcut to the form you want to work with.
2. Both Windows and Macintosh users can open a file by double-clicking it.
   i. Use **My Computer** or **Windows Explorer** (Windows XP or Vista) or the **Finder** (Macintosh) to go to the **Workplace Issues Resources** folder.
   ii. Double-click the file you want to open.

3. Windows and Macintosh users can open a file from within their word processor.
   i. Open your word processor.
   ii. Go to the **File** menu and choose the **Open** command. This opens a dialog box.
   iii. Select the location and name of the file. (Navigate to the version of the **Workplace Issues Resources** folder that you've installed on your computer.)

Editing Your Document

Here are tips for working on your document:

- Refer to the book's instructions and sample agreements for help.
- Underlines indicate where to enter information, frequently including bracketed instructions. Delete the underlines and instructions before finishing your document.
- Signature lines should appear on a page with at least some text from the document itself.

Editing Forms That Have Optional or Alternative Text

Some forms have optional or alternate text:

- With optional text, you choose whether to include or exclude the given text.
- With alternative text, you select one alternative to include and exclude the others.

When editing these forms, we suggest you do the following:

Optional text. Delete optional text you do not want to include and keep that which you do. In either case, delete the italicized instructions. If you choose to delete an optional numbered clause, renumber the subsequent clauses after deleting it.

Alternative text. Delete all the alternatives that you do not want to include first. Then delete the italicized instructions.

Printing Out the Document

Use your word processor's or text editor's **Print** command to print out your document.

Saving Your Document

Use the **Save As** command to save and rename your document. You will be unable to use the **Save** command because the files are read only. If you save the file without renaming it, the underlines that indicate where you need to enter your information will be lost, and you will be unable to create a new document with this file without recopying the original file from the CD-ROM.

Listening to the Audio Files

This section explains how to play the audio files using your computer. All audio files are in MP3 format. For example, the manager interview with an employee complaining of harassment is on the file "ComplaintInterview.mp3." At the end of this appendix, you'll find a list of the audio files and their file names.

Most computers come with a media player that plays MP3 files. You can listen to files that you have installed on your computer or directly from the CD-ROM. See below for further information on both.

The following are general instructions. Because every media player is different, refer to your media player's **Help** files for more specific instructions. Please do not contact Nolo's technical support if you are having difficulty using your media player.

Playing the Audio Files Without Installing

If you don't want to copy 26.1 MB of audio files to your computer, you can play the CD-ROM on your computer. Here's how.

Windows

1. Insert the CD-ROM to view the **Welcome to the Workplace Issues CD** window.
2. Click **Listen to Audio**.

If nothing happens when you insert the CD-ROM:

1. Double-click the **My Computer** icon.
2. Double-click the icon for the CD-ROM drive you inserted the CD-ROM into.
3. Double-click the file "Welcome.exe."

Macintosh

1. Insert the CD-ROM. (If the **Workplace Issues CD** window does not open, double-click the **Workplace Issues CD** icon).
2. Double-click the **Audio** folder.
3. Double-click the audio file you want to hear.

Listening to Audio Files You've Installed on Your Computer

There are two ways to listen to the audio files that you have installed on your computer.

1. Windows users can open a file by selecting its shortcut.
   i. Click the Windows **Start** button.
   ii. Open the **Programs** folder.
   iii. Open the **Workplace Issues Resources** folder.
   iv. Open the **Audio** subfolder.
   v. Click the shortcut to the file you want to work with.
2. Both Windows and Macintosh users can open a file by double-clicking it.
   i. Use **My Computer** or **Windows Explorer** (Windows XP or Vista) or the **Finder** (Macintosh) to go to the **Workplace Issues Resources** folder.
   ii. Double-click the file you want to open.

Files on the CD-ROM

The following files are in RTF:

Form Title	File Name
Litigation Calendar	Calendar.rtf
Intake Form—Employee Complaint	IntakeForm.rtf
Policy Distribution Log	Log.rtf
Policy Prohibiting Discrimination and Harassment	Policy.rtf
Acknowledgment of Receipt of Policy	Receipt.rtf

The following files are in MP3:

Form Title	File Name
Common Harassment and Discrimination Questions (interview with author)	01_AuthorIntrvw.mp3
Manager Interview with Employee Complaining of Harassment	02_HarassIntrvw.mp3
Bad Job Interview Scenario	03_BadIntrvw.mp3
Good Job Interview Scenario	04_GoodIntrvw.mp3

State Laws on Discrimination and Harassment

State Laws That Prohibit Discrimination and Harassment 286

State Enforcement Agencies 298

State Laws That Prohibit Discrimination and Harassment

State and Statute	Covered Employers	Protected Categories	Training Law	Training: Covered Employers	Training Requirements
Alabama *Alabama Code §§ 25-1-20; 25-1-21*	20 or more employees	Age	None	N/A	N/A
Alaska *Alaska Stat. §§ 18.80.220; 18.80.300(10); 47.30.865*	1 or more employees	Race, national origin, gender, pregnancy, age, disability, religion, AIDS/HIV, marital status, parenthood	None	N/A	N/A
Arizona *Arizona Rev. Stat. Ann. §§ 41-1461; 41-1463; 41-1465*	15 or more employees	Race, national origin, gender, age, disability, religion, HIV/AIDS, genetic testing	None	N/A	N/A
Arkansas *Arkansas Code Ann. §§ 11-4-601; 11-5-403; 16-123-102(6); 16-123-107*	9 or more employees	Race, national origin, gender, pregnancy, disability, religion, genetic testing	None	N/A	N/A
California *California Government Code §§ 12920; 12926.1; 12940; 12941; 12945*	5 or more employees	Age, race, national origin, gender, pregnancy, sexual orientation, gender identity, disability, religion, genetic testing, HIV/AIDS, marital status, political activities/ affiliations	*California Government Code § 12950.1*	50 or more employees	2 hours of interactive sexual harassment training by qualified trainer every 2 years for all supervisors; new supervisors must be trained within 6 months of hire or promotion

State Laws That Prohibit Discrimination and Harassment (cont'd)

State and Statute	Covered Employers	Protected Categories	Training Law	Training: Covered Employers	Training Requirements
Colorado *Colorado Rev. Stat. §§ 24-34-301, 24-34-401, 24-34-402, 24-34-402.5, 27-10-115*	1 or more employees	Age, race, national origin, gender, pregnancy, sexual orientation, disability, religion, HIV/AIDS, lawful off-duty conduct	*3 Colorado Code Regs. § 708-1, Rule 80.11(C)*	1 or more employees	Sexual harassment training of all employees "encouraged" but not required
Connecticut *Connecticut Gen. Stat. Ann. §§ 46a-51, 46a-60, 46a-81a, 46a-81c*	3 or more employees	Age, race, national origin, gender, pregnancy, sexual orientation, disability, religion, HIV/AIDS, genetic testing, marital status	*Connecticut Gen. Stat. Ann. § 46a-54(15)(B)*	50 or more employees	2 hours of sexual harassment training of all supervisors; new supervisors must be trained within 6 months of hire or promotion. Retraining not required but encouraged every 3 years. Qualifications of trainers not specified.
Delaware *Delaware Code Ann. Tit. 19, §§ 710, 711, 724*	4 or more employees	Age, race, national origin, gender, disability, religion, HIV/AIDS, genetic testing, marital status	None	N/A	N/A
District of Columbia *District of Columbia Code Ann. §§ 2-1401.01 through 2-1402.13.*	1 or more employees	Age, race, national origin, gender, sexual orientation, gender identity, disability, religion, HIV/AIDS, genetic testing, marital status, family duties, personal appearance, political affiliation, victim of intrafamily offense	None	N/A	N/A

State Laws That Prohibit Discrimination and Harassment (cont'd)

State and Statute	Covered Employers	Protected Categories	Training Law	Training: Covered Employers	Training Requirements
Florida *Florida Stat. Ann.* *§§ 760.01, 760.02,* *760.10, 760.50,* *448.075*	15 or more employees	Age, race, national origin, gender, disability, religion, HIV/AIDS, marital status, sickle cell trait	None for private sector employers	N/A	N/A
Georgia *Georgia Code Ann.* *§§ 34-1-2, 34-5-1,* *34-5-2, 34-6A-1,* *45-19-20*	1 or more employees (age); 15 or more employees (disability); 10 or more employees (gender)	Age, gender, disability	None	N/A	N/A
Hawaii *Hawaii Rev. Stat.* *§§ 378-1, 378-2,* *378-2.5*	1 or more employees	Age, race, national origin, gender, pregnancy, sexual orientation, disability, religion, HIV/AIDS, genetic testing, marital status, arrest and court record	None	N/A	N/A
Idaho *Idaho Code.* *§§ 39-8303,* *67-5902, 67-5909,* *67-5910*	5 or more employees	Age, race, national origin, gender, pregnancy, disability, religion, genetic testing	None	N/A	N/A

State Laws That Prohibit Discrimination and Harassment (cont'd)

State and Statute	Covered Employers	Protected Categories	Training Law	Training: Covered Employers	Training Requirements
Illinois *410 Illinois Comp. Stat. § 513/25; 775 Ill. Comp. Stat. §§ 5/1-102, 5/1-103, 5/1-105, 5/2-101, 5/2-102, 5/2-103; 820 Ill. Comp. Stat. §§ 105/4, 180/30; Ill. Admin. Code tit. 56 § 5210.110*	15 or more employees; 1 or more employees (disability)	Age, race, national origin, gender, pregnancy, sexual orientation, gender identity, disability, religion, HIV/AIDS, genetic testing, marital status, citizenship status, military status, arrest record, domestic violence victim	None for private sector employees	N/A	N/A
Indiana *Indiana Code Ann. §§ 22-9-1-2, 22-9-2-1, 22-9-2-2, 22-9-5-1*	6 or more employees; 15 or more employees (disability)	Age, race, national origin, gender, disability, religion	None	N/A	N/A
Iowa *Iowa Code §§ 216.2, 216.6, 729.6*	1 or more employees	Age, race, national origin, gender, pregnancy, sexual orientation, gender identity, disability, religion, HIV/AIDS, genetic testing	None for private sector employees	N/A	N/A
Kansas *Kansas Stat. Ann. §§ 44-1002, 44-1009, 44-1112, 44-1113, 44-1125, 44-1126, 65-6002(e)*	4 or more employees	Age, race, national origin, gender, disability, religion, HIV/AIDS, genetic testing, military status	None	N/A	N/A
Kentucky *Kentucky Rev. Stat. Ann. §§ 207.130, 207.135, 207.150, 342.197, 344.010, 344.030, 344.040*	8 or more employees	Age, race, national origin, gender, pregnancy, religion, disability, HIV/AIDS	None	N/A	N/A

State Laws That Prohibit Discrimination and Harassment (cont'd)

State and Statute	Covered Employers	Protected Categories	Training Law	Training: Covered Employers	Training Requirements
Louisiana *Louisiana Rev. Stat. Ann. §§ 23:301 to 23:368*	20 or more employees	Age, race, national origin, gender, pregnancy, disability, religion, genetic testing, occupational pneumoconiosis (coal dust exposure)	None	N/A	N/A
Maine *Maine Rev. Stat. Ann. tit. 5, §§ 19302, 4552, 4553, 4571–4576, tit. 26, § 833; tit. 39-A, § 353*	1 or more employees	Age, race, national origin, gender, pregnancy, sexual orientation, gender identity, disability, religion, genetic testing, past workers' compensation claim, past whistleblowing	*Maine Rev. Stat. Ann. tit. 26, § 807(3)*	15 or more employees	Sexual harassment training of all new employees within one year of hire. Supervisors and managers to be trained in specific responsibilities of positions. No retraining required. Qualifications of trainers not specified.
Maryland *Maryland code, Art. 49B, §§ 15, 16, 17; Labor and Employment § 3-704*	15 or more employees	Age, race, national origin, gender, pregnancy, sexual orientation religion, marital status, disability, genetic testing	None	N/A	N/A
Massachusetts *Massachusetts Gen. Laws ch. 149 § 24A; ch. 151B, §§ 1, 4*	6 or more employees	Age, race, national origin, gender, sexual orientation, disability, religion, HIV/AIDS, genetic testing, marital status, military status, arrest record	None	N/A	N/A

State Laws That Prohibit Discrimination and Harassment (cont'd)

State and Statute	Covered Employers	Protected Categories	Training Law	Training: Covered Employers	Training Requirements
Michigan *Michigan Comp. Laws §§ 37.1103, 37.1201, 37.1202, 37.2201, 37.2202, 37.2205a, 750.556*	1 or more employees	Age, race, national origin, gender, pregnancy, disability, religion, HIV/AIDS, genetic testing, marital status, height, weight, misdemeanor arrest record	None	N/A	N/A
Minnesota *Minnesota Stat. Ann. §§ 144.417, 181.81, 181.974, 363A.03, 363A.08*	1 or more employees	Age, race, national origin, gender, pregnancy, sexual orientation, gender identity, disability, religion, HIV/AIDS, genetic testing, marital status, local commission membership, public assistance receipt	None	N/A	N/A
Mississippi *Mississippi Code Ann. § 33-1-15*	1 or more employees	Military status, breast-milk expression breaks	None	N/A	N/A
Missouri *Missouri Rev. Stat. §§ 191.665, 213.010, 213.055, 375.1306*	6 or more employees	Age, race, national origin, gender, disability, religion, HIV/AIDS, genetic testing	None	N/A	N/A
Montana *Montana Code Ann. §§ 49-2-101, 49-2-303, 49-2-310*	1 or more employees	Age, race, national origin, gender, pregnancy, disability, religion, marital status	None	N/A	N/A

State Laws That Prohibit Discrimination and Harassment (cont'd)

State and Statute	Covered Employers	Protected Categories	Training Law	Training: Covered Employers	Training Requirements
Nebraska *Nebraska Rev. Stat. §§ 20-168, 48-236, 48-1001 to 48-1010, 48-1102, 48-1104*	15 or more employees; 20 or more employees (age); 1 or more employees (genetic testing)	Age, race, national origin, gender, pregnancy, disability, religion, genetic testing, HIV/AIDS, marital status	None	N/A	N/A
Nevada *Nevada Rev. Stat. Ann. §§ 613.310 and following*	15 or more employees	Age, race, national origin, gender, pregnancy, sexual orientation, disability, religion, HIV/AIDS, genetic testing, service animal use, whistleblowing	None	N/A	N/A
New Hampshire *New Hampshire Rev. Stat. Ann. §§ 141-H:3, 354-A:2, 354-A:6, 354-A:7*	6 or more employees	Age, race, national origin, gender, pregnancy, sexual orientation, disability, religion, genetic testing, marital status	None	N/A	N/A
New Jersey *New Jersey Stat. Ann. §§ 10:5-1, 10:5-4.1, 10:5-5, 10:5-12, 10:5-29.1, 34:6B-1, 43:21-49*	1 or more employees	Age, race, national origin, gender, pregnancy, sexual orientation, gender identity, disability, religion, HIV/AIDS, genetic testing, marital status, atypical hereditary trait, military status, service dog use	None	N/A	N/A

				Training:	
State and Statute	**Covered Employers**	**Protected Categories**	**Training Law**	**Covered Employers**	**Training Requirements**
New Mexico *New Mexico Stat. Ann. §§ 24-21-4, 28-1-2, 28-1-7*	4 or more employees; 15 or more employees (gender identity discrimination)	Age, race, national origin, gender, pregnancy, sexual orientation, gender identity, disability, religion, genetic testing, marital status, serious medical condition	None	N/A	N/A
New York *New York Exec. Law §§ 292, 296; Labor Law § 201-d*	4 or more employees	Age, race, national origin, gender, pregnancy, sexual orientation, disability, religion, HIV/AIDS, genetic testing, marital status, lawful off-duty conduct, military status, observance of Sabbath, political activities, service dog use	None	N/A	N/A
North Carolina *North Carolina Gen. Stat. §§ 95-28.1, 127B-11, 130A-148, 143-422.2, 168A-5*	15 or more employees	Age, race, national origin, gender, disability, religion, HIV/AIDS, genetic testing, military status, sickle cell or hemoglobin C trait	None for private sector employees	N/A	N/A
North Dakota *North Dakota Cent. Code §§ 14-02.4-02, 14-02.4-03, 34-01-17*	1 or more employees	Age, race, national origin, gender, pregnancy, disability, religion, marital status, lawful off-duty conduct, public assistance receipt	None	N/A	N/A

Table title: **State Laws That Prohibit Discrimination and Harassment (cont'd)**

State Laws That Prohibit Discrimination and Harassment (cont'd)

State and Statute	Covered Employers	Protected Categories	Training Law	Training: Covered Employers	Training Requirements
Ohio *Ohio Rev. Code Ann. §§ 4111.17, 4112.01, 4112.02*	4 or more employees	Age, race, national origin, gender, pregnancy, disability, religion	None	N/A	N/A
Oklahoma *Oklahoma Stat. Ann. tit. 25, §§ 1301, 1302; tit. 36, § 3614.2; tit. 40, § 500; tit. 44, § 208*	15 or more employees	Age, race, national origin, gender, disability, religion, genetic testing, military status	None	N/A	N/A
Oregon *Oregon Rev. Stat. §§ Hampshire Rev. Stat. Ann. §§ 25.337, 659A.030, 659A.100 and following, 659A.303*	1 or more employees	Age, race, national origin, gender, pregnancy, sexual orientation, disability, religion, genetic testing, marital status, parent w/court-ordered medical support	None	N/A	N/A
Pennsylvania *43 Pennsylvania Cons. Stat. Ann. §§ 954-955*	4 or more employees	Age, race, national origin, gender, pregnancy, disability, religion, GED, service animal use, association with disabled person	None for private sector employees	N/A	N/A
Rhode Island *Rhode Island General Laws §§ 12-28-10, 23-6-22, 28-5-6, 28-5-7, 28-6-18, 28-6.7-1*	4 or more employees; 1 or more employees (gender-based wage discrimination)	Age, race, national origin, gender, pregnancy, sexual orientation, gender identity, disability, religion, HIV/AIDS, genetic testing, domestic abuse victim	None for private sector employees	N/A	N/A

State Laws That Prohibit Discrimination and Harassment (cont'd)

State and Statute	Covered Employers	Protected Categories	Training Law	Training: Covered Employers	Training Requirements
South Carolina *South Carolina Code §§ 1-13-30, 1-13-80*	15 or more employees	Age, race, national origin, gender, pregnancy, disability, religion	None	N/A	N/A
South Dakota *South Dakota Codified Laws Ann. §§ 20-13-1, 20-13-10, 60-12-15, 60-2-20, 62-1-17*	1 or more employees	Race, national origin, gender, disability, religion, genetic testing, preexisting injury	None	N/A	N/A
Tennessee *Tennessee Code Ann. §§ 4-21-102, 4-21-401 and following, 8-50-103, 50-2-201, 50-2-202*	8 or more employees; 1 or more employees (gender-based wage discrimination)	Age, race, national origin, gender, pregnancy, disability, religion, service dog use	None for private sector employees	N/A	N/A
Texas *Texas Lab. Code Ann. §§ 21.002, 21.051, 21.082, 21.101, 21.106, 21.402*	15 or more employees	Age, race, national origin, gender, pregnancy, disability, religion, genetic testing	None for private sector employees	N/A	N/A
Utah *Utah Code Ann. §§ 26-45-103, 34A-5-102, 34A-5-106*	15 or more employees	Age, race, national origin, gender, pregnancy, disability, religion, HIV/AIDS, genetic testing	None for private sector employees	N/A	N/A

				Training:	
State and Statute	Covered Employers	Protected Categories	Training Law	Covered Employers	Training Requirements
Vermont *Vermont Stat. Ann. tit. 21, §§ 495, 495d; tit. 18, § 9333*	1 or more employees	Age, race, national origin, gender, sexual orientation, disability, religion, HIV/AIDS, genetic testing, birthplace	None	N/A	N/A
Virginia *Virginia Code Ann. §§ 2.2-3900, 2.2-3901, 40.1-28.6, 40.1-28.7:1, 51.5-41*	1 or more employees	Age, race, national origin, gender, pregnancy, disability, religion, genetic testing, marital status	None	N/A	N/A
Washington *Washington Rev. Code Ann. §§ 38.40.110, 49.60.040, 49.60.172, 49.60.180, 49.12.175, 49.44.090, 49.76.120*	8 or more employees; 1 or more employees (gender-based wage discrimination)	Age, race, national origin, gender, pregnancy, sexual orientation, gender identity, disability, religion, HIV/AIDS, genetic testing, marital status, Hepatitis C, state militia member, service animal use, domestic violence victim	None for private sector employees	N/A	N/A
West Virginia *West Virginia Code §§ 5-11-3, 5-11-9, 16-3C-3, 21-5B-1, 21-5B-3*	12 or more employees; 1 or more employees (gender-based wage discrimination)	Age, race, national origin, gender, disability, religion, HIV/AIDS	None	N/A	N/A

State Laws That Prohibit Discrimination and Harassment (cont'd)

State Laws That Prohibit Discrimination and Harassment (cont'd)

State and Statute	Covered Employers	Protected Categories	Training Law	Training: Covered Employers	Training Requirements
Wisconsin *Wisconsin Stat. Ann. §§ 111.32 and following*	1 or more employees	Age, race, national origin, gender, pregnancy, sexual orientation, disability, religion, HIV/AIDS, genetic testing, marital status, arrest/ conviction record, state or national guard/military status	None	N/A	N/A
Wyoming *Wyoming Stat. §§ 27-9-102, 27-9-105, 19-11-104*	2 or more employees	Age, race, national origin, gender, pregnancy, religion, military status	None	N/A	N/A

State Enforcement Agencies

Alabama
EEOC District Office
Birmingham, AL
205-212-2100
800-669-4000
www.eeoc.gov/birmingham/index.html

Alaska
Commission for Human Rights
Anchorage, AK
907-274-4692
800-478-4692
http://gov.state.ak.us/aschr

Arizona
Civil Rights Division
Phoenix, AZ
602-542-5263
877-491-5742
www.azag.gov/civil_rights/index.html

Arkansas
Equal Employment Opportunity
   Commission
Little Rock, AR
501-324-5060
www.eeoc.gov/littlerock/index.html

California
Department of Fair Employment and
   Housing
Sacramento District Office
Sacramento, CA
916-478-7200
800-884-1684
www.dfeh.ca.gov

Colorado
Civil Rights Division
Denver, CO
303-894-2997
800-262-4845
www.dora.state.co.us/Civil-Rights

Connecticut
Commission on Human Rights and
   Opportunities
Hartford, CT
860-541-3400
800-477-5737
www.state.ct.us/chro

Delaware
Office of Labor Law Enforcement
Division of Industrial Affairs
Wilmington, DE
302-761-8200
www.delawareworks.com/
   industrialaffairs/welcome.shtml

District of Columbia
Office of Human Rights
Washington, DC
202-727-4559
http://ohr.dc.gov/ohr/site/default.asp

Florida
Commission on Human Relations
Tallahassee, FL
850-488-7082
http://fchr.state.fl.us

State Enforcement Agencies (cont'd)

Georgia
Atlanta District Office
U.S. Equal Employment Opportunity
 Commission
Atlanta, GA
404-562-6800
800-669-4000
www.eeoc.gov/atlanta/index.html

Hawaii
Hawai'i Civil Rights Commission
Honolulu, HI
808-586-8636
www.hawaii.gov/labor/hcrc

Idaho
Idaho Commission on Human Rights
Boise, ID
208-334-2873
www2.state.id.us/ihrc

Illinois
Department of Human Rights
Chicago, IL
312-814-6200
www.state.il.us/dhr

Indiana
Civil Rights Commission
Indianapolis, IN
317-232-2600
800-628-2909
www.in.gov/icrc

Iowa
Iowa Civil Rights Commission
Des Moines, IA
515-281-4121
800-457-4416
www.state.ia.us/government/crc

Kansas
Human Rights Commission
Topeka, KS
785-296-3206
www.khrc.net

Kentucky
Human Rights Commission
Louisville, KY
502-595-4024
800-292-5566
www.kchr.ky.gov

Louisiana
Commission on Human Rights
Baton Rouge, LA
225-342-6969
www.gov.state.la.us/HumanRights/
 humanrightshome.htm

Maine
Human Rights Commission
Augusta, ME
207-624-6050
www.maine.gov/mhrc

Maryland
Commission on Human Relations
Baltimore, MD
410-767-8600
800-637-6247 (in-state only)
www.mchr.state.md.us

Massachusetts
Commission Against Discrimination
Boston, MA
617-994-6000
www.mass.gov/mcad

State Enforcement Agencies (cont'd)

Michigan
Department of Civil Rights
Detroit, MI
313-456-3700
www.michigan.gov/mdcr

Minnesota
Department of Human Rights
St. Paul, MN
651-296-5663
800-657-3704
www.humanrights.state.mn.us

Mississippi
Department of Employment Security
Jackson, MS
601-321-6000
www.mdes.ms.gov

Missouri
Commission on Human Rights
Jefferson City, MO
573-751-3325
www.dolir.mo.gov/HR

Montana
Human Rights Bureau
Employment Relations Division
Department of Labor and Industry
Helena, MT
406-444-2884
800-542-0807
http://erd.dli.mt.us/HumanRight/
  HRhome.asp

Nebraska
Equal Opportunity Commission
Lincoln, NE
402-471-2024
800-642-6112
www.neoc.ne.gov

Nevada
Equal Rights Commission
Reno, NV
775-823-6690
www.detr.state.nv.us/nerc.htm

New Hampshire
Commission for Human Rights
Concord, NH
603-271-2767
www.nh.gov/hrc

New Jersey
Division on Civil Rights
Newark, NJ
973-648-2700
www.nj.gov/oag/dec/index.html

New Mexico
Human Rights Division
Santa Fe, NM
505-827-6838
800-566-9471
www.dws.state.nm.us/dws-humanrights.
  html

New York
Division of Human Rights
Bronx, NY
718-741-8400
www.dhr.state.ny.us

North Carolina
Employment Discrimination Bureau
Department of Labor
Raleigh, NC
919-807-2796
800-NC-LABOR
www.nclabor.com/edb/edb.htm

State Enforcement Agencies (cont'd)

North Dakota
Human Rights Division
Department of Labor
Bismarck, ND
701-328-2660
800-582-8032
www.nd.gov/labor/services/human-
rights

Ohio
Civil Rights Commission
Columbus, OH
614-466-5928
888-278-7101
www.crc.ohio.gov

Oklahoma
Human Rights Commission
Oklahoma City, OK
405-521-2360
888-456-2885
www.ok.gov/ohrc

Oregon
Civil Rights Division
Bureau of Labor and Industries
Portland, OR
971-673-0764
www.oregon.gov/BOLI/CRD

Pennsylvania
Human Relations Commission
Harrisburg, PA
717-787-4410
www.phrc.state.pa.us

Rhode Island
Commission for Human Rights
Providence, RI
401-222-2661
www.richr.state.ri.us/frames.html

South Carolina
Human Affairs Commission
Columbia, SC
803-737-7800
800-521-0725
www.state.sc.us/schac

South Dakota
Division of Human Rights
Pierre, SD
605-773-4493
www.state.sd.us/dol/boards/hr

Tennessee
Human Rights Commission
Knoxville, TN
865-594-6500
www.tennessee.gov/humanrights

Texas
Commission on Human Rights
Austin, TX
512-463-2642
www.twc.state.tx.us/customers/jsemp/
jsempsubcred.html

Utah
Anti-Discrimination and Labor Division
Labor Commission
Salt Lake City, UT
801-530-6801
800-222-1238
http://laborcommission.utah.gov/
AntidiscriminationandLabor/
employmentdiscrimination.html

State Enforcement Agencies (cont'd)

Vermont
Attorney General's Office
Civil Rights Division
Montpelier, VT
802-828-3171
www.atg.state.vt.us

Virginia
Council on Human Rights
Richmond, VA
804-225-2292
http://chr.vipnet.org

Washington
Human Rights Commission
Seattle, WA
206-464-6500
800-233-3247
www.hum.wa.gov

West Virginia
Human Rights Commission
Charleston, WV
304-558-2616
888-676-5546
www.wvf.state.wv.us/wvhrc

Wisconsin
Equal Rights Division
Madison, WI
608-266-6860
www.dwd.state.wi.us/er

Wyoming
Department of Employment
Cheyenne, WY
307-777-7261
http://wydoe.state.wy.us

Forms

Policy Prohibiting Discrimination and Harassment

Acknowledgment of Receipt of Policy

Policy Distribution Log

Intake Form—Employee Complaint

Litigation Calendar

Policy Prohibiting Discrimination and Harassment

1. Our Company's Commitment

The Company is committed to providing a workplace free of discrimination and harassment for all employees and employment applicants. The Company has a policy of zero tolerance of discrimination and harassment, which means that we will not tolerate workplace discrimination or harassment of our employees by any coworker, company officer, manager, or supervisor or any other person.

2. What Constitutes Discrimination or Harassment

Discrimination means treating someone differently, in a way that negatively affects the terms or conditions of employment, based on his or her gender, race, color, national origin, religion, age, disability, genetic information, or any other category protected by state or federal law.

Harassment is workplace conduct that creates an intimidating, offensive, or hostile working environment and is based on someone's gender, race, color, national origin, religion, age, disability, genetic information, or any other category protected by state or federal law. Sexual harassment includes all of these prohibited acts, as well as the conditioning of work benefits upon an employee's consent to, or rejection of, sexual conduct.

3. Prohibited Conduct

All discriminatory or harassing acts, behavior, and conduct are prohibited, including, but not limited to, comments, jokes, gestures, unwelcome physical contact, drawings, cartoons, videos, emails, name-calling, slurs, or use of derogatory terms. Prohibited sexual harassment includes all of these actions as well as other unwelcome sex-based conduct, such as unwanted sexual advances, requests for sexual favors, or sexually suggestive gestures, jokes, and propositions. These lists are intended as illustrations only. Conduct not listed may be considered discriminatory or harassing if it otherwise meets the definition above.

Company officers, managers, and supervisors are prohibited from basing any employment decision upon an employee's consent to, or rejection of, sexually harassing conduct as described above.

4. Prohibited Employment Decisions

Any employment decision that is based on an employee's gender, race, color, national origin, religion, age, disability, genetic information, or any other category protected by state or federal law is strictly prohibited. Any employment decision that is based on an employee's consent to, or rejection of, sexually harassing conduct is strictly prohibited. Employment decisions include, but are not limited to, acceptance or rejection of a job application, granting or denial of an interview, hiring, job or position assignment, shift or work hours assignment, project assignment, office or equipment assignment, promotion or demotion, award or denial of bonuses, granting or denial of raises, disciplinary actions, granting or denial of leave, granting or denial of job benefits, downsizing, reductions in force, layoff, offers of resignation, and termination.

5. General Standard of Conduct

In addition to following this policy as described above, all employees are expected to behave professionally and treat others with courtesy and respect at all times, whether in the workplace or while engaged in company business of any kind, including work-related trips, after-work events, and business or social functions relating to the Company.

6. Violations of This Policy

The Company will not tolerate violations of any provision of this policy. Anyone found to have violated this policy will be subject to immediate and appropriate disciplinary action, up to and including termination.

7. Complaints and Reporting

Any employee who experiences or observes any incident that he or she believes may constitute discrimination or harassment should immediately report the incident to his or her direct supervisor, the Human Resources Director, any department head, or any Company officer.

Managers or supervisors who observe, learn of, or receive complaints of possible discrimination or harassment must promptly inform the Director of Human Resources.

8. Investigation Procedure

The Company will immediately investigate all alleged complaints of discrimination or harassment. All complaints will be handled as confidentially as possible by a neutral investigator appointed by the Company. The investigator will take all necessary steps to ensure a complete investigation and may interview employees or others who may have knowledge relevant in the investigation and review physical evidence related to the complaint. When the investigation is complete, the Company will take corrective action, if appropriate.

The Company will not engage in or tolerate retaliation against any employee who makes a good-faith complaint or participates in an investigation, regardless of the outcome of the investigation. If any employee believes that he or she is being subjected to any kind of negative treatment because of making a complaint, assisting in a discrimination or harassment investigation, or filing an administrative charge or lawsuit alleging discrimination or harassment, the employee should report the conduct immediately to his or her immediate supervisor, or the human resources director, any department head, or any Company officer.

Acknowledgment of Receipt of Policy

I, _____, acknowledge that on

_____, 20_____, I received and read a copy of the

attached company policy against discrimination and harassment.

Date: _____

Employee Signature: _____

Policy Distribution Log

Name of Person Completing Log: _____

Employee Name	Date Policy Provided to Employee	Acknowledgement Received? (Yes/No)	Date Acknowledgment Received

Intake Form—Employee Complaint

To: _____

From: _____

Date: _____

Name of reporting employee: _____

Telephone number (work): _____

Telephone number (home): _____

Reporting employee's supervisor: _____

Employee: ___ has ___ has not reported incident(s) to his/her supervisor.

Summary of reporting employee's description of reported incident(s), with dates:

_____

_____

_____

_____

_____

Names of others who participated in the incident(s):

_____

_____

_____

Witnesses to reported incident(s):

_____

_____

_____

Names of anyone employee has told about the incident(s):

_____

_____

_____

Location of reported incident(s):

_____

_____

_____

Documents relating to the incident(s), if any:

_____

_____

_____

Reporting employee described the incident as:

___ Discrimination based on:

      ___ gender   ___ race   ___ age   ___ religion   ___ disability

      ___ national origin   ___ other (specify): _____

___ Harassment based on:

      ___ gender   ___ race   ___ age   ___ religion   ___ disability

      ___ national origin   ___ other (specify): _____

___ Neither discrimination nor harassment

Date: _____

Intake person signature: _____

Litigation Calendar

Case Name: _____

Event	Event Date or Deadline	Tickler Date	Reserve Conference Room? (Yes/No)	Participants	Reminder Sent? (Yes/No)

Index

A

Accommodate, failure to, 14, 232
Accommodation
  of disabilities, reasonable, 31–32, 232
  of religious observance, 27–29
Accused employee
  communicating findings of
    investigation to, 146–147, 151
  confidentiality and protection of
    privacy of, 148
  denials by, 140
  discipline report placed in personnel
    file of, 170
  interviewing, special considerations for,
    136–140
  justifications/rationalizations by, 140
  removal from premises in sexual assault
    allegations, 135
  repeat offenders, 180–181
  transfer of, 135
  See also Supervisors, harassment by
Acknowledgment forms, 89–90, 168
Active-listening strategies, 121
ADA (Americans with Disabilities Act),
  11, 198
ADEA. *See* Age Discrimination in
  Employment Act (ADEA)
Admission, requests for, 241
Adverse action, requirement to show, 15
Affirmative defense
  defined, 56
  employee failure to report, 56–58, 76
  requirements for, 56–57
  written policies as necessary to, 75

Age-based discrimination
  benefits, 25–26
  defined, 25
  discovery in lawsuits on, 243–244
  government agency findings and, 212
  hiring advertisements and, 34
  hiring applications and, 34
  investigation of, 139
  law governing, 11, 25–26, 198
  waiver and release of employment
    claims, 26
Age Discrimination in Employment Act
  (ADEA)
  and benefits protection, 25–26
  EEOC as enforcement agency for, 198
  overview, 11
  and waiver and release of employment
    claims, 26
Agency complaints
  actions available to agency, 208–209
  attorney for, assistance to, 217–218,
    219, 220
  attorney recommended for, 193,
    196–197, 202, 210, 214, 215–216,
    222
  attorney-requested documents as
    privileged, 218
  clarification requested for, 205
  company response alerting agency to
    weaknesses in, 206
  company written response to, 202–208
  complaint by employee, 200–202
  complaint process, overview, 199–200
  documentation and, 218

Fact sheet to track company response to, 206–207
finding of, 211–213
lawsuit by agency, 209, 211
organization of information in preparation for, 217–218
overview, 196
professionalism in face of, 219, 221, 224
as required before employee files lawsuit, 197–198
right to sue letter, 200, 208, 211
role of agencies, 197–198
standard forms and, 208
statement of position and, 207–208
time for, 203, 209
time, request for additional, 205
See also Investigations, of agency complaints; Mediation
Alabama, 286, 298
Alaska, 186, 298
Americans with Disabilities Act (ADA), 11, 198
Ancestry. *See* National origin discrimination
Annual reminders of the policy, 90
Answer, 237–239
Antifraternization policies, 65
Apologies, 232, 233
Arbitration, 251–253
Arizona, 286, 298
Arkansas, 286, 298
Attorney–client privilege
confidentiality required for, 220
defined, 220
and depositions, 265
and documents requested by attorney creating, 218, 255–256

Attorneys
agency complaints, recommended for, 193, 196–197, 202, 210, 214, 215–216, 222
assistance to, in agency complaints, 217–218, 219, 220
for discipline of reporting employee (appearance of retaliation), 189
as investigators, 86–87, 193–194
for mediation, 214, 215–216, 217
for multistate employers, 46
for personal liability lawsuits, 269–272, 274
present at interview of witnesses, 132
privacy of communications. *See* Attorney–client privilege
for repeat patterns, 181
requests for updates from, 257
separate, for investigating and litigating, 86–87, 193
See also Lawsuits
Authority
job titles to match, 59, 61
settlement, 216–217, 223

B

Bench trials, 249
Benefits
age-based discrimination and, 25–26
as area of discrimination, 37
Bias, of customers, 40
Blonde jokes, 91
Breach of contract lawsuits, 201
Burden of proof, 248

C

Calendar, litigation, 246, 256–257

California
enforcement agency, 298
laws, 286
size of employer, 45
training requirements in, 97, 101, 106–108

CD-ROM
creating documents from files, 280–282
editing a document, 281
files list, 284
installing, 279
listening to audio files, 282–283
opening a file, 280–281
overview, 278
printing a document, 282
README file, 278
saving a document, 282

Chronology (timeline) in documentation, 164–166, 218, 219, 254–256

Circumstantial evidence, defined, 15

Citizenship status discrimination
defined, 23
law governing, 12

Civil Rights Act of 1866 (Section 1981), 11–12

Civil Rights Act of 1964, Title VII, 10–11, 27, 45

Closure letters, 151

Colorado, 287, 298

Communication of policies to employees
acknowledgment forms, 89–90, 168
distribution log of policy, 168
lead by example, 91
necessity of, 89

reinforcement of policy, 90, 98
See also Policies prohibiting discrimination and harassment

Company-wide actions, 232–233

Compensatory damages, 45

Complaint procedures
affirmative defense where employee doesn't follow, 56–58, 76
confidentiality concerns and, 84–85, 105–106
fair hearing, importance of, 121
multiple complaints indicating problem with, 180
necessity of, 82
overview, 79
participation of employee in, 106
retaliation, policy against, 80
training of employees in, 105–106
training of supervisors in, 104
when to report, 106
whom to report violations to, 83–84, 105
See also Complaints, receiving; Investigation procedures; Policies prohibiting harassment and discrimination

Complaints in lawsuits. *See* Lawsuits, process of

Complaints, receiving
active-listening strategies, 121
awareness of the problem, 118
checklist of what to say to reporting employee, 122
confidentiality issues, 121
emotions, handling of, 120–122
hypersensitive employees and, 120
information gathering, 121–123

initial response as critical, 118
intake form for, 164
judgment, refraining from, 120
multiple complaints, 179–182
neutrality in, 121
patience in, 121
pattern among incidents, 180–182, 190
policy assured to be followed, 122
resolution desired by reporting
  employee, 123
respectful treatment of reporting
  employee, 119–121
retaliation assured to be prohibited, 122
summary of the complaint, 158–159
See also Complaint procedures
Computers, tracking or blocking uses of,
  167, 180
Confidentiality issues
  attorney–client privilege dependent on,
    220
  and communication of findings to
    reporting employee, 148
  and communication of results to other
    employees, 183–184
  complaint procedures and, 84–85
  and complaints, receiving, 121
  discipline report and, 170
  and gossip, dealing with, 176–177, 178
  management of documents and, 171
  mediation and, 214
  overview, 80
Conflicts of interest, personal lawsuits
  and, 269–271, 272, 274
Connecticut
  enforcement agency, 298
  laws, 287
  training requirements in, 97, 101

Consensual relationships
  endings of, 66–67
  personnel policies and, 65–66
  with subordinates, 68–69
  and witnessing employees, 66
Consent issues
  humor and, 52
  touching and, 50
Constructive discharge, 40, 50, 231
Contracts, race discrimination and, law
  governing, 11–12
Coworkers
  harassment by, overview, 63
  presence at interview, 132
Credit checks, race discrimination and, 23
Customer bias, 40

D
Damages
  cap on federal, 236
  compensatory, 45
  as goal in lawsuits, 231
  for personal liability lawsuits, payment
    of, 274–275
  punitive, 45, 77
  state laws not limiting, 45
  Title VII limits on, 45
  See also Lawsuits; Settlement
Decisions made during employment. *See*
  Employment, decisions made during
Defamation claims, 146–147, 177, 201,
  236, 269
Defenses
  affirmative. *See* Affirmative defense
  Kolstad, punitive damages and, 77
  See also Liability
Delaware, 287, 298

Depositions
    answer only what is asked, 259–261
    attendance at, in personal liability suits, 273
    breaks, requesting, 265
    changes to statements, 266
    defined, 241
    educational preparation for, 263
    objections to testimony, 264–265
    privileged communications and, 265
    testimony in, 263–266
    transcripts of, 265–266, 268, 273
    trials and use of, 268
    videotaped, 268
    See also Lawsuits, process of
Diabetes, 32
Directors. *See* Management and directors
Disability discrimination
    complaint to government agencies on, 206
    defined, 30
    definition of disability, 30–31
    investigation of, 137
    law governing, 11, 198
    reasonable accommodation and, 31–32, 232
    undue hardship and, 32
Discipline
    communicating decision for, to accused, 146–147
    communicating decision for, to reporting employee, 149
    discrimination claims for unfair, 38–39
    of employee involved in a complaint, retaliation and, 188–189
    follow up on, 150
    guidelines for, 38–39

for inappropriate vs. illegal behavior, 13–14
    investigation procedures outlining range of possible, 87
    policy advising repercussions of prohibited behavior, 79
    written report on decision for, 170
Discovery
    assisting the attorney during, 243–245
    defined, 239–240
    desire to hide evidence, 243–244
    disagreements during, 243
    methods of information exchange in, 240–242
    redaction (blocking out) of documents, 242
    types of records, 240
    See also Depositions
Discrimination
    circumstantial evidence, 15
    defined, 3, 10, 13
    elements required to show, 15–16
    forms of, 14, 232
    gossip becoming, 178
    harassment as form of, 44
    inappropriate but not illegal behaviors, 13–14, 16
    "smoking gun" cases, 14
    when occurring. *See* Employment, decisions made during; End of employment; Hiring
    See also Complaints; Discipline; Documentation; Investigations; Laws; Lawsuits; Policies prohibiting discrimination and harassment; Training; *specific types of discrimination*

Dismiss, motion to, 237–238, 273
Disparate impact, 14
Disparate treatment, 14
District of Columbia, 297, 298
Diversity
  challenges of, 2
  training in, 109–112
Diversity jurisdiction, 62
Documentation
  and agency complaints, 218
  attorney copies of, 220
  attorney-requested, as privileged, 218
  backup copies of, 172
  benefits and objectives of, 154–155
  changes to statements of witnesses,
    memos describing, 160–161
  complaint, summary of, 158–159
  discipline report, 170–171
  final report, 168–170
  index of documents, 254–256
  information to include in, 155–157
  intake form for reporting employee,
    164
  interview notes, 162–164
  lawsuit potential and retention of,
    172–173
  lawsuit potential guiding content of,
    155, 156, 166, 206–207
  legal protection through, 154
  management of documents, 171–172
  organization of, 171–172
  of physical evidence, 166–167, 171–172
  policy distribution log, 168
  retention and storage of, 172–173
  timeline of reported incident(s),
    164–166, 218, 219, 254–256
  types of documents to be used, 155,
    158

  where to keep documents, 172
  witness statements, 159–162
Document index, 254–256
Documents, discovery and
  demands for document production, 241
  redaction (blocking out information),
    242
  types of documents, 240
Dress codes, 18–19
  medical issues and, 19
  uniform requirements, and religious
    observances, 27

E

Education requirements, race
  discrimination and, 22
EEOC. *See* Equal Employment
  Opportunity Commission (EEOC)
Elements required to show discrimination
  adverse action suffered, 15
  improper motive of employer, 15–16
  and pretexts for discrimination, 16
  protected class, member of, 15
  qualification for job, 15
Ellerth/Faragher standard. *See* Affirmative
  defense
Email
  discovery and, 240, 243–244
  source of, for documentation, 156
Emotional distress, lawsuit for infliction
  of, 201
Emotions
  lawsuit remedies sought and, 232
  personal liability suits and, 273
  professionalism and control of, 219,
    221, 224
  testimony and, 261
  See also Morale

Employee liability. *See* Personal liability of supervisors

Employment claims, waiver and release of, 26

Employment, decisions made during
benefits and pay, 37
changes during employee's tenure, 40
customer bias, 40
job assignments, 37
performance evaluations, 37–38
policy statement of, 79
promotions, 38
training and mentoring, 37
See also Discipline; End of employment; Hiring

End of employment
exit interviews and, 41
references, providing, 41
termination, layoff, reorganization, or reduction in force, 40, 230–231
See also Resignation; Wrongful termination claims

English-only rules, 23–24

EPA (Equal Pay Act), 11, 198

Epilepsy, 30

Equal Employment Opportunity Commission (EEOC)
complaints to. *See* Agency complaints
duplicate complaints sent to, 199
overview, 198–199
retention of documents, requirements for, 172–173

Equal Pay Act (EPA), 11, 198

Ethnicity, discrimination based on, the law and, 11–12

Evidence
burden of proof, 248
circumstantial, 15
desire to obscure, 243–244, 262
documentation of physical evidence, 166–167, 171–172
lawsuits and preparation of, 246
mediation and, 214
motion to exclude, 249
See also Discovery

Exclude evidence, motion to, 249

Executives. *See* Management and directors

Exit interviews, 41

F

Facial jewelry, 29

Fact sheet on allegations, 206–207, 219

Failure to accomodate, 14, 232

Fair Credit Reporting Act, 140

Fair Employment Practices Agencies (FEPAs, state agencies)
complaints to. *See* Agency complaints
duplicate complaints sent to, 199
listing of state enforcement agencies, 298–302
overview, 199

Federal laws
age, 11, 25–26, 198
cap on damages, 236
contracts, race and, 11–12
difference from state, summary of, 44–46
disabilities, 11, 198
gender, 10–11, 198
genetics, 11, 33, 198
personal liability of supervisors and, 62
table summarizing, 12
Title VII of the Civil Rights Act of 1964, 10–11, 27, 45
See also Agency complaints

Florida, 287, 298
Food, religious accommodation for, 28
Friends, present at interview, 132

G
Gender discrimination. *See* Sex-based discrimination
Gender identity discrimination
    defined, 21
    sex-changes, 22
    sex stereotyping and, 21
    state laws forbidding, 45
Genetic discrimination
    defined, 33
    law governing, 11, 33, 198
Genetic Information Nondiscrimination Act (GINA), 11, 33, 198
Georgia, 288, 299
GINA (Genetic Information Nondiscrimination Act), 11, 33, 198
Gossip and rumors, 176–179
Government agencies. *See* Agency complaints
Group-wide actions, 232–233

H
Handbook. *See* Personnel policies
Harassment
    by coworkers, overview, 63
    defined, 3, 44, 48
    forms of. *See* Hostile work environment; Tangible employment action
    by nonemployees, 63, 124
    off-work events and locations, 69–70, 185–186
    by supervisors. *See* Supervisors, harassment by

witnessing employees and, 64, 66
    See also Complaints; Consensual relationships; Discipline; Documentation; Investigations; Lawsuits; Policies prohibiting discrimination and harassment; Training; *specific types of harassment*
Hawaii, 288, 299
Hiring
    advertisements, 33–34
    applications, 34
    dos and don'ts of, 42
    interviewing, 35–36
    overview, 33
    screening, 35
    testing, 35
    See also End of employment
Hostile work environment harassment
    avoiding liability. *See* Affirmative defense
    coworker harassment, 63
    defined, 49, 51
    nonemployee harassment, 63, 124
    protected status and, 52–54
    severe and pervasive, requirement for, 54–56
    by supervisors, 60
    unwelcome conduct, 51
    and witnessing employees, 64
Humor
    and harassment, 52, 91
    and respect for reporting employee, 119

I
Idaho, 288, 299
Illegal discrimination. *See* Discrimination
Illinois, 288, 299

Immigration Reform and Control Act, 12

Index of documents, 254–256

Indiana, 288, 299

Insurance for personal liability, 274

Interrogatories, 240

Interview questions, discrimination in hiring, 35–36

Interviews in investigation
  of accused employee, 136–140
  changes to story after interviews, 160–161
  facts, gathering of, 126–131
  information, providing, 131
  notes of, 162–164
  plan for investigation, 125–126
  policy on, 87
  subsequent interviews to clarify inconsistencies, 129
  third parties present for, 132
  witness statements, 159–162

Investigation procedures
  attorney investigators, 86–87, 193–194
  corrective action policy, 87
  interview policy, 87
  necessity of, 82
  neutral investigators, 86–87, 121
  overview, 79, 86
  retaliation suspicions and, 88
  sample policy, 89
  separation of persons. *See* Separation of the reporting and accused employees
  solution, crafting of, 145
  See also Complaint procedures; Investigations, conducting; Policies prohibiting harassment and discrimination

Investigations, conducting
  attorneys, hiring to conduct, 86–87, 193–194
  botched, 194
  closure letters to communicate findings, 151
  communication of findings to accused, 146–147, 151
  communication of findings to reporting employee, 148–151
  conclusions, arriving at, 140, 141–145, 154
  conclusions, management pressing for premature, 192
  discipline report, 170–171
  disputed facts, chart to organize, 142
  disputed facts, credibility of, 143–144
  failure to conduct, and desire to lie, 262
  follow up on corrective action, 150
  goal of, 141
  in good faith, protecting from defamation or wrongful termination claims, 146–147
  "he said, she said" cases, 142, 144
  inconclusive results, communication of, 150
  laws violated, reporting to company management, 141
  of multiple complaints, 179–182
  outside investigators, 140, 191, 192
  overview, 124–125
  planning, 125–126
  policy assured to be followed, 131, 151
  of retaliation, 190
  rumors and gossip, dealing with, 176–179

solution, crafting of, 145
timeliness of, 124–125, 145
written final report, 168–170
See also Confidentiality issues;
    Documentation; Interviews
    in investigation; Investigation
    procedures; Investigations, of agency
    complaints; Retaliation
Investigations, of agency complaints
    cooperating with agency investigators,
        221–222
    copy of agencies files, request for, 213
    dismissal of complaint following, 209
    employee requests closing of, 208
    finding of, 211–213
    interviews of witnesses, company
        preparation for, 209–211, 220, 225
    invalid complaint not investigated, 208
    mediation and, 213, 214, 217
    overview, 208–209
    protecting company interests during,
        210–211
    "right to sue" letter issued following,
        200, 208, 211
    See also Agency complaints
Iowa, 289, 299

J
Jerks, behavior of as not illegal, 13–14, 16
Jury vs. judge (bench) trials, 249

K
Kansas, 289, 299
Kentucky, 289, 299
Kolstad defense, 77

L
Language, English-only rules, 23–24
Laws
    employees protected by federal, state,
        and local, 46
    enforcement of. *See* Agency complaints;
        Equal Employment Opportunity
        Commission; Fair Employment
        Practices Agencies
    retaliation prohibited by, 54, 184–185
    violation of, investigator reporting to
        company management, 141
    See also Federal laws; State laws
Lawsuits
    agencies filing, 209, 211
    agency file, request copy of, 213
    agency findings not binding on, 211,
        212–213
    alternatives to. *See* Arbitration;
        Mediation; Settlement
    anxiety and, 229, 258, 267
    attorney, requests for updates from, 257
    for breach of contract, 201
    claims for both federal and state
        violations, 46, 62
    complaint to agencies required prior to,
        197, 201, 234–235
    and confidentiality violated because of
        physical threat, 183
    for defamation, 146–147, 177, 201,
        236, 269
    dividing up a case, 255
    documentation as protection from, 154
    documentation content guided by
        potential of, 155, 156, 166, 206–207
    goals and objectives of plaintiff,
        229–233

jurisdiction for, 62

mediation limiting right to, 214

other types not requiring agency
involvement, 201

pattern of complaints, response to as
legal protection from, 181–182

remedies desired, 231–233

retention of documents in case of,
172–173

"right to sue" letter from agencies, 200,
208, 211

warning of impending, 234–235

for wrongful termination, 146–147, 201

See also Damages; Lawsuits, process
of; Liability; Personal liability of
supervisors; Settlement

Lawsuits, process of

amended complaints, 238

burden of proof, 248

complaint filed by plaintiff, 235–237

complaint to agencies required prior to,
197, 201, 234–235

evidence, nature of, 248–249

jury vs. judge (bench) trials, 249

liaison role of assisting employee,
253–257, 258–268

litigation calendar and tickler system,
246, 256–257

motion for summary judgment,
246–247, 273

motion to dismiss, 237–238, 273

motion to exclude evidence, 249

motion to strike, 238

multiple claims in complaint, 236–237

objections to testimony, 264–265,
267–268

overview, 234–235

pretrial preparation, 245–247

response by company to complaint,
237–239

trials, 248–250

witness testimony in depositions,
263–266

witness testimony in trials, 266–268

witness tips, 258–262

See also Depositions; Discovery

Layoffs, 40, 207, 230–231

Leading by example

intervention through, 104

reinforcement of policy through, 91

Liability

defense to. *See* Affirmative defense

of individual employees. *See* Personal
liability of supervisors

mediation and nonadmission of, 215

strict, 49, 51

supervisors and greater employer risk
of, 58–59, 102, 145, 194

See also Lawsuits; Settlement

Listening

active, in investigations, 121

to questions while testifying, 259

Louisiana, 289, 299

Lying under oath, 261–262

M

Maine

enforcement agency, 299

laws, 290

training requirements in, 97

Management and directors

and agency complaints, preparation for,
219, 223

complaints against executives, 191, 192

informing of, 191–192
and mediation, preparation for, 223
pressing for a conclusion prematurely, 192
reporting repeat patterns to, 181
tracking patterns, 190
See also Supervisors
Marital status discrimination, state laws forbidding, 45
Maryland, 290, 299
Massachusetts, 290, 299
Mediation
    agencies facilitating, 208, 211, 213, 214
    attorney for, 214, 215–216, 217
    confidentiality and, 214
    defined, 214
    finding a mediator, 214
    of a lawsuit, compared to agency complaint, 251
    lawsuits limited following, 214
    and liability, nonadmission of, 215
    location of, 216
    preparation for, 223–224
    process of, 216–217
    settlement authority and, 217–218, 223
    written statement of facts, 214
Michigan, 290, 300
Minnesota, 291, 300
Mississippi, 291, 300
Missouri, 291, 300
Montana, 291, 300
Morale
    and controlling inappropriate but not illegal behavior, 16
    harassment and discrimination, effects on, 4
    inconsistent enforcement of rules and, 39

and need for addressing situation publicly, 183
and need to alert company officers or directors, 190
professionalism sustaining, 221
See also Emotions
Motion for summary judgment, 246–247, 273
Motion to dismiss, 237–238, 273
Motion to exclude evidence, 249
Motion to strike, 238
Multiple complaints, 179–182
Multistate employers
    attorney advice recommended for, 46
    policy listing protected classes for, 78
    sexual orientation discrimination and, 13, 47

N

National origin discrimination
    defined, 23
    English-only rules and, 23–24
    law governing, 12
    lawsuits vs. settlement and, 230
    sample final report involving, 169–170
Nebraska, 291, 300
Nevada, 292, 300
New Hampshire, 292, 300
New Jersey, 292, 300
New Mexico, 292, 300
New York, 293, 300
Nonadmission statement, 215
Nonemployees
    harassment by, 63, 124
    protection of, state laws for, 46
North Carolina, 293, 300
North Dakota, 293, 301

O

Off-work events and locations
    harassment or discrimination incidents
        and, 69–70
    retaliation and, 185–186
    See also Consensual relationships
Ohio, 293, 301
Oklahoma, 293, 301
Older Workers Benefit Protection Act
    (OWBPA), 25–26
Online resources
    California trainer qualifications,
        107–108
    storage of electronic documents, 172
    trainings, 107
Oregon, 294, 301
Out-of-pocket losses, awarding of, 45
OWBPA (Older Workers Benefit
    Protection Act), 25–26

P

Paid leave, of employee accused of sexual
    assault, 135
Peer pressure, 52
Pennsylvania, 294, 301
Performance evaluations
    discrimination claims based on unfair,
        37–38
    poor, retaliatory accusations and,
        143–144
    reinforcing the policy during, 90
Perjury, 261–262
Personal liability of supervisors
    attorney for, 269–272, 274
    attorney's fees for, 269, 271–272
    conflicts of interest with company
        attorney, 269–271, 272, 274

damages, payment of, 274–275
    and dating subordinates, policies
        against, 68
    federal laws and, 62
    insurance for, 274
    limiting exposure, 273–275
    overview, 269
    reasons for lawsuits, 62, 269, 270
    role as defendant in, 272–273
    settlement of, 272, 274
    state laws for, 46, 62
    training to prevent, 102
Personnel files, discovery and, 240
Personnel policies
    and consensual relationships, 65–66
    monitoring of computers revealed in,
        167
    supervisors dating subordinates, 68
Pervasive and severe, requirement for,
    54–56
Photographs of evidence, 172
Physical assaults or threats
    attorney as investigator in cases of, 193
    and public discussion of investigation,
        183
    and separation of reporting and
        accused employees, 135, 193
Physical evidence, documentation of,
    166–167, 171–172
Physical examination, 241
Piercings, display of, 29
Policies, personnel. *See* Personnel policies
Policies prohibiting discrimination and
    harassment
    as affirmative defense, 56–58, 75–76
    assurance policy is followed, 122
    benefits of, 74–77

commitment to prevention, 77

confidentiality, 80, 84–85

distribution log of, 168

elements of, 77–80

employment decisions, 79

gossip and need to reiterate, 177–178

necessity of, 81

prohibited conduct statement, 78

protected classes statement, 78

punitive damages, as defense against, 77

repercussions for prohibited behaviors, 79

retaliation investigations and distribution of, 188

retaliation prohibited, 80

review of, 92

standard of behavior, 79

See also Communication of policies to employees; Complaint procedures; Investigation procedures

Pornographic material on computers, 167, 180

Position statement, 207

Pregnancy discrimination

and agencies, complaints to, 224

investigation of, 130

overview, 19–20

Pretexts for discrimination, defined, 16

Prevention

policy committing to, 77

supervisors intervening, 91, 103–104, 123

See also Training

Privacy of employees

of accused employee, 148

computer monitoring and, 167

See also Confidentiality issues

Privileged communications. *See* Attorney–client privilege

Promotions

lawsuits and, 232

overview, 38

Protected classes

federal, 12

hostile work environment and, 52–54

illegal discrimination as based on, 10

person in same class as harasser, 53–54

policy statement of, 78

requirement to be member of, 15

states, 45, 286–297

Psychological examination, 241

Punitive damages

good-faith effort as defense against (Kolstad defense), 77

limits on, 45

Q

Quid pro quo harassment, 49

R

Race discrimination

affirmative defense and, 57

agencies, complaints to, 201, 222

credit checks and, 23

defined, 22

discovery in lawsuits for, 242

dress codes and medical issues, 19

educational requirements and, 22

interview techniques, 128

investigation of, 128, 143, 144

law governing, 10–12, 45

receiving complaints of, 119

rumors in aftermath of complaint, 179

and separation of reporting and
accused employees, 133
specificity of disputed facts and, 143
Reasonable accommodation, of
disabilities, 14, 31–32, 232
Recovery. *See* Damages
Redaction, 242
References, providing, 41
Reinstatement, 232
Relationships. *See* Workplace relationships
Religious discrimination
accommodation of observances, 27–29
beliefs, defined, 26
defined, 26
observances, defined, 27
religious entities and, 29
training in avoidance of, 109
Reorganizations, 40, 207, 230–231
Repeat offenders, 180–181
Reporting employee
communication of findings to, 148–151
inconclusive results, communicating
to, 150
See also Complaints, receiving;
Confidentiality; Lawsuits;
Retaliation; Witnesses
Reporting harassment. *See* Complaint
procedures; Complaints, receiving
Requests for admission, 241
Resignation
exit interviews and, 41
forced, as constructive discharge, 40,
50, 231
See also End of employment
Retaliation
agency complaints, and prevention of,
224–225

appearance of, and separation of
reporting/accused employees,
135–136
changes of witness statements, and fear
of, 160–161
complaint procedures prohibiting, 85,
106
defined, 185, 187
interviews and assurances against, 131
investigation/responding to, 190
laws barring, 54, 184–185
and lawsuit witnesses, 245
legal definition of, 187
management of documents and, 171
in non-work environments, 185–186
policy prohibiting, 80
prevention of, 188–189
receiving complaints and assurances
against, 122
reporting of, 106
restoration of employee to former
position, 190
supervisors seeming to condone, 186
suspicions of, investigation and, 88
Rhode Island, 294, 301
Rumors and gossip, 176–179

S

Section 1981 (of the Civil Rights Act of
1866), 11–12
Separation of the reporting and accused
employees
level of distance of, 133–134, 149
overview, 133–135
physical assault or threats and, 135, 193
and retaliation, appearance of, 135–136
supervisors accused, 133, 134

Settlement
  apologies and, 233
  conference for, 250
  defined, 250
  motion for summary judgment and
    potential for, 247
  of personal liability lawsuits, 272, 274
  reasons for, 230–231
  times for, 246, 250–251
  types of agreements, 250
  See also Lawsuits
Settlement authority, 216–217, 223
Severe and pervasive, requirement for,
  54–56
Sex-based discrimination
  circumstantial evidence and, 15
  defined, 17
  documentation requirements, 157, 158
  dress codes, 18–19
  investigation of, 138
  law governing, 11, 198
  personality issue vs., 18
  by person in same protected status,
    53–54
  pregnancy, 19–20, 130, 224
  strength requirements and, 14
  See also Gender-identity discrimination;
    Sexual harassment; Sexual orientation
    discrimination; Sexual stereotyping;
    Workplace relationships
Sex changes, 22
Sexual assault, and paid leave/removal of
  accused, 135
Sexual harassment
  in academia, 60
  answer to complaint in lawsuit, 239
  depositions in lawsuits for, 260

documentation and, 156
gossip about complaint becoming, 178
multiple claims in lawsuit for, 236–237
plausibility of disputed facts and, 143
retaliation for complaints of, 187
training mandated by states, 101,
  106–107
witnessing employees and, 64
Sexual orientation discrimination
  defined, 21
  disability discrimination and, 30
  multistate employers and, 13, 47
  separation of reporting and accused
    employees and, 134
  sex stereotyping and, 21
  state laws forbidding, 45
Sexual stereotyping
  defined, 17
  gender identity and, 21
  sexual orientation and, 21
Size of employer
  federal requirements, 12
  state requirements, 45, 286–297
  state training requirements, 97
"Smoking gun" cases, 14
South Carolina, 294, 301
South Dakota, 294, 301
Spouses, present at interview, 132
Standards of behavior
  consensual relationships, 65–66
  dating subordinates, 68
  policy stating, 79
  training establishing, 98, 105
State laws
  difference from federal, summary of,
    44–46
  enforcement agencies, 298–302

indemnification of employees, 271–272

personal liability of supervisors and, 46, 62

table summarizing, 286–297

for training, 45, 97, 101, 106–108

See also Agency complaints

Strength requirements, 14

Strict liability, 49, 51

Strike, motion to, 238

Subpoenas, 242

Summary judgment, motion for, 246–247, 273

Supervisors

complaints by, 104

failing to report incidents, 181–182

permitting retaliation to occur, 196

prevention and intervention by, 91, 103–104, 123

retaliation seemingly condoned by, 186

training to deal with complaints, 101–102, 104

See also Management and directors; Supervisors, harassment by

Supervisors, harassment by

attorney as investigator in, 194

authority of, and liability, 59–61

authority of, deference to not warranted, 140

dating subordinates and, 68–69

definition and interpretation of "supervisor," 45–46, 58–59

empty threats, 60–61

federal law holding employer responsible, 45–46

liability risk to employer, 58–59, 102, 145, 194

off-work events and locations and, 69–70

removal of managerial authority generally, 145

removal of managerial decisions affecting reporting employee, 134, 145

separation from reporting employee, 133, 134

training to prevent. *See* Training

See also Personal liability of supervisors

T

Tangible employment action

constructive discharge, 40, 50, 231

defined, 48, 49–50

by supervisors, 60

Tennessee, 295, 301

Termination, layoff, reorganization, or reduction in force, 40, 207, 230–231

Texas, 295, 301

Tickler system and litigation calendar, 246, 256–257

Timeline, in documentation, 164–166, 218, 219, 254–256

Title VII (of the Civil Rights Act of 1964), 10–11, 27, 45

Touching as harassment, consent issues, 50

Training

benefits of, 96–99

content and conducting of, 106–107

diversity training, 109–112

follow up on requirements for, 150

goals of, 112

joint sessions, 99, 100–101

out-of-court settlement requiring, 103

policy reinforced during, 90, 98

prevention and intervention by supervisors, 103–104

separate sessions for accused supervisor, 103

separate sessions for employees, 99, 101, 105–106

separate sessions for supervisors, 99, 101–104

state laws requiring, 45, 97, 101, 106–108

states not requiring, liability avoidance in, 45, 98–99

who conducts, 107–109

written form, need for, 100

Transsexual change, 22

Truth

credibility of disputed versions, 143–144

and good-faith investigations, 125, 141–142

need for, 243–244, 261, 262

U

Undue hardship

disabilities and, 32

religious accommodation and, 27–29

Union members, 132

Utah, 295, 301

V

Vegans/vegetarians, 28

Vermont, 295, 302

Virginia, 295, 302

W

Washington, DC, 297, 298

Washington state, 296, 302

Webinar trainings, 107

West Virginia, 296, 302

Wisconsin, 296, 302

Witnesses

attorney interviews with, in lawsuits, 244–245

preparation by company, for agency interviews, 209–211, 220, 225

statements of, preparation of, 159–162

tips for, in lawsuits, 258–262

trial testimony of, 266–268

See also Depositions; Retaliation

Witnessing employees, reporting by

consensual relationships and, 66

harassment, 64

Workplace relationships

consensual, 65–69

favoring a paramour, 19, 68–69

mentoring lunches, 38

personnel policies on, 65–66, 68

touching, 50

See also Supervisors, harrassment by

Wrongful termination claims

agency complaints and, 201

good-faith belief of employer defeating, 146–147

Wyoming, 296, 302

Z

Zero tolerance policy, 77

NOLO *Keep Up to Date*

Go to **Nolo.com/newsletter** to sign up for free newsletters and discounts on Nolo products.

- **Nolo Briefs.** Our monthly email newsletter with great deals and free information.

- **Nolo's Special Offer.** A monthly newsletter with the biggest Nolo discounts around.

- **BizBriefs.** Tips and discounts on Nolo products for business owners and managers.

- **Landlord's Quarterly.** Deals and free tips just for landlords and property managers, too.

And don't forget to check **Nolo.com/updates** to find free legal updates to this book.

Let Us Hear From You

Comments on this book? We want to hear 'em. Email us at feedback@nolo.com.

HDAB1

NOLO and USA TODAY

Cutting-Edge Content, Unparalleled Expertise

The Busy Family's Guide to Money

by Sandra Block, Kathy Chu & John Waggoner • $19.99

The Busy Family's Guide to Money will help you make the most of your income, handle major one-time expenses, figure children into the budget—and much more.

The Work From Home Handbook

Flex Your Time, Improve Your Life

by Diana Fitzpatrick & Stephen Fishman • $19.99

If you're one of those people who need to (or simply want to) work from home, let this book help you come up with a plan that both you and your boss can embrace!

Retire Happy

What You Can Do NOW to Guarantee a Great Retirement

by Richard Stim & Ralph Warner • $19.99

You don't need a million dollars to retire well, but you do need friends, hobbies and an active lifestyle. This book shows how to make retirement the best time of your life.

The Essential Guide for First-Time Homeowners

Maximize Your Investment & Enjoy Your New Home

by Ilona Bray & Alayna Schroeder • $19.99

This reassuring resource is filled with crucial financial advice, real solutions and easy-to-implement ideas that can save you thousands of dollars.

Easy Ways to Lower Your Taxes

Simple Strategies Every Taxpayer Should Know

by Sandra Block & Stephen Fishman • $19.99

Provides useful insights and tactics to help lower your taxes. Learn how to boost tax-free income, get a lower tax rate, defer paying taxes, make the most of deductions—and more!

First-Time Landlord

Your Guide to Renting Out a Single-Family Home

by Attorney Janet Portman, Marcia Stewart & Michael Molinski • $19.99

From choosing tenants to handling repairs to avoiding legal trouble, this book provides the information new landlords need to make a profit and follow the law.

Stopping Identity Theft

10 Easy Steps to Security

by Scott Mitic, CEO, TrustedID, Inc. • $19.99

Don't let an emptied bank account be your first warning sign. This book offers ten strategies to help prevent the theft of personal information.

ORDER ANYTIME AT WWW.NOLO.COM OR CALL 800-728-3555

Prices subject to change.

NOLO® *Online Legal Forms*

Nolo offers a large library of legal solutions and forms, created by Nolo's in-house legal staff. These reliable documents can be prepared in minutes.

Online Legal Solutions

- **Incorporation.** Incorporate your business in any state.
- **LLC Formations.** Gain asset protection and pass-through tax status in any state.
- **Wills.** Nolo has helped people make over 2 million wills. Is it time to make or revise yours?
- **Living Trust (avoid probate).** Plan now to save your family the cost, delays, and hassle of probate.
- **Trademark.** Protect the name of your business or product.
- **Provisional Patent.** Preserve your rights under patent law and claim "patent pending" status.

Online Legal Forms

Nolo.com has hundreds of top quality legal forms available for download—bills of sale, promissory notes, nondisclosure agreements, LLC operating agreements, corporate minutes, commercial lease and sublease, motor vehicle bill of sale, consignment agreements and many, many more.

Review Your Documents

Many lawyers in Nolo's consumer-friendly lawyer directory will review Nolo documents for a very reasonable fee. Check their detailed profiles at **lawyers.nolo.com**.

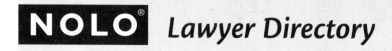